POLICEWOMEN AND EQUALITY

Policewomen and Equality

Formal Policy v Informal Practice?

Sandra Jones

Research Fellow, Centre for the Study of Community and Race Relations
Brunel University

MACMILLAN

First published 1986

Published by
THE MACMILLAN PRESS LTD
Houndmills, Basingstoke, Hampshire RG21 2XS
and London
Companies and representatives
throughout the world

Typeset by Latimer Trend & Company Ltd, Plymouth
Printed in Hong Kong

British Library Cataloguing in Publication Data
Jones, Sandra
Policewomen and equality : formal policy
v informal practice.
1. Policewomen—Great Britain   2. Sex
discrimination in employment—Great
Britain
I.   Title
331.4′133   HV8023

ISBN 0–333–41802–6
ISBN 0–333–42441–7 Pbk

Contents

List of Tables and Figures

FIGURES

Foreword

Only ten years ago, even though the Commissioner of Police for the Metropolis was openly engaged in a battle against entrenched corruption within the London CID, there was little public interest in the nature and quality of policing. Yet over the past ten years, a whole series of developments has transformed the perspective in which policing is seen. Not only have the police themselves been brought from the shadows to the centre of attention, but they have also been close to the centres of conflict and social change in society at large, for example in industrial and race relations.

A number of events have been the focus of increasing criticism of standards of police conduct; the clearest examples are the death of Blair Peach during a demonstration in Southall in 1979, the urban riots of 1981 and 1985 and the policing of the miners' strike in 1984–5. Also, criticisms have been expressed more forcefully and coherently than before, often by bodies like the GLC Police Committee which exist to develop and propagate a critical view. There have been more serious and more extensive public disturbances over the past five years than in the previous fifty. Although public order policing is a small part of all policing, it has become the most visible part, and it can expose the police in a physical and apparently hostile role. There has been an enormous increase in the number of official and unofficial reports, assessments and comments on policing, public order and crime; examples are the Scarman report on the Brixton disorders of 1981, the PSI report on police and people in London (published in 1983), the British Crime Survey, the television series on policing in the Thames Valley (transmitted in 1981) and the reports on policing in Merseyside (published in 1985). The Royal Commission on Criminal Procedure, both through its own report (published in 1981) and through the research it commissioned, stimulated a more intensive examination than ever before of the powers and actual practices of the police following an arrest. The Commission's report was followed by two Bills (debated in successive Parliamentary sessions) which eventually resulted in the Police and Criminal Evidence Act 1985. The Royal Commissions also prepared the way for the introduction of an independent prosecution service in 1986.

An important development has been the re-examination of the relation between the police and the other institutions of a democracy.

The arrangements whereby the Home Secretary is the police authority for London has again been called into question. Following a recommendation in Lord Scarman's report, the Police and Criminal Evidence Act requires that there should be arrangements for consultation between police managers and local communities; in response, police consultative committees are being set up in many parts of the country. Some police authorities (notably Merseyside before its abolition) have started to explore the potential for exercising more influence or control over policing and practice. Pilot schemes have been introduced whereby lay visitors observe at police stations.

Conflicts in industrial relations such as the Grunwick dispute and the miners' strike have been searching tests of the policing system and particularly of the independence and neutrality of the force. Race relations issues have been an even more difficult challenge. The prevalence of racial attacks was highlighted by a Home Office report published in 1981, which also pointed to the small success of the police in dealing with this kind of offence. The police handling of the investigation into the Deptford Fire in which 13 black people died in January 1981 was met by vocal protests from black people. The riots of 1981 and 1985 were in large part acts of protest, specifically against the police, by black people in the main.

All of these developments have created the conditions in which there can be a fundamental rethinking of the functions and status of the police, a redefinition of their relationship to democratic institutions and a new assessment of the ways in which policing can be shaped either by enlightened management or by external controls (the law, police regulations, the complaints system as reformed in 1985). Since the Edmund Davies settlement in 1979, police pay has been radically increased and recruitment has picked up; there has been an increase in other resources available to the police. The Home Office is in a position to expect a return from this increased expenditure, and this expectation of results is a further pressure for change.

Another fundamental social change over the past ten years has been the incorporation of some of the principles of equality into the institutional structure, as signalled by the Sex Discrimination Act 1975 and the establishment of the Equal Opportunities Commission. There is, in fact, a close link between the rethinking of policing and the rethinking of the role of women. A specific point is that women have rightly complained about the way police deal with sexual attacks and about the inadequacy of crime prevention policy in this field. But a more fundamental issue is the restricted role traditionally allotted to women within the police force itself. Parliament decided, after explicitly considering the matter, that the police should not be excluded from the provisions of the Sex Discrimination Act. This meant that police forces had to abolish the separate women's police sections that existed up to 1975 and begin the process of integrating women police officers on an equal basis with men. It should also have meant that quotas restricting the total number of women police officers were abandoned.

This book reports the results of pioneering research on the position of women in one police force at this time of change. It should not be thought that this is a small subject at the corner of policing or of feminism. On the contrary, because of the visible and symbolic role of the police and because of the authority they carry, the position of women in the force is of cardinal importance for the women's movement. Equally, women in the force are central to constructive thinking about policing reform. Many of the kinds of policing that need to be strengthened are ones to which women can and should make a significant contribution. This study about women in a police force is therefore about the interaction between two vital areas of social change. It is also about the effects of legislation; and here it gives us an insight into the different ways in which the law can be used in social policy (for example, to stimulate change or to legitimate changes already taking place) and into the severe problems of implementing equal opportunity legislation. The study shows that while changes in some formal structures have been rapid, the functions and opportunities of women police officers have changed more slowly, and in trying to open up opportunities to women, formidable obstacles are encountered. For police officers, social scientists and anyone with an interest in the women's movement, this is a fascinating story.

David J. Smith
Policy Studies Institute, April 1986

Acknowledgements

When I first suggested, to a senior policeman, the possibility of a research study of the present role of policewomen, the idea was greeted with amused scepticism. So it was with the mixed feelings of trepidation and determination that I began this study, not knowing quite what support I would receive.

In the event, the response by all involved has been positive and supportive, even by those within the police service who openly declared that they held traditional views about the most suitable role for policewomen. No doubt their expectations about the outcomes of this study were somewhat different from those who support and encourage the new 'modus operandi' of policewomen. Amongst this latter group are several senior policewomen who gave me advice in the pilot stages of this work and who suggested various lines of enquiry – all of which proved subsequently to be of central value and importance.

I would like to take this opportunity to thank publicly everybody who has helped me complete this study by offering their support, encouragement and time. Some people deserve a special mention. First and foremost, my thanks are due to the Equal Opportunities Commission who funded the research. Christine Jackson and Ron Barrowclough were particularly encouraging and, it must be said, waited patiently for a research report delayed by its ever-increasing length and my move to a new research post.

Special thanks are also extended to the Chief Constable of 'Medshire' who generously allowed me to interview, survey and patrol with his police officers. Many of his staff were involved at various times in the distribution and collection of questionnaires and arranging interviews and visits. All of these activities were ably and efficiently coordinated by Linda, who acted as liaison officer for the force. Thank you.

I would like to mention some of the other people who made crucial personal contributions to this study. My colleague Mike Levi provided constant encouragement and advice, as well as enriching my 'working life' with his wit and humour. Lesley Culverhouse helped with the interviewing and typed up most of the tapes – a task which at times seemed never ending. My daughter, Tania, did a sterling job helping me to code the questionnaires and verify the punching.

Richard Joss was bullied into reading the manuscript and did so with a critical police eye, as well as correcting my split infinitives along the way. Ian Mackay was a constant source of personal support who, by reminding me that the work was overdue and refusing to let me get too distracted by my new job, ensured that the book was completed.

I am indebted to all the people already mentioned. However, the study would have been impossible without the cooperation of all the men and women officers in 'Medshire' who participated, and it is to them that my debt is greatest.

S.J.J.

1 Women in Policing

MAJOR MILESTONES: 1900–75

Although the foundations of today's police service were laid with the introduction of Peel's 'New Police' in 1829, it was not until after the end of the First World War that the first women were officially recognised as police officers. These early years of women in policing are revealing not only for the strength of feeling characterised by 'the grudging admission of a limited number of female officers',[1] but also because they demonstrate the origin of the sexual division of labour which has in a large part persisted at least up until the passage of the Sex Discrimination Act. It was during these first years of the women police that their caring, nurturing and feminine role as 'moral guardians' to children and to fellow members of the weaker sex was established. Acceptance of even this restricted contribution to policing initially met with hostility and resentment, not least from the Police Federation who were 'jealous of the introduction of women into a traditionally male occupation'.[2] Indeed, the more recent debate which surrounded the inclusion of the police service within the Sex Discrimination Act was reminiscent of this earlier struggle to establish a role for women in policing.

In policing, as in industry, women's involvement was initially the result of several social reform movements (for example, the Penal Reform League) which were given impetus by the huge depletion of manpower[3] caused by the First World War and the consequent need to draw upon the reserve army of female labour. One extremely important factor was a particular brand of social problem, precipitated by the war, which was seen as threatening to the moral well-being of girls and young women: the escalation in the supply and demand of prostitutes. The combined effect of this, and the entry of women into the labour force on a large scale, generated public concern about the social and moral conditions of women and girls who, as the weaker sex, were seen to need special protection and guidance.

This prompted various voluntary organisations to set up preventive patrols. For example, the Women's Auxillary Service evolved from a vigilante organisation, the Women Police Volunteers, set up to 'assist with the care of refugees and to protect girls from the attentions of the brutal and licentious soldiery'.[4] The objective of this organisation was to 'prove by its work and reliability that there is a permanent sphere for policewomen in every county, city and borough throughout the United Kingdom'.[5] Almost simultaneously the National Union of Women Workers in response to 'the danger and excitement which possessed much of the girlhood and womanhood of the country'[6] established Voluntary Women's Patrols who did preventive work among women and girls in the vicinity of military camps, munition factories and in parks.

Although these groups had no official status the work they did was noticed and in 1918, the new Commissioner of the Metropolitan Police, Nevil Macready, obtained Home Office approval for an officially recognised number of patrols to be known as the Women Police Patrols, under their own superintendent. One hundred patrolwomen were employed in 1919 under the direction of ten sergeants, one assistant superintendent and one superintendent. At this time they had neither the status nor the powers of attested constables because of a clause in the existing Police Acts which stated that only 'fit men' could be sworn in. Their initial reception by both the police service, particularly the neonate Police Federation, and the public was hostile. This reaction is partly attributed by one police historian[7] to the alienation caused by a rival private-enterprise organisation evolved out of the Women's Auxilliary Service patrols, whose leaders had earlier been active as suffragettes. Their militaristic style is believed to have contributed to the eccentric and feminist reputation attributed to policewomen in their early days.[8] Much of the flavour of these early tensions is present in a recent account of her experiences as a policewoman given by Lock.[9]

The role of the Women's Police was formally considered in 1920 by the Baird Committee who concluded that women had proved their value during the war. However, despite the committee's recommendations that they should be fully attested, highly trained, form an integral part of the police force, and that an assistant inspector of constabulary should be appointed to inspect policewomen and to promote their welfare and efficiency, very little progress was made. This was mainly due to the fact that discretion as to whether or not policewomen should be employed was left to the local police authorities and consequently very few were recruited by forces other than the Metropolitan Police. Some encouragement for the Women's Police came when they were incorporated by the new Commissioner Macready into the Metropolitan Police and when, in 1922, the full powers of a sworn constable were granted to women. This was soon overshadowed by the short but harsh judgement on policewomen delivered by the Geddes Committee on

National Expenditure, as a result of which many forces dispensed with their policewomen entirely. Even those employed by the Metropolitan Police were drastically cut from 112 to 24, and these remaining pioneers would also have been abolished had it not been for the determined efforts of Lady Astor. Despite an unsympathetic Home Secretary who, according to Lock[10] held the view that 'their work ... was not police work, no matter how noble', this small nucleus of policewomen was retained after her prolonged campaign.

Two other early inquiries considered the employment of policewomen and both – the Bridgeman Committee of 1924[11] and the Royal Commission on Police Powers and Procedures of 1929[12] – recognised the value of policewomen, particularly in connection with dealing with women and children. Nevertheless, despite the conclusion of the Royal Commission that 'the time is ripe for a substantial increase in their numbers, more particularly in cities for patrol work in uniform',[13] and their usefulness in relation to interviewing victims of sexual cases, the employment of policewomen was again left to local discretion.

The 'specialist' contribution made by policewomen was however acknowledged in 1930 when the Home Secretary standardised the pay and conditions of service for policewomen and specified their main duties. These were to include patrolling, duties in connection with women and children found missing, ill, destitute or homeless, or in immoral surroundings, taking statements from women and children, and dealing with female prisoners. The Home Office had, in effect, defined what was to be the formal role of policewomen for the next forty-five years, in that they were to be mainly concerned with women and children who were victims of offences or were felt to be in 'moral danger'. This role was given legal reinforcement by the Children and Young Persons Act of 1933 which required that 'specialist' women officers should deal with juveniles. By actively developing this specialist role (at a time when being a specialist in the police service had not acquired its present day prestige) rather than seeking equality with policemen, the early policewomen demonstrated their acceptance of a division of labour based on sex. This ensured that they undertook duties considered more suited to their feminine skills and which were less dangerous and demanding of physical strength.

In the Metropolitan Police provisions were made in 1934 to employ and train policewomen in all districts for duties concerning women and children. Policewomen's departments were introduced as separate authorised establishments, with their own rank and promotion structure, administered by a separate branch at Scotland Yard with a woman commander. Although their role had been formally and legally recognised, general acceptance was less easily obtained, so that by 1939 only forty-five police forces out of a total of 183 were employing policewomen, and in London the number had only just returned to its pre-Geddes level. Whilst some of this slow rate of female recruitment was due to the differential effect of the depression on female labour, there is little doubt that it can also be attributed to the indifference of the Home Office and chief constables to the value of policewomen, and continuing resistance by operational policemen to the incursion of women into their erstwhile exclusively male occupation.

The outbreak of the Second World War boosted female recruitment once again in most occupations, including the police service. During the war period the Women's Police increased from 282 in 1940 to 418 in 1945. In addition, a campaign by the National Council of Women resulted, in 1939, in the foundation of the Women's Auxiliary Police Corps, which by the end of the war had over 3000 full-time unattested members. Initially their duties were restricted to the driving and maintenance of vehicles and clerical, radio, telephone and canteen work, but as the shortage of manpower worsened, their role expanded to include keeping order in the vicinity of military camps – a function reminiscent of the 'moral watchdog' role of the Voluntary Women's Patrols during the First World War. A further 342 women, however, were sworn in and, along with the regular policewomen, performed the whole range of law-enforcement duties.

The war-time contribution made by both the regular policewomen and the auxilliaries had a substantial effect on changing police and public attitudes towards their value in police work. The praise and acclaim extended by the Inspectors of Constabulary in their report at the end of the war also included mention of the Women's Police and auxilliaries. This was echoed in a report by the Postwar Committee,[14] set up in 1944, which recommended the employment of policewomen on a wide range of duties. Their increasing acceptability was only partially reflected in the period following the war which saw a slow but steady increase in their numbers. During 1949–59, for example, their establishment (total authorised strength) virtually doubled, and continued to rise slowly during the 1960s. In 1966, for example, there were 4000 women out of 95 000 officers.[15]

Their reputation was considerably enhanced during this period by the sustained efforts of Barbara Denis de Vitre, who was appointed Assistant Inspector of HM Constabularies in 1948. However, this recognition of the value of policewomen was restricted to the role originally defined in 1930 which was rooted in the traditional concept of what was acceptable as 'women's work'. Although a limited number of women were assigned to duties which were seen as the prerogative of their male colleagues, such as investigation work in the CID (where, for example, there were only three women in the Metropolitan Police in 1933),[16] the majority continued to perform duties which were based on this original sexual division of labour. This persisted right into the early 1970s and was reinforced by the rise in female and juvenile crime during the post-war years, particularly during the 1960s. For example, according to Smart, since 1959 'women are engaging more frequently in more varied forms of crime'.[17] This led to the increasing involvement of policewomen in the interviewing and searching of female and juvenile offenders and served to emphasise the traditional stereotype of the feminine gender role.

By 1971 there were 3884 female officers, representing 3.9 per cent of the total national police strength. Although their basic training was the same as for the men, they were still employed in separate policewomen's departments and they received additional training in the skills and knowledge required for their specialist work. By this time the principal duties of the women's departments were:

 (i) an involvement in enquiries concerning offences commited against female and to a lesser extent against male juveniles;
 (ii) attending interviews of female offenders and to a lesser extent of male juvenile offenders;
 (iii) escort duties for female offenders and to a lesser extent male juveniles;
 (iv) investigations concerning female missing persons and to a lesser extent missing male juveniles;
 (v) all aspects of child neglect cases and involvement with local care orders;
 (vi) liaison with social agencies concerned with missing persons and child neglect cases;
 (vii) interviewing, acquiring information and maintaining records regarding families, females and children with domestic and personal problems, either separate from or in liaison with social agencies.

As well as their duties, conditions of service were different for policewomen. Policewomen's departments had their own rank and promotion structure and their own inspectorate, and although there were local variations, their rate of pay was less, at nine-tenths of that of male officers. In general, although they worked morning and afternoon shifts, women did not work night shifts, but were on call on a rota basis in case they were required, for example to take a statement from a victim of an alleged offence of indecency.

These, then, were the main features of the position and function of women in policing which existed well into the early 1970s. At that time, in response to a combination of economic and social trends which increasingly challenged the female stereotype in America and in Europe, the Equal Pay Act (1970) and the Sex Discrimination Act (1975) gave legal recognition to women's employment rights. The Sex Discrimination Act also heralded a major change in the formal role of women police.

THE SEX DISCRIMINATION ACT AND THE POLICE SERVICE

The political decision to include the police service within the provisions of the Sex Discrimination Act was a subject of considerable controversy both before and after the passage of the Bill through parliament. As a result of the Act, no further distinction was to be made in either recruitment or deployment on the grounds of sex, thus challenging the notion that policing should be a mainly masculine occupation and heralding the removal of the traditional and well-established sexual division of labour. Most policewomen's departments (with their associated rank, promotion and separate inspection arrangements) were abolished. Some forces, however, did interpret the provisions of the Act so that some work dealing with women and children was continued as a specialist function, and others (for example, Leicestershire, Avon and Somerset, and Lincolnshire) have subsequently re-introduced units to deal with this kind of work. The general trend, however, was that women were to be fully integrated into the main stream of general police duties, on equal terms with men, including night-shift work and all aspects of patrol and specialist work.

Some significant changes in the employment status of policewomen had already begun to occur in the lead-up period before the passage of the Sex Discrimination Act. Perhaps the most notable was Sir Robert Mark's independent decision in 1972 to disband policewomen's departments in the Metropolitan Police and the subsequent integration of his women officers into general police work. The following year promotion lists were combined, and in 1974, probably as a result of the Equal Pay Act of 1970, women's salaries were made up to the same level as those of male officers on a national basis. Although they retained their policewomen's departments, some police forces had already begun to employ policewomen on more general duties. As one woman sergeant from Suffolk recalled:

> I think there is a false assumption made that all women in the force before the Act were tied up in PW departments. This is not so. For eight years I was a PC on a sub-division dealing with women, children and juveniles first and then taking the vehicle out to patrol the town centre, perhaps. It wasn't until I was promoted sergeant that I went into a policewoman's department.[18]

Indeed, in some cases the introduction of the Act was actually felt to have restricted the work women were able to do in that it brought to notice the fact that some women were already being allowed to do Panda and foot patrols alone at night. Attention was drawn to these women by the media debate surrounding the Act, with its associated and dramatically portrayed fears for women's safety, as a consequence of which, it is claimed that supervisors became *more* careful about allowing them to patrol alone.[19]

Nevertheless, whether the Act prompted radical change or merely accelerated a process that had already begun, it represented the first official redefinition of the role of women in policing and a major change in the formal and legal context within which women operate. Although service within the police is covered by the employment provisions of the Act, certain adaptations have been made (S.17.1 (a) and (b)) to take account of the constable as an independent office-holder. For the purposes of the provisions of the Act, he or she is treated as an employee of the chief officer and/or the local police authority, rather than of the sovereign to whom the police constable swears allegiance on appointment. (This same provision is also applied to cadets).

Certain specific exemptions were also made. Consequently the Act provides that police regulations made under sections 33, 34 and 35 under the Police Act 1964[20] shall not treat men and women officers differently, except in relation to the requirements relating to height,[21] uniform or equipment, or allowances in lieu of uniform or equipment (S.17.2 (a)). Other exceptions provided for include special treatment for women in connection with pregnancy and childbirth (S.17.2 (b)) and in relation to pensions for special constables and cadets (S.17.2 (c)). The Act also provides for compensation arising out of a case brought against a chief officer or police authority to be paid out of the police fund.

However, with the possible exception of the height requirement, these special adaptations in respect of the police service do not alter the essence of the Act. In fact, the exemption of the height requirement can be seen as protective towards women applicants since it allows for the fact that the average woman is shorter than the average man. The inclusion of this exemption in the Act was an implicit recognition of the *possibility* of future discrimination and as such it could be construed as the first example of positive action. However, as we shall see presently, this motive is not always apparent in the way in which this exemption is used in the recruitment of women.

The application of the Act to policing was almost guaranteed to generate debate. Chief officers and the Police Federation were, 'shoulder to shoulder'[22] in their attempt to secure exemption (already granted to the Armed Forces) from the provisions of the Act. Their main arguments for exemption were the physical demands of police patrol duties and the increased risk of violence that women performing general patrol work would be subject to. Underlying this protective attitude was the belief that police work is somehow unfeminine. Some of this feeling is reported by Whittaker who states:

> The Federation confidently pronounced that 'the very nature of the duties of a police constable is contrary to all that is finest and best in women'.[23]

As this demonstrates, the tenor of the debate was again at the level of an instinctive belief that 'the real job of policing' should be left to the men. The masculine ethos and anxiety underlying these arguments were repeatedly evident in the *Police Review* and in the Police Federation's own magazine *Police* in the years that followed the Act, along with 'fears of the police force being swamped by women'.[24]

Though many policewomen publicly welcomed the change,[25] a substantial number of women were also opposed to integration for varying reasons. Some were concerned about the long-term effects of the loss of their specialist role on the service they were able to provide the public, whilst others were worried about the effects of integration on their career prospects. The claim was that promotion opportunities would be increased by the Act. Suitably qualified women would be eligible for all the promotions within the service instead of the limited number of 'dead women's shoes' that sometimes characterised promotion opportunities in policewomen's departments; but some women were not convinced. For example, one woman inspector is reported as saying: 'Women already have to be better at their jobs than men to get anywhere if they are at all ambitious, and now it will be harder because of the competition.'[26] Some women resigned rather than face reorganisation.[27]

These arguments persisted and even at the time of Lord Edmund-Davies's Report, in 1979, on police pay and representative bodies,[28] they were still very much alive. The loss of expertise in relation to the traditional policewomen's skills and their social service role was acknowledged, as was the very real danger that this expertise would be lost 'for ever as experienced women officers leave the service'. Recommendation 81 suggests that consideration should be given to the specialist departments staffed by suitable women *and* men.[29] It was also suggested that the practical implications of integration, such as the difficulties inherent in combining child-rearing with working the same shift pattern as male officers, have been such as to adversely affect women's ability to pursue a career in the police service.

In the same report submissions from the Federation and the Superintendents' Association made it clear that they still felt that the police service should be exempted from the Act. The Federation said that they would continue to press for its removal, using this policy as a justification for the continuation of the practice of separate representation for male and female officers; a practice which though perfectly *legal*[30] could be construed as against the *spirit* of the Act. It is also significant perhaps that whilst the Association of Chief Police Officers 'expressed no strong views' on the Act, they also felt that 'a great deal of anxiety about the full integration of women officers could be eased by sensible deployment'.[31] The question of what is 'sensible deployment' is a crucial concern of this study and is dealt with in Chapter 4.

Whatever the strengths and weaknesses or rights and wrongs of these arguments, it is nevertheless the case that since 1975 the police service *is* subject to the Sex Discrimination Act, the purpose of which is to prevent discrimination on the grounds of sex and marriage and to ensure equality of opportunity and treatment in employment. Indeed, the sentiment expressed by Smith, in relation to discriminatory practice in the recruitment of female officers in the Metropolitan Police, neatly encapsulates these legal obligations and might well be used to describe the wider provisions of the Act:

If parliament is persuaded that the Force is right, then it should amend the legislation; if not, then the Force should bring its selection policy into conformity with the law.[32]

Given this background of controversy it would not be surprising if policewomen, despite their theoretically equal status, were uncertain about their modern role; it is the way in which this role has changed and the contribution made by the Sex Discrimination Act which is the central theme of this book.

2 Setting the Scene

This study has its origins in a previous research project, directed by the author, during which attitudes towards policewomen were surveyed as part of a more extensive inquiry into police–public relationships[1] and police officers' attitudes towards organisational aspects of the police service.[2] One general finding, supported and corroborated by informal observations and discussions with police officers, was that the attitudes of many male officers (and, indeed, some female officers) remain coloured by their limited views about the role of policewomen; views which often reflect their more general attitudes towards women in society.

Although at the time of the study the police service had been subject to the provisions of the Sex Discrimination Act (1975) for almost five years, we found considerable resistance to the idea that women should perform general police duties, or that they could do so as effectively as their male counterparts. Some of the more commonly expressed beliefs were that women as police officers are physically and emotionally inferior to men, policework is not women's work and is unfeminine, and they are not career-minded and do not stay in 'the job' for any length of time. This latter objection has been voiced in more forceful terms by implying that women only join 'the job' as a romantic interlude before marriage.[3]

On the other hand, there was also considerable concern amongst older policewomen about what they felt to be the ill-considered way in which their integration into the main stream of policing was implemented. More specifically, there was a feeling that the loss of their specialist and expert role in relation to those duties that were their traditional and almost exclusive domain had had an adverse effect on the service that the police could give to the public. This traditional work included, as documented earlier, offences involving alleged indecency, and dealing with female victims and offenders, juveniles and missing persons.

Some of the other questions raised included whether younger women joining the police hold the same views as their older female colleagues, or whether, from their perspective, the loss of the specialist role had been adequately compensated for by the more varied activities afforded by general police work and by the increased career opportunities, including promotion, that were assumed to be a consequence of integration.

A previous questionnaire survey of British policewomen, conducted in 1977, addressed the question of what policewomen thought about the effects of integration on their careers and working lives.[4] However, although this study represented the first systematic attempt to evaluate the effect on the police service of this major piece of social policy legislation, it was conducted very soon after the implementation of the Act, perhaps before there had been time for the effects to be fully appreciated. It also relied entirely on the responses of policewomen and, as mentioned above, it was clear from previous work that male attitudes may contribute significantly to the spirit with which the provisions of the Sex Discrimination Act are adopted within the police service, and these attitudes may therefore be a prime factor in the uncertainty which surrounds the policewomen's role. This is of crucial importance should such attitudes translate into informal organisational barriers which result in disadvantage or discrimination against policewomen, and effectively make a myth out of the reality of integration.

Apart from the studies cited above, such other research evidence as exists does indeed point to the significance of policemen's attitudes towards policewomen as a prime factor in the development and maintenance of this ambiguity. Although there have been some major studies of this topic in America,[5] the equivalent information in the British context is relatively scarce. And although there are some compelling similarities in the policing sub-cultures of the two countries, there are (quite apart from the differences in the relevant legislature) some cultural differences deriving from the unarmed, and arguably predominantly 'peace-keeping' rather than 'law-enforcement', status of the British police officer which warrant independent analysis.[6] A recent study by the Police Studies Institute on the Metropolitan Police provides some limited comparable information about the influence of male attitudes. In their observational study of the police in action, Smith and Gray examine the treatment of women officers by their male colleagues, and policewomen's reactions to it. They state:

What women police officers say is amply confirmed by our observations of the way in which they are treated. In informal conversations, most of them say that policemen are prejudiced against them, that they greatly over-emphasise the importance of physical strength in the job so as to argue that women cannot do it adequately, that women are effectively excluded from some of the more interesting kinds of work and that men will not accept them as full members of the working group or as colleagues on an equal basis ... There is no doubt that a majority of policemen do have broadly the attitudes that policewomen ascribe to them.[7]

The recent case of discrimination, discussed in Chapter 7, brought by PC De Launay against the Metropolitan Police bore out the findings of this research.

Several studies[8] document these male attitudes and relate them to the unique occupational sociology of policing, though there are divergent opinions on the way in which these value patterns and attitudes are formed. According to Brown[9] there are three major schools of thought. In the first of these it is argued that recruits to the police already hold distinctive attitudes and values whereby certain types are attracted by and are selected for police work. The second socialisation model attributes police attitudes to the occupational socialisation process within the police organisation. In this model the recruits' attitudes, values and opinions are shaped by the police experience during his early years as a police officer. The third approach argues that there is a strong interaction between environment and personality in determining behaviour and combines the recruitment versus socialisation propositions. The model is based on the premise that:

> there is a complex interaction between the entering personality characteristics at the recruitment stage and the environmental, organisational, social and work constraints which police officers experience on the job during the occupational socialisation process.[10]

Although opinions may differ about the way in which these attitudes develop, the general theme running through these studies is that not only is the police service a male-dominated organisation (both numerically and culturally), but it bears the responsibility of ensuring that social order, embodied in the Rule of Law, is maintained. The symbolic imagery associated with this order-maintaining function, and in the law-enforcement role, reflects and reinforces the belief in the 'natural order', in which men are strong and women are weak and need protecting. In simple terms this is interpreted as meaning that laws are made for the protection and control of society and therefore it is natural that the strong, protecting male should enforce these laws. The control element of this interpretation is fundamental to understanding the occupational culture of the police service and the way police officers construe their work. It leads to the generation of conflict between the belief in the necessary but legitimate use of coercion needed for control and the 'softness' implicit in the notion of 'giving' a service.

The ideology developed from this belief in the concept of the natural order and the need to control is encapsulated in what Skolnick[11] calls the 'working personality' of policemen. In his socialisation model analysis it is the twin elements of danger and authority which isolate the police officer and creates the sub-culture. Most of the documented attitudinal correlates of this 'working personality'[12] have a traditionally masculine flavour, such as for example, physical courage, suspiciousness, self-assertiveness, authoritarianism and loyalty.

The notion that women are able to perform the same duties as men challenges these basic concepts and threatens to undermine the masculine identity and social importance of this apparently masculine controlling role. Though some of the obstacles and difficulties encountered by women trying to enter policing on equal terms are shared with other traditionally male occupations and are well documented,[13] in some respects policing poses unique problems and dilemmas, not least of which is that embodied in the concept of 'dangerousness'. The significance of the danger and violence is that it is a part of 'real' police work, with all the immediacy of action, and this also derives from the much valued law-enforcement, order-maintaining role.

The prevalence of these related notions might lead one to think that real-life police work justified the images portrayed by the media,[14] particularly the many television dramatisations. In fact, much of the routine work of a police officer is very mundane and can be boring[15] involving repetition of seemingly pointless activities. Part of this is an inevitable consequence of the structure of police work. Demand is unpredictable but personnel have to be available just in case.[16] Boredom can actually generate low-level, but hardly dangerous or exciting, law-enforcement activities (such as arresting drunks), and other practices (for example, 'easing' behaviour) such as those documented in the study, already referred to, by Cain.

Numerous studies[17] have examined the composition of the calls that police respond to, and attitude surveys have assessed the extent and nature of public demand and preferences for service.[18] Whilst it is clear from these studies that the public act as role definers for the police, it is also the case that the majority of work resulting from this public demand is not related to law-enforcement. Although there are variations according to the rural/urban characteristics of the area policed, it is nevertheless the case that up to 70 per cent of all calls for service have what might be called a broad social-welfare function. This was amply borne out by our study of police–public relationships referred to earlier. For example, it was found that 43 per cent of all public initiated calls (based on aggregated replies from a sample of just under a thousand people from two contrasting police force areas) were for 'crime and related' reasons. Of all the contacts with the public initiated by the police themselves, only 30 per cent were crime related. 'Service' calls accounted for the majority of the rest of the contacts. These involved the police in many diverse activities ranging from seeking information or signing documents (for example, passport application forms), enquiries about lost property, stray dogs and missing persons, to helping to settle family rows, all of which were seen by the public to be legitimate police activities.

It was also quite clear that the relative proportions of 'service' and 'crime' related police activity, whether intiated by the public or the police, was linked to the style of policing adopted and general public satisfaction with the police. The 'community oriented' policing adopted by the Southern force was characterised by high proportions of 'service' related activities, and high public satisfaction. Though it would be wrong to make any 'cause and effect' generalisations it is fair to say that, even allowing for higher criminal victimisation rates, the more action-oriented reactive (or 'fire-brigade') style of policing practised by the Northern police force studied, was associated with a lower proportion of public and police initiated contacts for 'service' related reasons and lower levels of public satisfaction.

It would seem, then, that not only is the dramatic crime-fighting view of what constitutes 'real' police work far removed from the reality of the daily lives of the majority of police officers, but the routine and unexciting 'service' work which forms their staple diet is a fundamental correlate of public views of police effectiveness. When one also considers the facts about the non-spectacular nature of the bulk of crimes reported to the police and the evidence about who actually *detects* most crime (up to 80 per cent of detections are as a direct result of public involvement),[19] another touchstone of police beliefs becomes questionable. Clearly, the police sub-culture perception of their work exists in spite (or perhaps because) of the facts, supported by research evidence, that most policework, including patrol, is not dangerous or exciting and that exposure to violent situations is likely to be very limited.

Nevertheless, the anxieties surrounding the physical aspect of policing persist and whilst there are undoubtedly risks involved and it is possible to sympathise with them, the extent to which they exist and therefore can be used to justify the exclusion of women from general patrol duties is questionable. This is all the more so in the light of the observation[20] that an officer of either sex cannot subdue a struggling prisoner unaided, and that in a crisis, even a strong male officer would probably need help. Apart from the study of the Metropolitan Police, mentioned above, where women officers felt that policemen over-emphasise the importance of physical strength, the previously quoted survey of British female police officers also examined women's attitudes towards the possibility of violence. Although it was mentioned by the majority policewomen surveyed it did not emerge as an overriding worry. The study considered the ability of women to handle violence and concluded:

> it should be remembered that many violent encounters can be defused and avoided by verbal means by a skilled and well-trained officer. Thus, if sufficient emphasis is put on these negotiating skills in training young constables – males and females – the problem for women may not be so great as it appears at first.[21]

These findings along with the evidence about the actual composition of police work may well give credence to the argument[22] that these fears stem as much from a threat to male self-identity as from genuine concern for the welfare of female officers.

This is all the more so in the light of the way in which the public evaluate police performance. One major finding of our recent study was that it is the personal interactive skills of individual police officers that are one of the primary determinants of public satisfaction with the police. When the public were asked why they were satisfied or otherwise with the police, the qualitative reasons given reflected a concern with the personalised image of the police. Regardless of whether an individual's experience of the police has been in connection with service, traffic or crime, it was the interpersonal skills reflected in his/her helpfulness, courtesy, kindness and tolerance which 'personalise' the police image and by which 'the police' are collectively judged.

In comparison very few people (less than a quarter) actually gave clear instrumental reasons for their satisfaction which could be said to reflect the technically efficient, law-enforcement professional self-image held by the majority of the police officers interviewed. Police reasons for consumer satisfaction indicated their preoccupation with 'professional' efficiency. They stressed, for example, the quick (in terms of response rates) and efficient service that the police provide for the public and the fact that the police 'success rate', especially for major crimes, is good. In other words, the police falsely believed they were judged on their technical rather than personal, human interaction skills. Of course, it may well be that, as with other professionals, the 'public' take for granted police efficiency in their technical (law-enforcement) role and consequently use these other 'service delivery' criteria to judge overall effectiveness. Nor do these interpretations detract from the importance of the law-enforcement/control role, rather they point to the need for a balanced appreciation of the relative importance of all the various aspects of the police role.

Nevertheless, it is perhaps rather ironic, given sustained male opposition, that not only does the bulk of policework consist of precisely the kind of activity that policemen associate with a woman's role, i.e. that of help and support, service rather than control, but also the public value these social-welfare activities and see them as an integral and legitimate part of the police function. Also the public makes generalised judgements based on the associated interpersonal skills of caring. It could even be that the skills traditionally associated with women in policing are, in some respects, more in tune with public expectations of service delivered in a humane manner rather than control imposed with efficiency.

ATTITUDES, DEFINITIONS AND ORGANISATIONAL PRACTICE

The extent to which the formal and organisational changes have led to genuine equality of opportunity and treatment within the police service may be dependent on the way in which male attitudes translate into practice. The dominant concern of the research behind this book was to establish to what extent these male attitudes exist, whether they are shared by female officers, and, more importantly whether they are reflected in formal and/or informal organisational practice. It was hypothesised that if these attitudes are universally held by men, but not by women, and are consciously or unconsciously translated into practice, then they would effectively restrict the opportunities of women to play a fully integrated and equal role. In other words, the extent to which these attitudes result in prejudice, disadvantage or discrimination will be the key issue in describing the limits of the policewomen's role.

Before considering the possible consequences of certain male attitudes, it is useful to examine some of the terminology involved in the consideration of organisational practice, the Sex Discrimination Act and the implications for the modern policewomen's role. As stated above, the limits on this role will depend on three commonly used, but often confused and interchanged, terms. The first of these, prejudice, is the starting point for both disadvantage and discrimination. Formally, it is defined as a 'preconceived opinion, bias'.[23] Whilst the formal definition does not imply a direction to the bias, in our context a more accurate definition would include a negative dimension, such that it is an 'unfavourable opinion or feelings formed beforehand without knowledge or reason'.[24] Since we are also concerned with relations between people there is also an element of social comparison such that 'prejudice is a negative attitude toward a person or a group based upon a social comparison process in which the individual's own group is taken as the positive point of reference'.[25]

A consequence of prejudice is disadvantage since, according to Allport, 'the net effect of prejudice ... is to place the object of prejudice at some disadvantage not merited by his own conduct'.[26] Sexism is also a result of prejudice which, when combined with power, assigns a subordinate position to women such that it 'attributes an unchanging set of characteristics to a group of people [women] the inferior position of the whole group and therefore supports and benefits the group in power, in this case men'.[27]

When prejudice results in behaviour which is at the other person's or group's expense (and by implication to the advantage of the prejudiced person or group) then this is discrimination. In common usage the term discrimination has many meanings which 'extend from making simple, innocent distinctions between groups to depriving people of benefits because irrelevant criteria are used'.[28]

It is the notion of deprivation which is of central importance to the legislation embodied in the Sex Discrimination Act. The Act applies to discrimination against both women and men and defines two kinds, direct and indirect sex discrimination. These are:

> Direct sex discrimination arises where a person treats a woman, on the grounds of her sex, less favourably than he treats, or would treat, a man. (Section 1(1)(a))

> Indirect sex discrimination consists of treatment which may be described as equal in a formal sense as between sexes but discriminatory in its effect on one sex. (Section 1(1)(b))[29]

The Act details the various circumstances in which unlawful discrimination in employment may occur. In the case of direct discrimination it is necessary for the complainant to show that the treatment was both less favourable than the treatment which was (or would be) accorded to a man in the same or not materially different circumstances and that this treatment was on the grounds of her sex. Likewise, direct marriage discrimination occurs where a married person is treated less favourably, on the grounds of marital status, than an unmarried person of the same sex would be in the same or not materially different circumstances.

The conditions in relation to indirect sex discrimination are more complex. As detailed in the Equal Opportunities 'Code of Practice'

> Indirect sex discrimination occurs when an unjustifiable requirement or condition is applied equally to both sexes, but has a disproportionately adverse effect on one sex, because the proportion of one sex which can comply with it is much smaller than the proportion of the other sex which can comply with it.[30]

In this case the woman has to show that the condition or requirement with which she must comply in order to qualify for or obtain some benefit (e.g. a job) is applied, or would be applied, equally to men and to women; that it is such that the proportion of women who can comply with it is considerably smaller than the proportion of men who can comply with it; that it is to the detriment of the woman in question because she cannot comply with it; and that it cannot be shown by the person applying it to be justifiable, irrespective of the sex of the person to whom it is applied.

A central aspect of indirect sex discrimination is the notion of 'proportions' of people able to comply with a requirement and as such is an attempt to prevent discrimination occurring by conscious or unconscious use of criteria which disadvantage one or other sex.

Obvious examples relate to mobility or physical requirements for certain jobs. A requirement of mobility might bar more women than men. Likewise, if an employer is unable to show that certain physical requirements are necessary for the successful performance of a job, but that the application of the requirements equally to men and women leads to proportionately fewer women/men being able to comply, to the disadvantage of the applicant in question, then this would constitute indirect sex discrimination, whether or not the employer *deliberately* set out to disadvantage one sex. However, it should be noted that physical requirements can be lawful even though they may adversely affect women, provided they can be justified by the employer as necessary. Indirect marriage discrimination is a similar concept to indirect sex discrimination and may arise when a condition or requirement is applied equally to married and unmarried persons of the same sex but which is in fact discriminatory in its effect on married persons.

As applied to this study of policewomen, the effect of the translation of prejudiced male attitudes into *formal* policy and practice, such as for example in the recruitment and deployment of personnel, could well be such as to constitute potential indirect sex and marriage discrimination. For example, recruitment decisions based on formally stated criteria (or even informal criteria which are never stated but have acquired legitimacy through tradition) which have a disproportionate disqualifying impact on women, (such as 'length of potential service' considerations) could, if not proved to be a justifiable selection criterion, be examples of indirect discrimination. This is due to the fact that many women interrupt their careers to have children and may remain out of paid employment for several years.

Similarly, a policy which requires men and women who rejoin the police service to attend a long *residential* training course may have a disproportionate impact on married women, particularly if their reason for leaving the service was to have children. (Fewer women than men may be able to leave their family responsibilities for such an extended period.) In this latter case, it would be necessary to show that a residential course was a justifiable condition of re-appointment. In the recruitment example, it would be necessary for the employer to justify the prospects for long, uninterrupted service as a necessary criterion for the job of a police officer. In practice it is more likely that this type of decision would constitute an *implicit* policy, based on male belief, and if it subsequently restricted the proportion of female officers in a force, it would be an example of indirect discrimination.

In terms of the deprivation of benefit, discrimination in recruitment has considerable consequences for many women since the police service is now virtually the best paid job for a woman. In the examples given in *New Earnings Survey*[31] the police service has the highest hourly rate of pay for women and also the lowest gross differential (at 90.4 per cent) between male and female earnings. Evidently, the denial of entry has real financial consequences.

Similarly, direct discrimination might be evident in the existence of *informal* barriers or policies which have the effect of modifying or restricting the roles that women are able to fulfil, such as not allowing single policewomen to team-up on motor patrol with married male officers. In addition, deployment practices may have 'knock on' effects such as restricting the amount of experience a woman is able to gain with consequent implications for her promotion prospects, or, as in the case of policing public order situations, the relative amount of overtime she is able to earn. Because of the nature of policing discussed above it is probable that these informal barriers, if they exist, are the most prevalent. Similarly, there are good *prima facie* grounds for supposing that these attitudes will be more evident amongst older, higher ranking officers who, by virtue of their rank, may formally reinforce these barriers to role equality.

If this is the case then the net result of this process, particularly in respect of female deployment, will be that they are generally fitted in at the periphery of policing, undertaking the less interesting, onerous and dangerous work, and will be less evident in those specialist departments which are particularly associated with the 'masculine' ethos of police work. As a consequence, the effects of these barriers will be identifiable both in the deployment and, because experience (particularly in the prestigious male-oriented departments) is a recognised prerequisite, in the promotion of policewomen.

To summarise, the overall impression which emerges from previous research and discussion in the media is that although integration has occurred theoretically in the police service, the role of policewomen is ambiguous in that they are not fully accepted as equals by their male colleagues, and furthermore, they no longer have the recognition of being specialists in 'traditional' policewomen's work which in some sense might compensate for the lack of general equality with their male counterparts. At the heart of all these issues is the question of what kind of impact the Sex Discrimination Act has had on the career prospects of women in an organisation which is characterised by its predominantly male-oriented occupational culture in which physical strength and prowess are prized attributes.

It was against this background that the Equal Opportunities Commission agreed to support this research to examine the impact of the Sex Discrimination Act on the recruitment, deployment and promotion of policewomen, and both male and female officers' attitudes towards issues raised by the inclusion of women in the general duties of day-to-day policing. The Chief Constable of a medium-sized police force (referred to in this account as Medshire) agreed to the study in his area, and the pilot work was conducted in another force in order to avoid sample contamination.

Four related sources of information contributed to the study. These were:

(i) a series of in-depth interviews conducted with policemen and policewomen designed to provide a sensitive, qualitative examination of the issues surrounding the role of policewomen, with the aim of evaluating the extent to which informal barriers to role equality exist;

(ii) a general survey of male and female officers using a structured questionnaire to examine attitudes towards integration and related organisational factors, such as deployment and promotion opportunities;

(iii) a short period of observational work, both in police stations and on patrol with male and female officers; and

(iv) an examination of official sources of documentary information concerning the recruitment, deployment and promotion of police officers.

Full details of the research design, methodology, sample sizes and response rates can be found in Appendix A. An integral part of the study was the comparison between those officers (both male and female) who joined the police service before and after the implementation of the Sex Discrimination Act. In the text these are referred to as 'traditionals' and 'moderns', titles which reflect the dominant official female role at the time of recruitment rather than individual officer's role preferences.

As indicated above, the broad objective of the research was to examine the practice of equality within the police force and to evaluate the consequences of the Sex Discrimination Act in reality as well as in formal organisational terms. More specifically, this research objective had the twinfold aims of examining the role of women in the police service in terms of their recruitment (Chapter 3), deployment

(Chapter 4) and career prospects (Chapters 5 and 6) and the attitudes of both male and female officers towards the present and preferred roles of policewomen, in order to ascertain whether 'informal barriers' exist as a result of adverse male attitudes (Chapter 7). This second aim included an appraisal of whether these attitudes substantially modify the roles that women are able to fulfil.

3 Entering the Police

Until integration, the separate organisational arrangements which governed the employment of women police officers meant that in effect a quota system was operated such that women constituted only a small proportion (approximately 5 per cent) of the overall police workforce. The major consequence of the Sex Discrimination Act was that policewomen's departments were integrated into the main stream of policing thus removing the existing restriction on their numbers.

Furthermore, the Act indicated that women should be recruited on the same basis as men, be assigned to the same range of duties, including general patrol, and be considered eligible for specialist departments and promotion on the same grounds as male officers.

Since, in any examination of equality of treatment, the major hurdle is often the first one, this chapter examines the effects of the Act on the first of these aspects, namely the recruitment and selection of women officers compared with their male counterparts. It is arranged in four sections. The first examines recruitment from a national perspective and attempts to map out overall patterns in recruitment. This is followed by an assessment of local trends and the situation in Medshire and demonstrates that although there are local variations, the main features of the national pattern are constant. The final section considers the selection philosophy, strategy and issues which underpin the current practices revealed by this examination of recruitment patterns.

THE NATIONAL PERSPECTIVE

After the Sex Discrimination Act there was to be no further distinction made, on the grounds of sex, in the recruitment of police officers. Just how well have women fared nationally as a result? As shown in Table 3.1, prior to the implementation of the Act there were 5840[1] women police officers in England and Wales. This represents an increase of 2219 (61.2 per cent) over the 1970 figure of 3621. In an equivalent five-year period after the Act, the number of women officers increased by 78.6 per cent (or 4590) to 10 430 in 1980. At the end of 1982, when this study commenced, there were 11 015 policewomen, representing an increase of almost 90 per cent (5175) since the implementation of the Act. Between the same periods the number of male officers increased by 11 181 (12.4 per cent for 1970–5); 5694 (5.6 per cent for 1975–80); and 8635 (8.5 per cent for 1975–82).

TABLE 3.1 *Number of female and male officers in the police service in England and Wales, 1970–83*[2]

Year	Female	Male	Year	Female	Male
1970	3 621	90 014	1977	7 866	100 231
1971	3 865	92 869	1978	8 555	100 415
1972	4 187	95 385	1979	9 472	103 731
1973	4 394	96 061	1980	10 430	106 889
1974	4 767	97 213	1981	10 772	108 696
1975	5 840	101 195	1982	11 015	109 830
1976	7 066	102 303	1983	11 076	109 927
% increase in five years before Act	61·2	12·4			
% increase in five years after Act				78·6	5·6
% increase between Act and this study				88·6	8·5

At first sight these figures indicate a substantial percentage increase in the number of women officers since the Act. However, it should be borne in mind that in the five years prior to the Act there had already been a 61.2 per cent increase. It could be argued that had this rate of increase just been maintained there would have been an extra 3562 women officers recruited, independently of the Act. Seen in this light, the Act alone could be said to account for only an extra 1028 (17.4 per cent) women officers. This is a generous estimate, as it assumes no increase in the tendency to recruit women for other reasons, and it is apparent from the figures that there had already been some increase in the annual rate of female recruitment in the years leading up to the legislation.

There are two other important points to make about these figures. Firstly, in absolute terms it is quite clear that although by the end of 1982 the actual number of women officers had nearly doubled since the Act, there had been 3460 more *male* than *female* officers recruited in the same period. It is impossible to tell whether this is due to the larger 'pool'[3] of male applicants from which selection is made. In theory the proportion of male to female applicants should not influence the way recruits are selected since, under the terms of the Act, all applicants should be treated individually, regardless of sex. Nor is it possible to estimate whether this difference is due to fewer male applicants than females failing to meet the national and local published selection criteria. If this were the case it would imply that the advertising and recruitment literature has less impact on the self-selection process in females than in males, and that as a consequence fewer qualified females make initial applications. However, there is no reason to suppose that female applicants are any less self-selecting than male applicants.

In fact, if one were to assume an equitable selection process there would be a case, at least on the basis of what is known of the educational background of recruits, for arguing that female applicants are better qualified than their male counterparts. Although there has been a general and marked national increase in the educational standard attained by recruits over the last five years, there is a discrepancy between male and female qualifications. For example, in 1982 only 4.2 per cent of female, as compared with 10.8 per cent of male, recruits (excluding the Metropolitan Police) had *no* formal qualifications. Indeed 43 per cent of the males recruited had only the minimum requirements (one to four O-levels or a pass on the Police Initial Test) compared with 32 per cent of the female recruits. Of those with higher than minimum requirements, a higher proportion of women had five or more O-levels, and at degree level the difference is quite marked: 13.6 per cent of female compared with 10.3 per cent of male recruits were graduates in 1982. A simple comparison of male and female recruits, according to whether they have the minimum or higher than minimum educational requirements, demonstrates a marked difference which is statistically significant, yielding a χ^2 value of 33.2 (d.f. = 1).

The survey of Medshire officers confirms this national pattern. For example, 64 per cent of the policemen surveyed and 84 per cent of the policewomen had CSE or GCE O-level qualifications. Policewomen generally had a higher number of each of these: over three-quarters (76 per cent) of the women surveyed had five or more compared with 69 per cent of policemen. However, the difference is more pronounced when GCE A-levels and degree qualifications are compared. Whilst 8 per cent of the policemen surveyed had A-levels and just under 2 per cent had a degree, the equivalent figures for policewomen were 27 per cent and 11 per cent respectively. As Table 3.3 demonstrates, the difference between men and women has widened since the Sex Discrimination Act.

TABLE 3.2 *Educational background of male and female recruits in 1982 (excluding Metropolitan Police)*

	Male		Female	
	(%)	(no.)	(%)	(no.)
No formal qualifications	10·8		4·2	
1–4 O-levels	32·4		27·9	
Total		1406		265
5 or more O-levels	33·8		41˙	
2 or more A-levels	12·5		13·2	
Degree	10·3		13·6	
Total		1845		560

The second point of interest concerns the period immediately after the Act. This was a time of considerable discontent with pay and conditions of service within the police, which only ended with the implementation of the Edmund-Davies recommendations in 1979. This discontent was manifest in the numbers of officers leaving the service. Although 15 349 male officers were appointed between 1976 and 1978 there was actually a net reduction in the total male strength of almost two thousand (1888). The total number of male officers who resigned during this period was 9822, almost 2000 more than in the previous three-year period. The percentage of the total male personnel resigning in each of the years 1976 to 1978 were 2.38 per cent, 3.89 per cent, and, 3.46 per cent respectively. This high turnover was mainly amongst constables but was exacerbated by an unusually high number of retirements. Just over 10 000 male officers retired over the period though it is difficult to assess just how many of these officers actively chose early retirement. As a rough guide, a comparison with the previous three years indicates that up to 4000 men may have chosen this option.

There was also a considerable turnover of female personnel at this time but estimating the number of resignations which were entirely due to the pay dispute is complicated by a number of factors. One of these has already been mentioned, namely, the uncertainty about integration which prompted some women to resign rather than face reorganisation. Another is the higher 'natural' wastage of female officers. As will be discussed later, marriage and child-bearing contribute to this higher rate of resignation amongst female officers. Also, given the relatively rapid increase in female personnel during the early 1970s, it would be expected that some of this increase would be for personal reasons of this kind if

TABLE 3.3 *Educational qualifications of male and female police officers by time of joining Medshire police*

	O-level or CSE		A-level		Degree	
	Male (%)	Female (%)	Male (%)	Female (%)	Male (%)	Female (%)
'Traditionals'	5	11	—	2	—	—
'Moderns'	86	100	16	40	5	17·5

only because of the higher proportion of women in the 'vulnerable' age-group. (Female recruits aged eighteen plus joining in 1970, 1971 and 1972, having served five to seven years, would have reached prime child-bearing years in the mid to late seventies). Altogether, 3585 women resigned during 1976–8 (12 per cent, 16 per cent and 14.9 per cent of the total female strength in each of the three years respectively) compared with 1943 in the previous three years. A further 207 women retired on pension compared with 135 retirements in the previous three years. Nevertheless, because of the increased number of appointments made (4873 between 1976 and 1978 compared with 2569 between 1973 and 1975) there was an overall net increase of about 1500 female officers during this period.

It would be naive to suppose that this initial surge of female recruitment was solely due to the implementation of the Sex Discrimination Act, since it happened at a time when not only were the levels of resignations and retirements high but male recruitment was lower than normal. Recruitment of male officers in 1977 dropped to 4329, lower than the 1974 level at a time when losses were high. Evidently the problems of pay and conditions of service, were also a deterrent to possible applicants at a time when the employment market was still relatively buoyant (compared with present conditions). For female applicants, given the generally lower average wage levels for women outside the police service, the equal pay and opportunities offered by the police service appeared relatively attractive. Many forces were struggling to recruit sufficient numbers and were recruiting women in an attempt to reach their establishment levels. (The underlying principle was much the same as in the war periods, though the effect was much less dramatic.) This use of female labour was most noticeable in the larger, metropolitan forces outside of London. In Greater Manchester women comprised 6.9 per cent of the total actual strength in 1975, a figure which rose to 8.8 per cent in 1976 and 11.3 per cent by 1978. Similarly, the figures for Merseyside for these three years were 7.6 per cent, 9.5 per cent and 11.1 per cent, and for the West Midlands 6.8 per cent, 8.4 per cent and 11 per cent.

Since the implementation of Edmund-Davies the recruitment situation has changed completely. Not only is the police service a relatively well-paid occupation (and this is enhanced by the index-linked annual awards which have protected police salaries at a time of general pay restraint), it also offers security at a time of uncertainty in the labour market. A cynical interpretation might be that the increase in the level of unemployment has had some positive effect, if only in guaranteeing an increasing market for police officers' law-enforcement skills. One of the officers interviewed in Medshire, expressing a commonly held view, quipped, '. . . more secure than ever. High unemployment means more crime and disorder, so we at least get to keep our jobs!' (Case No. MA02).

The consequence of the pay settlement was that recruitment increased markedly in 1979 with 7192 male and 1630 female officers appointed compared with 4963 and 1575 in the previous year. The numbers of male and female appointments made during this period can be seen in Table 3.4. Since the annual comparability of *actual* numbers

TABLE 3.4 *Police officer appointments made in England and Wales since the Sex Discrimination Act*

Year	Female (No.)	Female (% change)	Male (No.)	Male (% change)
1976	1 648	+ 40·8	6 057	− 4·0
1977	1 650	+ 0·1	4 329	− 28·5
1978	1 575	− 4·5	4 963	+ 14·6
1979	1 630	+ 3·5	7 192	+ 44·9
1980	1 384	− 15·0	6 318	− 12·0
1981	510	− 63·1	4 629	− 26·7
1982	854	+ 67·0	4 325	− 6·5

of officers appointed is affected by increases in authorised establishment, they are also displayed as *proportions* of all appointments made in Figure 3.1. This also includes the information for the five years immediately before the Act to demonstrate the trends in the data more clearly.

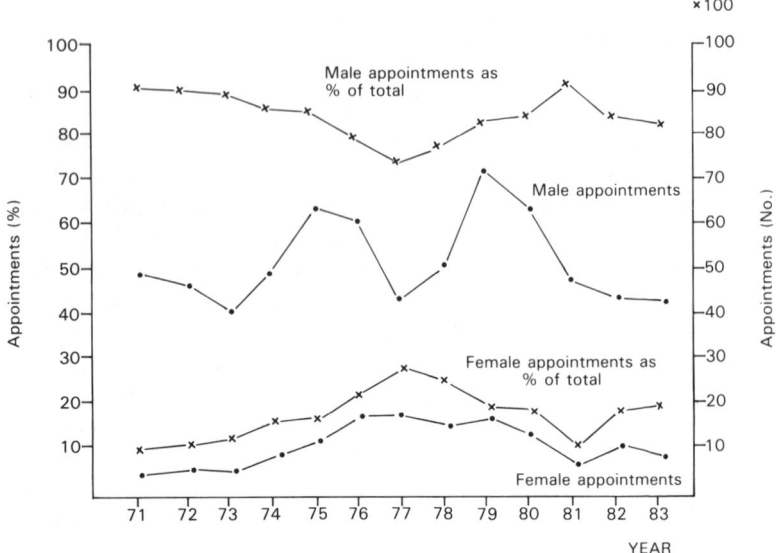

FIGURE 3.1.   Male and female appointments in the police service, 1971–83

Whilst the information displayed in the figure demonstrates a decrease in the actual number of male officers during the years immediately following the Act, it also shows that, except for an initial surge in female appointments at this time, the level remains fairly constant from 1976 to 1979 and then begins to fall off. However, what is noticeable, both from the figure and Table 3.4, is that they show that the improved pay and conditions of service resulted in a substantially greater recruitment of *male* rather than *female* police officers.

The increase in male appointments (2229) represented a 44.9 per cent rise over the previous year compared with a 3.5 per cent (55) increase in female officers for the same period. For the following two years (1980 and 1981) the appointment figures show that although the rate had slowed down from the 1979 peak, this also affected female recruitment more than male. Compared with 1979, 12 per cent fewer male officers were appointed in 1980 but 15 per cent fewer female officers. In 1981 the difference was more pronounced with 26.7 per cent fewer males and 63.1 per cent fewer females appointed than in 1980.

Some redress to this situation occurred in 1982 when 6.5 per cent fewer males were appointed but 67 per cent more females. But again it should be remembered that this apparent dramatic percentage increase only represents 344 more *actual* appointments over the 1981 figure. Indeed, as Figure 3.1 shows, the proportional increase in 1982 of 16.5 per cent and in 1983 of 18.7 per cent[4] is not substantially greater than in the two years before the Act, when female appointments accounted for 15 per cent and 15.6 per cent of the total made.

The general pattern which emerges from this examination of the national figures is one which indicates that the Act in itself has had comparatively little direct impact on the recruitment of female officers. While the abolition of separate female establishment figures did allow forces to recruit female officers in order to compensate for the higher rate of resignations, at a time when male recruitment was depressed, it is clear that once the 'crisis' was over and the police service became a relatively attractive occupation, male recruitment took precedence over that of female. This pattern of recruitment of female labour is not restricted to the police service. Traditionally female labour has been used when wage levels fail to attract male personnel.[5] There is also a relationship between high unemployment and a decline in the percentage of females in the labour market[6] and/or the relative proportion of women recruited.[7] What is of interest in the case of the police service is that this has happened almost in spite of legislation, introduced during the same period, which was specifically designed to disallow this.

LOCAL TRENDS

The increase in the proportion of female officers in the police service on a national basis (from 5.2 per cent at the end of 1975 to 8.5 per cent in 1982) masks considerable variation between the different forces in England and Wales. Thus, by the end of 1982, the proportion of female officers in the total actual strength had risen, for example, in the West Midlands Police by 6.5 per cent, in the Kent Constabulary by 5.6 per cent, and, in the Metropolitan Police by 5.2 per cent. By way of contrast, during the same period, the proportion had risen by only 0.1 per cent in the Durham Constabulary, 0.9 per cent in the Northamptonshire and Northumbria police forces and in Medshire by 0.8 per cent. Table 3.5 demonstates the distribution and range of this data for all forces in England and Wales. It is arranged in quartiles[8] in order to demonstrate the extent of local variation between forces.

As can be seen from the table, not only is there a wide range in the percentage increase since 1975 (with an average increase of 5 per cent for those forces in the first quartile, and only 1.4 per cent for those in

TABLE 3.5. *Relative growth in the proportion of women officers in England and Wales, 1975–82*

	Proportion of females in force 1975	(%)	1976	(%)	1978	(%)	1982	(%)	Overall increase (%)
1st Quartile									
Highest	Derbyshire	8.0	Merseyside	9.5	Greater Manchester	11.3	West Midlands	13.3	5.3
Lowest	Kent	4.9	Leicester	6.3	Surrey	8.2	Derbyshire	9.9	5.0
Mean		5.9		7.8		9.8		10.9	5.0
2nd Quartile									
Highest	West Yorkshire	6.6	West Yorkshire	9.8	Cleveland	9.9	West Yorkshire	9.9	3.6
Lowest	Metropolitan Police	4.1	Devon & Cornwall	6.2	Thames Valley	8.6	Devon & Cornwall	8.6	3.3
Mean		5.6		7.7		9.2		9.2	4.5
3rd Quartile									
Highest	Sussex	6.5	Cambridge	8.4	Bedfordshire	8.4	Bedfordshire	8.4	1.9
Lowest	Dyfed Powis	4.3	Hampshire	5.7	Hampshire	6.8	Dyfed Powis	6.8	2.5
Mean		4.6		7.0		7.7		7.7	3.1
4th Quartile									
Highest	Durham	6.4	Durham	6.7	Nottinghamshire	6.7	North Yorkshire	6.7	1.4
Lowest	Norfolk	3.7	Cumbria	4.4	Medshire	4.9	Medshire	4.9	0.8
Mean		5.1		5.9		6.2		6.2	1.7
Overall mean		5.2		6.3		7.6		8.5	3.3

the fourth quartile) but there was, in any case, a considerable variation in the proportion of women (from 3.2 per cent in Norfolk to 8.0 per cent in Derbyshire) in the forces just prior to integration.

Similarly, at the end of 1982, these proportions vary widely between forces, with 13.3 per cent in the West Midlands and just under 5 per cent in Medshire.[9] This latter figure puts this force in the bottom quartile of the table, along with Lincolnshire and Northumbria (6.1 per cent each) and Durham (6.2 per cent), and is lower than the national average proportion of women in the police *before* the Sex Discrimination Act.

Interestingly, all the forces in England and Wales (including those not shown in the table) increased their proportional female strength immediately prior to the Edmund-Davies settlement but in only fourteen forces was the increase between 1978 and 1982 *greater* than between 1976 and 1978. In twenty-eight forces the increase was *lower* between 1978 and 1982 (often substantially) and in nine of these forces the percentage of women in their actual strength was actually *less* than in 1978.

To summarise it is quite clear that both the proportion of female officers as a percentage of the total actual strength varied from force to force at the time of the Act, and that the subsequent rate of increase in female recruitment has also varied considerably. However, it is also apparent that the national trend in female recruitment (of a pre-Edmund-Davies bulge overtaken by greater male recruitment *after* the settlement) is not restricted to a few exceptional forces but is reflected by the majority of individual forces. The next section gives a more in-depth examination of local trends as exhibited in Medshire.

Trends in Medshire Police

As we have already seen, the proportion of women officers in Medshire places this force in the bottom quartile of the national distribution. At the end of 1982 the total authorised strength of the research force was about 3000, of whom just under 5 per cent were female. In the five-year period prior to integration the number of female officers increased from 2.6 per cent in 1971 to 4.1 per cent by the end of 1975, a rate of increase which is similar to several other forces such as the Metropolitan Police (2.9 per cent to 4.1 per cent), Devon and Cornwall (2.9 per cent to 4.4 per cent) and Gloucestershire (3.0 per cent to 4.8 per cent). However, since integration the rate of increase in Medshire force is the second lowest in England and Wales (at 0.8 per cent) and the force now has the lowest proportion of female officers (just over half of the national average of 8.5 per cent).

Medshire was also one of the few forces which did not dramatically increase female recruitment to compensate for the high turnover of personnel between 1977 and 1979, though some increase in female recruitment for this reason did occur in 1978 (See Table 3.6). Only about a dozen forces altogether had an increase of less than 1 per cent in their proportion of female officers during this period and, of these, only six had a less than 0.5 per cent increase. On balance, then, Medshire was very similar in its recruiting pattern to many other forces before integration, when the size of the policewomen's department was subject to separate establishment and inspection arrangements. However, the proportion of female officers in the force has subsequently grown at a comparatively slower rate than for most other forces.

TABLE 3.6 *Application and appointment statistics in Medshire since the Sex Discrimination Act*[22]

Year	Appointments as % of applications pursued		% applicants 'selected out' (education, age or physical)		Appointments as % of applications after 'selecting in' process	
	Male	Female	Male	Female	Male	Female
1976	34·0	10·9	21·0	31·8	65·6	75·0
1977	21·2	5·8	14·5	15·9	43·7	20·0
1978	23·8	14·3	36·8	43·6	65·7	39·7
1979	20·9	6·2	30·4	34·6	72·2	27·1
1980	10·3	3·9	20·0	20·3	53·6	19·2
1981	10·9	0·9	15·4	25·0	61·2	23·0
1982	6.3	6.2	18.8	18.3	45.8	41.5
Average	18·2	6·9	22·4	27·0	58·2	35·0

PRELIMINARY IMPLICATIONS OF NATIONAL AND LOCAL TRENDS

The main conclusions which may be drawn from these national and local figures are:
  (i) Not only have far fewer women officers been appointed in absolute terms but the proportion of females appointed is, even

allowing for fluctuations, actually declining from a peak reached in 1977.

(ii) It is possible to show that much of the extra female recruitment that has occurred would have done so for other reasons as policewomen's departments progressively increased their establishment.

(iii) The initial surge of female recruitment following the Act was mainly in response to an acute personnel shortage due to the pay dispute.

(iv) Since the Edmund-Davies settlement, male recruitment has dramatically outstripped that of females.

The fact that the proportion of females appointed has actually begun to decline since the Act raises the question of whether there is some form of internal mechanism which is consciously being used to limit the proportion of females in the total workforce. If so, the variability between forces suggests that this would be primarily the product of local autonomy and discretion in the recruitment process. The issue of whether or not these mechanisms, should they exist, result in effectively producing informal quotas which operate to restrict the proportion of women to a 'comfortable' (or comforting!) 10 per cent, follows from this initial question.

In this respect it is interesting to note that when the authors of the study of the Metropolitan Police, referred to earlier, indicated their belief in such an illegal quota, this was firmly denied. In explanation of the discrepancy between male and female appointments they consider it unlikely that there is a significant difference in the quality of male and female applicants. They state:

> In any case we have been told that it is 'unofficially' Force policy to keep the proportion of women in the Force down to about 10 per cent (which is roughly the present level).[10]

They note, however, that on current trends the proportion of women in the Metropolitan Police would rise to about 25 per cent within ten years if there were no discrimination in selection as a result of this unofficial policy. Of even more note is the fact that several months after the publication of the study it was announced in the House of Commons that 'the commissioner dropped the restrictive quota on the recruitment of women last December'.[11] Clearly it would seem that, at least until the results of this study, the Metropolitan Police have been operating some form of recruiting mechanism which regulates the intake of females.

Outside of the Metropolitan Police, the figures also suggest the existence of some local form of regulatory mechanism. If this is the case, there remains the issue of identifying how, and at which stage in the recruitment process, it occurs. The local nature of the mechanism suggests that it is a function of 'selecting in' procedures which operate independently of national policy embodied in either the Sex Discrimination Act or the selection criteria arising from the statutory regulations. In order to analyse the possible nature of this 'selecting in' process and the way in which it can be used to achieve this regulatory function, it is first necessary to examine the philosophy, strategy and issues underlying the recruitment process.

SELECTION PHILOSOPHY, STRATEGY AND ISSUES

(i)   'One Point of Entry'

All recruits into the police service join as police constables and, following an initial training course of fourteen weeks (plus a Local Procedures course of about two weeks and a series of three Progress and Monitoring courses) serve a two-year probationary period.[12] This 'one point of entry'[13] system has its origins in the policy formulated in 1829 by Rowan and Mayne, the first two commissioners of the Metropolitan Police. Apart from establishing minimum recruitment standards as regards age, height, physique, character and education, they made it a deliberate policy to recruit men 'who had not the rank, habits or station of gentlemen'. There was to be 'no caste system as in the Army or Navy', and promotion to higher rank was to be given to men from within the service. The rate of pay was deliberately fixed at a level low enough to deter ex-officers.[14]

The fact that all police officers have begun their careers on the beat as constables is seen as a virtue in the police service. Although an officer entry scheme was introduced by Lord Trenchard in 1934 in order to recruit a limited number of more highly qualified personnel, it did not last and ended in 1939. The idea of direct entry at inspector level has been suggested since, but has been consistently rejected on the grounds that the creation of an 'officer class' could have a disruptive effect on relations between ranks. In order to overcome this objection, while at the same time recruiting potential 'command quality' personnel, a special scheme for graduate entrants was introduced. This guarantees a place on the Special Course (run at the Bramshill Staff College) and accelerated promotion to inspector for a limited number of graduates (usually 25–30 per year), providing they successfully complete their probationary period as constables and pass their examination to sergeant rank at the first attempt. However, the scheme retains the essential traditional element, that of all officers serving as constables on the beat.

The necessity and desirability of this 'one point of entry' is further justified on the grounds that (i) the position of the constable is itself an office of unique responsibility, and (ii) only officers with experience of basic patrol duties can have sufficient understanding as a supervisory officer to lead the officers under his command. In relation to the uniqueness of the office of constable, the recruitment literature prepared by the Home Office in 1979 states:

> Well educated young men and women considering a police career are often surprised that they can only join at the lowest rank, as a police constable. But the constable has a key role in all police operations and unlike the lowest ranks of, for example, the armed services, has considerable freedom of action and does not simply act under orders. Each officer, as holder of an independent office of trust, is personally responsible for enforcing the law and must take decisions that the situation requires.

It is clear from this statement that the discretionary element of the police officer's role is seen to put him apart from the Armed Forces in that it requires the use of independent initiative.

The central importance of the second point, emphasising the value of experience as a necessary prerequisite to leadership is demonstrated by the graduate recruiting literature produced in 1982:

> In order to develop the necessary qualities of leadership for the future you will need a sound training in the everyday problems of police-work. And it is for this reason that *all* police officers start their careers as constables.

The 'one point of entry' policy of recruitment is therefore seen to have the combined virtues of egalitarianism, recognition of the uniqueness of the office of constable and perpetuation of the subculturally valued notion of 'learning through experience'.

(ii) The Dual Function

Whatever the benefits in terms of working relationships between ranks and the development of leadership qualities, this policy has implications for the procedures of police officer selection and poses some interesting problems. These arise out of the dual function inherent in the recruitment and selection strategy. On the one hand, the hierarchical structure of the police organisation is such that the majority of entrants will remain in the lower ranks throughout their career. On the other hand, the same selection procedure has also to ensure that sufficient people are recruited who have the qualities and potential to rise through the ranks up to and including that of chief officer.

The selection process thus has to cover a broad spectrum of ability and potential, within the context of a disciplined service. It has to ensure that the majority of those selected are able to fulfil a wide range of day-to-day police duties, ranging from the mundane to the extraordinary, whilst at the same time generating a pool of potential managers. The disciplined nature of the organisation requires that recruits should be willing to act under orders from senior officers, often without question as, for example, in public order situations; but, paradoxically, the considerable discretion inherent in the role of constable also implies the ability to act independently and with initiative.

In addition to these seemingly contradictory qualities, the limited promotion opportunities require that the selection process also identifies those officers as being, in the main, *content* to serve in the lower ranks. Certainly, the consequences of a recruitment drive in the mid-seventies which offered the prospect of a professional 'career' is itself becoming a focus of concern within the police service as it becomes increasingly difficult for people to fulfil their career expectations. It is somewhat ironic that the surge in recruitment, following the favourable pay award recommended by Edmund-Davies, should have compounded the problem by attracting a substantial number of highly qualified recruits into the service with possibly more ambition and heightened career expectations. This trend towards better qualified personnel has been accelerated by the fact that most forces are currently up to their establishment figures and are only recruiting minimum numbers.

The subsequent contraction of the labour market has also had an effect on the police service by producing a relatively stable employment situation and comparatively stagnant career patterns, as evidenced by a lower turnover of personnel and fewer promotion opportunities. This reduction in promotion opportunities has been exacerbated by the increasing financial restraints now being applied to the police service. The quest for efficiency and effectiveness means that chief officers will be denied any increase in formal establishments unless they can show that their personnel are being properly deployed.

At the same time as the decline in recruitment, relatively favourable rates of pay have made it more difficult for police officers to find equally well-paid occupations outside of the police service, (in turn exercerbated by a shrinking job market governed by the laws of supply and demand), so there are less opportunities for the ambitious officer. The importance of selection of officers who are content to remain in the lower ranks obviously becomes more of an issue against this economic background, but is further complicated by the effects of the progressive downgrading of the beat officers' role during the mid-sixties to the late-seventies.

As argued elsewhere[15] the trend in policing during this time was towards the development of a professional self-image which stressed the technically efficient aspects of the role of the police officer. Specialisation became an essential integral part of this police self-image. Whilst it was possible to use specialisation as an accepted and acceptable substitute for promotion and as a means of job-enrichment (and, indeed, this was encouraged), this is no longer the case. In the wake of Scarman, the prevailing zeitgeist is that of community involvement which requires a return to the generalist role which, over the last two decades, has become systematically devalued. The problem now being faced is how to enhance the status of the beat officer given the combination of selection, economic and attitudinal factors which have, in the past, generated discontent with the basic patrol officer's 'lot'.

(iii) Selection and Representation

Added to all these factors is the overriding consideration restated by Scarman that the recruitment and selection process should ensure that 'the composition of our police forces must reflect the make-up of the society they serve'.[16] Although his comments were made specifically in relation to the under-representation of members of minority ethnic groups within the police service, they might legitimately be applied to the recruitment of women into the police. However, this presupposes that this concern reflects a desire (all other things being held constant) for equitable proportional representation.

It could be argued that this desire will be dependent on the subtle distinction, discussed in Chapter 2, which can be drawn between 'serve' and 'control', and whether in reality service to the community takes precedence over control. In the former case, there would seem at the very least to be compatibility with the notion of equitable representation. The 'control' concept, however, fits more comfortably into the symbolic imagery associated with the 'order-maintaining function' and which, as we have seen, is assumed to be the 'natural' prerogative of the male. Certainly, our previous examination of this topic indicates a wealth of evidence to suggest that although the service function constitutes a major part of the police role, primacy is given both in attitude and reality to control and order maintenance.

In terms of its implications for the recruitment of women (and a similar thread of argument could be applied to the colonial, patriarchal attitude extended by the dominant white male group towards some minority ethnic groups), the ascendency of the notion of 'control' rather than 'service' would be such as to shape the choice of selection criteria. Conceivably, even objective criteria based on characteristics associated with 'control' (such as physical strength, height, etc.) could put certain groups, including women, at a disadvantage. When considered in combination with prejudicial attitudes, either unconscious or conscious, the catalytic effect could be such as to transform disadvantage into discriminatory practice. The issue to be addressed is whether the recruitment and selection process *does* involve an element of disadvantage due to the *de facto* importance placed upon 'control' rather than 'service' in the objective and subjective criteria used for selection; and whether recruiting officers do have the discretion implied by national and local figures on female recruitment and; consciously or unconsciously, use it to evaluate the qualities they subjectively believe to be required of the 'good' police officer.

(iv) Objective Selection Criteria

It is evident even from the brief discussion above that there are problems in establishing selection criteria which: (i) adequately fulfil the multiple and often conflicting expectations inherent both in the dual function of recruitment policy and in the nature of the police officer's role; and (ii) are free from biases which could lead to disadvantage. The approach generally adopted, both at a national and local level, has been initially to use what appear go be objective criteria to 'select out' rather than to 'select in'. Thus, at a national level, recruitment into the police service is governed by the Police Regulations 1979, and the qualifications for appointment are governed by Regulation 14. These cover character references (and require that the applicant must give information regarding previous history or employment), lower and upper age limits, physical and mental fitness, height, and educational standards. Regulations 12 and 13 also prohibit (except at the discretion of the Chief Officer) the appointment of people with certain business interests in the force area or who have close relatives with business interests. Regulations 12, 13 and 14 are given in Appendix B.

Some of these regulations clearly 'select out' certain members of the population, such as those relating to height and age (particularly the upper age limit, which is set at 30 years) unless the applicant has previous whole-time service in the Armed Forces or as a seaman, when the limit is set at 40 years). Thus, in the case of the height requirement, for which the police service is exempt from the Sex Discrimination Act under Section 17, the Regulations state that:

> A candidate for appointment to a police force . . . must, . . . unless the chief officer of police otherwise decides, be not less in height than, in the case of a man 172 cms, or in the case of a woman, 162 cms.

So although a candidate may be suitable in all other respects he/she will not, except at the discretion of the chief officer be selected. In practice, chief officers have used this power to raise, rather than to lower, the height requirements for their own forces so that some forces have higher height requirements than others. For example, the City of London requires that men shall be 180 cm (5 ft 11 in), and women 167.5 cm (5 ft 6 in). In effect this regulation 'selects out' a large proportion of the population, which might contain 'suitable material', right at the beginning of the selection procedure and actually puts members of some groups at a disadvantage. For example, the average height of women is less than that of men, and therefore raising the height limit by the *same* amount for men and women means the pool to recruit from is automatically reduced more for women than for men. So that although it is possible that the exemption was conceived of as positive action, in *reality* the discretion this allows police forces can (and is) used to minimise this effect.

The actual validity of the height requirement as an objective selection criterion is questionable, however, since it is based on the professional opinion, from within the police, that 'shorter men are unfitted to perform duty in the streets, since they lack the necessary air of authority'[17] and rests on the untested presupposition that height and the qualitative (and probably unmeasurable) variable, 'air of authority' are strongly and positively correlated. The relationship between height and 'air of authority' has, interestingly, an almost implicit 'control' dimension. Also, quite apart from the difficulties of measurement and the questionable deduction that certain heights go with certain levels of authority, there are well known historical precedents which run contrary to this supposition.

The height regulation is used here merely as an illustration of criteria which 'select out' and which may not have the validity attributed to them. 'Selecting out' is not unique to the police service but forms an essential part of many selection procedures in both the public and private sector of industry. However, the important point about such criteria is that they should be shown to be closely related to the ability to actually perform the job and not presumed to be related to qualitative aspects of job performance which have not been objectively assessed as necessary.

In the case of the police service, although there are some grounds for questioning the job-relatedness of some of the statutory selection criteria (and, in fact, some groups may consequently be at an automatic disadvantage), they do generally ensure some national uniformity by individual forces in the way they 'select out' unsuitable applicants. Presumably, there is also a process of self-selection as a result of the advertising and recruitment literature, which ensures that the majority of applicants fulfil these basic standard requirements. Whilst, as noted previously, there may be no reason to suppose that women are normally less self-selecting than men, some factors do have a determining effect.

Advertising itself can significantly influence the type of person who applies for a particular job, and can attract members of one sex rather than the other. In the context of the police, the slogan adopted in the national campaign of 1980, four years after the implementation of the Act, 'Does the man make the job, or does the job make the man?', would not seem, in terms of self-selection, to be very effective in making the police service equally attractive to both women and men! (See Appendix B).

Although national figures on the self-selection issue are not available, in Medshire it was found that less than 19 per cent of those whose applications were processed[18] in 1982 (a total of 1634 males and females) were selected *out* on the basis of the standard age, education and physical requirements. What this also means is that there is considerable local responsibility for selecting police recruits. Evidently, the 'selecting in' procedure at local level is very important in determining who is appointed, and this is discussed in more detail presently.

At this local level there may also be additional 'objective' criteria, so that, in the case of the research force the minimum Home Office requirements with regard to health/physique[19] are accepted but a higher than minimum educational standard is set. In other words, unless exempt by possession of recognised educational qualifications, a candidate for appointment is required to obtain a score of at least 100 on the standard entrance examination (Police Initial Recruitment Test), compared with the Home Office minimum of 85. Current force policy also dictates that, with the exception of applications made under the graduate entry scheme, applicants must reside in the force area.[20]

It is at the local level that enquiries 'as to the candidate's suitability, attitude to work and life in general are made with referees, schools, previous employers and police of the area in which he resides or has resided previously'. Convictions of a criminal nature also 'select out' though this is to some extent dependent upon the nature of the offence and the time that has elapsed since the conviction. All candidates, unless they fail the standard entrance examination or the medical examination, are 'given the benefit of an interview'. Local responsibility for selection can, therefore, apply in up to 80 per cent of all applications received.

(v) The Selection Interview

At the selection interview different criteria are used for assessing candidates and there is also a change in the way this assessment is conducted. Although the composition of the interview panel is laid down by the Home Office Code of Practice on Selection Procedures and the members are trained to the required Home Office standard,[21] the selection criteria are essentially qualitative and are used to 'select in' rather than 'out'. In other words, rather than candidates being excluded because they do not meet the required standards, they are now included if they are assessed as having the desired qualities. The responsibility for specifying desirable qualities in a police officer is that of the local force and they are derived from the multiple expectations of the constable's role already discussed. In Medshire they are detailed in the Recruitment Policy document:

> ... when the interviewing panel looks at a potential recruit they are looking for a person who:
> accepts discipline,
> accepts responsibility,

shows a willingness to learn,
shows personal integrity,
can take decisions on his/her own initiative,
displays intelligence and common-sense,
has good judgement,
has a well-balanced personality,
is tolerant of people from differing backgrounds,
has the ability to influence and motivate others.

The interview form used to assess these qualities is given in Appendix B. At first sight it would seem fairly evident from this list of desirable qualities (and the specific criteria representing them on the interview form) that none of them apparently reflect a local emphasis on the 'control' rather than 'service' distinction discussed in Chapter 2; nor do they appear to put female applicants at a disadvantage. However, they are highly subjective in nature and thus assessments of candidates' suitability at the selection interview are open to the exercise of discretion.

It is important to emphasise that the point about these criteria is not that they are necessarily invalid or that they are exclusive to the police service; merely that their subjectivity indicates a high level of discretion at the disposal of the recruitment staff. Also, it is clear that the accuracy of the assessment could be open to criticism. Both these factors must be borne in mind when considering the differential 'success' rates of male and female applicants. Two arguments arise from this discretionary flexibility:

(i) It is this considerable discretionary element at the local level which has the greatest influence on the choice of recruits since it determines the way in which these subjective criteria are translated and applied.

(ii) There are other unwritten, possibly subliminal, criteria which because of this discretion and the inherently subjective nature of the local selection interview can be, and are, applied.

Since, as we have seen, the statutory regulations account for such a small proportion of those applicants who are *not* recruited (by the process of selecting out) they are evidently less significant overall than the qualitative criteria used at force level to 'select in'. Consequently they have less relative impact on female recruitment. Support for the argument that it is the use of subjective criteria to 'select in' candidates which regulates the level of female intake is provided by an examination of the applications and appointments made in Medshire.

As can be seen from Table 3.6, female applicants are only marginally more likely than males to be rejected on standard educational, physical or age requirements. Since integration, an average of 22 per cent of male and 27 per cent of female applications have been 'selected out' for these reasons. Nevertheless, the number of actual appointments made as a percentage of applications 'actually pursued' (some applications are withdrawn or no further action is taken by the applicant) shows that fewer female applications are successful. On average since integration, 18 per cent of male compared with just under 7 per cent of female applications result in appointment. These are similar proportions as reported by Smith and Gray in their study of the Metropolitan Police which examined the selection process. They found that the discrepancy in the Metropolitan Police arises *before* the selection board. Applicants in the Metropolitan Police have, according to Smith and Gray, roughly the same chance of being selected once they go before a selection board. They suggest that in the Metropolitan Police 'stiffer criteria are applied to female than to male applicants at the stages of selection prior to the interview.'[23]

In other words, in terms of the Sex Discrimination Act the Metropolitan Police appeared to be directly discriminating against women applicants, since under S.1 (1)(a) women applicants were being treated, on the grounds of sex, less favourably than male applicants. As part of the preliminary work to the present study, several interviews were conducted with women officers in the Metropolitan Police. One fairly senior officer mentioned that she believed that an additional, more stringent paper sift of women applicants was conducted before the selection board stage. This would be in line with the findings of Smith and Gray.

In the case of the present study, however, the 'extra' stringency for women applicants occurs at the interview. Since the difference in successful applications is not due, as we have already seen, to a disproportionate number of females failing to meet standard requirements at the pre-interview stage, as in the Smith and Gray study, then it follows that it is the result of local selection procedures. This is hardly surprising, given the recruitment policy of the force researched here which aims to give interviews to all the applicants who meet the minimum regulations. When the number of appointments made is calculated as a percentage of all those eligible applicants[24] after the 'selecting out' process is complete, the influence of the local procedure becomes apparent.

As can be seen from Table 3.6, since 1976 an average of 35 per cent of female compared with 58 per cent of male applications are successful after the local 'selecting in' stage of the recruitment process. In some years, particularly immediately after the pay settlement, male applications were almost three times more likely to result in appointment. Thus, in 1979, the proportion of appointments as a percentage of applications was 72 per cent for males compared with only 27 per cent for females. The pattern revealed in the table suggests a strong relationship between the increase of male, rather than female, recruitment and the improved attractiveness of the police service as an occupation. The figures obviously raise the issue of whether this is the result of discrimination in the application of local qualitative criteria, and whether it is due to the effect of recruiting officers' attitudes on the discretion they are able to exercise. On the evidence of this examination of the data there are positive grounds to support the idea that recruiting officers do have sufficient discretion to influence the selection of recruits; and we have already seen what impact this has, despite the Sex Discrimination Act, on female recruitment.

SUMMARY AND IMPLICATIONS

This analysis of the national and local trends in recruitment demonstrate quite clearly that despite appearances to the contrary, female recruitment has not increased dramatically as a result of the Sex Discrimination Act. Indeed other factors, and in particular the pay dispute of the late seventies, has had a far more substantial, though temporary, influence on female appointments.

The considerable variation that exists in the proportion of female officers between forces indicates that local autonomy and discretion is used to regulate the numbers of females within individual forces. The consequence of this discretionary practice is an informal (but unlawful) quota system which operates at a local level. In the forces outside London, the selecting-in stage of the recruitment process is where this discretion can be effectively and invisibly used. This is particularly true of the interview when qualitative judgements are made about a candidate's suitability, and this was certainly the case in the force studied. The question which remains, and which is discussed in Chapter 7, concerns the beliefs and the nature of the attitudes which underlie this differential use of discretion.

4 Doing 'the Job'

The earlier examination of recruitment amply demonstrates the way in which local autonomy and the consequent discretion allowed in recruitment and selection can generate informal organisational practices which circumvent the equal opportunities legislation. The effect of this is, as we have seen, to restrict the number of women joining the service. This chapter is concerned with what happens to those men and women who do become police officers, and examines the experience of doing 'the job'.

Focusing on the constraints and dilemmas which surround the employment of women in the service, it seeks to compare and contrast the expectations, experiences and attitudes of men and women actually employed on police duties. Deployment issues are examined from the point of view of the impact that the provisions of the Act have had on the role of policewomen. As such it examines the extent to which the operational role of women has changed in reality as a result of integration. Because of their symbolic importance, part of this examination will inevitably be concerned with those attitudes and beliefs which are cited by police officers as ritual 'evidence' of the unsuitability of women for an equal role in policing. However, whilst these will contribute to the substance of this commentary, a fuller discussion of the nature and extent of these attitudes is postponed until Chapter 7. The practical issue dealt with here is the role which women both want and/or are able to fulfil since the Act and whether the reality of integration matches these expectations.

As discussed earlier, the legislation had considerable implications for the police service. In effect, it meant that there was no longer to be any distinction between the way in which men and women were deployed on police duties. Instead of being specialists in those tasks felt to be suitable to the 'feminine nature', women were to be employed as generalists undertaking all aspects of police work, including patrol duties. In effect, the Act represented the first legal redefinition of the policewoman's role since her formal acceptance into the service, even though some limited extension had already begun in a piecemeal fashion in various individual forces. Nevertheless, it paved the way for integration and meant the abolition of the traditional division of duties; duties which were rooted in the classic stereotype of the feminine gender role, originally fought for and accepted by policewomen over half a century earlier.

The feelings that prevailed nationally at the time of integration have already been discussed, and at this stage it is important to restate the fact that many women as well as male officers were against the change. The various reasons for policewomen's opposition have been discussed in Chapter 1. However, before going on to examine the reality of integration in Medshire it seems pertinent to establish current feelings towards the change even though, as Lock has commented, 'some women like integration; others do not. Just how it is working is another story'.[1] At the very least this will allow some evaluation at a local level of the degree to which integration has been accepted, as well as providing a backdrop against which deployment issues can be considered. It will also allow an examination of any change of attitudes between those men and women who joined the service before integration and those who have joined since. It will allow a test of the hypothesis that recent male recruits share their older male colleagues attitudes which, in turn, are less positive towards a fully integrated role for women than those of female police officers. Indeed, the way in which 'it is working' may to some extent depend upon the degree to which integration has been accepted.

ROLE PREFERENCES

For comparative purposes the role preference questions developed by Southgate[2] and included in his questionnaire survey of policewomen in five police forces (Merseyside, Hampshire, Durham, North Wales and Wiltshire) were used. This survey was conducted in 1977 in order to assess the views of policewomen (no policemen were surveyed) towards integration. It compared the replies of women who had joined before and after the implementation of the Act. By comparing this data with information from the present study, some estimate of the way in which attitudes have changed can be made.

As shown in Table 4.1, a third of all the men and women surveyed in Medshire were in favour of a fully integrated role for women, compared with 40 per cent in favour of a modified role (in which women take on similar duties to men except where violence is anticipated). Only just under a quarter (24.6 per cent) felt that women should specialise in traditional duties concerning women and children. However, as the table also demonstrates, there are considerable differences between male and female officers' views on this issue. Almost 58 per cent of the women but only 23 per cent of the male officers felt that women should have a fully integrated role. This proportion of women does, in fact, represent quite a change in the degree of acceptance compared with the 1977 survey conducted by Southgate. Two years after the implementation of the Act, only 31 per cent of his sample were in favour of a fully integrated role, with the majority (47 per cent) in favour of a modified role. There was little support then (22 per cent) and even less at the time of the present research for a return to the traditional specialist role. Most of the policemen in the present survey preferred a modified role for women (46 per cent) and a substantial 30 per cent were in favour of the traditional role. There is clearly a marked difference in male and female views about the role women should fulfil which is statistically significant, yielding a χ^2 value of 41.4 (d.f. = 2). Also, on the basis of the comparison exercise, it is clear that there has been a substantial change in policewomen's views over the last six years. No doubt some of this change is due to the increased proportion of women who have joined since integration and who, it could reasonably be expected, joined because of the prospect of equal opportunities in pay and conditions of service.

It might also be expected that women who joined the service before integration would be more in favour of either the traditional role or the modified role than those who joined in expectation of a fully integrated role. Just under 43 per cent of the female respondents in this survey joined the service before integration and although this was the case, there was still considerable support amongst 'traditionals' (48 per cent) for a fully integrated role, compared with 65 per cent of the 'moderns'. This difference in views of the preferred female role was not significant, yielding a χ^2 value of 3.44 (d.f. = 2). Again, the difference between the earlier survey and the present research is quite evident since in that survey only 27 per cent of pre-Act intake, and 36 per cent of post-Act intake, preferred this role. Whilst there was more support amongst longer-serving women for the traditional role (17 per cent) than among their younger female colleagues (9.5 per cent), both these figures represent a decline in support for this role since 1977.

TABLE 4.1 *Male and female role preferences[3] for policewomen, whole sample and by time of joining (Southgate data included for comparison)*

	Whole sample 349 (%)	Total			'Traditionals'			'Moderns'		
		M (%)	F (%)	1977 680 (%)	M (%)	F (%)	1977 409 (%)	M (%)	F (%)	1977 271 (%)
N										
Fully integrated role	33	23	58	31	20	48	27	29	65	36
N		55	63							
Modified role	40	46	29	47	43	35	45	53	25	49
N		111	32							
Traditional role	25	30	16	22	36	17	26	18	9·5	15
N		73	14							
Don't know	0·3	0·4	—	—	0·6	—	2	—	—	—

Altogether 68.4 per cent of the policemen who completed a questionnaire had joined the service before integration and as expected almost twice as many of these officers were in favour of a traditional role (36 per cent) than those policemen who joined after the Act. However, the majority of both these groups were in favour of a modified role for policewomen. More 'moderns' (53 per cent) than 'traditionals' (43 per cent) felt this way. This could possibly be because these officers, being younger and lower in the hierarchy, are at the 'front line' of policing, and are consequently more involved and committed to the sub-cultural mores that stress action, physical strength and courage, loyalty and masculine prowess. This modified concept of the policewoman's role is not, however, shared by their female colleagues. Only 25 per cent of the women who joined after the Act would prefer a modified role. So whilst there is slightly more support amongst younger male officers for a fully integrated role than amongst their older pre-integration male colleagues, and little support either for the traditional role, this group also differs substantially from both groups of policewomen. Indeed, χ^2 comparisons demonstrate significant differences between both groups of male and female officers ($\chi^2 = 14.5$, d.f. = 2, for 'traditionals', and, $\chi^2 = 18.6$, d.f. = 2, for 'moderns').

PREFERRED ROLE OPTIONS: MALE AND FEMALE VIEWPOINTS

The difference between male and female officers is highlighted by their responses to a question concerning the re-establishment of policewomen's departments. Male opinion was split between a fully integrated role for women (35 per cent), the re-establishment of the old-style policewomen's departments with a separate career structure (37 per cent) and, the establishment of a specialist department staffed by male and female officers, though this latter option had less support at 26 per cent. By way of contrast, as Table 4.2 demonstrates, only 11 per cent of the women surveyed wished to see the return of policewomen's departments, though 35 per cent supported the idea of a specialist department staffed by males and females. Overall, this difference between men and women was statistically significant, yielding a χ^2 value of 25.5 (d.f. = 2). As Table 4.2 also shows, there was some slight (but, given a χ^2 value of 1.9, d.f. = 2, not significant) difference in preferences between the two groups of male officers with more 'moderns' choosing full integration rather than the re-establishment of policewomen's departments.

TABLE 4.2 *Prefered role options in Medshire*

	Both (%)	Total Male (%)	Female (%)	'Traditionals' Male (%)	Female (%)	'Moderns' Male (%)	Female (%)
Fully integrated role	41	35	53	33	32	40	68
Old style policewomen's department	29	37	11	40	13	31	9·5
New style department staffed by · men and women	29	26	35·5	25	55	29	21

What is noticeable from this table is the difference between the two groups of policewomen. Although neither group would wish, given the choice, to see the return of the old-style departments, the 'traditional' policewomen evidently feel the need for some kind of specialist department to take on the tasks concerned with women and children. (This difference between the two groups is significant giving ($\chi^2 = 16.0$, d.f. = 2). Some of the reasons for this perceived need are discussed in more depth later on in this chapter. In fact, about two-thirds of both male and female officers with pre-integration experience would opt for some kind of specialist department, the difference in opinion being about its form and staffing. There is, in this respect, a much wider discrepancy amongst younger male and female officers, with 31 per cent of males with no actual pre-integration experience nevertheless choosing to see the re-establishment of policewomen's departments, compared with only 9.5 per cent of their female counterparts.

Of those police officers interviewed, over half (52 per cent) were also against the re-establishment of policewomen's departments but for a variety of reasons. It is clear from these that it is the practicalities and personal implications which are of paramount importance rather than any ideological commitment to equality, though one atypical 'modern' policeman was worried about issues of this kind. He believed that, as a matter of informal policy, policewomen were not allowed a fully integrated role, and that they were still mainly used to fulfil duties associated with their traditional role. He made the observation that even if a specialist department staffed nominally by men and women was created:

> I think you would have policewomen being moved into that particular department ... I think it would be retrograde to the women. It might benefit the police force, in its way, but I think the women would suffer. (Case No. AM08)

Other reasons for opposition, however, were less altruistic and ranged from the practical and operational difficulties associated with taking women off reliefs, etc. and finding the manpower to replace them, to the monotony involved in dealing with the same kind of work (i.e. women's work) all the time. As one female constable, with five years' service, explained:

> I don't like the idea of a policewomen's department. I think if I just had to deal with juveniles and females I'd go potty. That's all they used to do. I didn't join the job to work 9 to 5 ... I think if I had to go into a policewomen's department I would leave. (Case No. AF03)

Another 'modern' woman officer gave a similar explanation but also commented on the excitement of not knowing what might happen from day to day – a theme that runs through many of the male officers' interviews in the different context of the attractions of policework.

As with the survey, more women were against re-establishment than men (62 per cent of all those against were women), though most of these women, particularly those who joined before integration, were concerned about the way 'traditional' tasks are now performed, a sentiment echoed by the only 'traditional' woman, with twenty-one years' service, who thought that policewomen's departments should be re-established. Asked how she felt at the time of integration, she said:

> we didn't want it. It meant that the department, which as I say was a specialist department, was being disbanded. I think we felt that the force was losing a valuable asset, and I think if you look at the other forces, some of them realise that they have lost a valuable asset, and I think they've partly reintroduced that department, but not solely as a policewomen's department. They have men working in there as well. (Case No. BF03)

She felt that since integration her work was less interesting, she was more office bound and had less chance to meet the public. However, even this officer would see a re-established department having a wider role than previously. Her concern was also shared by a male officer (who joined before integration) who was, nevertheless, against re-establishment. He said:

> What I think was wrong was to do away with it completely. I felt it worked, perhaps I was wrong ... It was always handy to get in touch with a PW to take a statement in relation to indecency cases. I think also a lot of the older PWs are far more capable of taking statements in relation to indecency cases than the younger PWs because they had more experience of it. (Case No. BM03)

Generally speaking most of the 'traditional' policewomen would share this officer's concern about the way these tasks are now performed, whilst at the same time not wishing to see the return of the women's departments. However, many of them also recognised some personal drawbacks as a result of integration but felt that on the whole they were better off (and not just financially). For example, a long-serving woman sergeant felt that integration had meant that women had lost out by having to work longer shifts but that this was compensated for by the opportunities for women to deal with various aspects of police work. She said:

> I think if we would have stayed as a WPC department we'd have been so specialised they wouldn't have given you the opportunity to try anything. But with integration I think it's good and bad. It widened everyone's horizons and gives you more opportunity for everything.

Included in the bad aspects was the 'bitchiness' that women had to put up with from the men. In her own words:

> They said women will never work on the same money, they will never do the same shifts and they'll never do the same jobs. But we've done it . . . It used to take the cream off it, you know, when you feel, 'Oh I've done a good job there', and you get a bit of bitchiness, such as, 'Oh yes, so and so done that, and a man would have done it better', and *you* know there was no improvement to be made. (Case No. BF11)

Some of the arguments used by the men about integration reflect this male attitude. For example, the 'equal pay, equal work' argument was used by men both for and against re-establishment. On the one hand the argument was 'women don't do the same work, they can't, but at the moment they get the same pay', implying both that they should be in a separate department dealing with work they can manage and that this should be accompanied by a reduction in their pay. The alternative argument was that since they *are* getting the same pay, they should be *made* to do the same work and suffer the same discomforts! One officer was particularly distressed by what he felt was an unfair pension advantage[4] enjoyed by policewomen which, in effect, meant that they were better paid than men.

The other reasons for re-establishment given by men (three 'moderns' and one 'traditional') also concerned women's ability to perform all police duties. One officer felt that general duties could be too gory for women, particularly road traffic accidents, and that they 'show their emotions more than blokes'. Adding, 'it's going to get worse crime-wise before it gets better', he felt that, on balance, 'I think we could do with a woman police department where they could be on call if we needed them' (Case No. AF07).

Only a minority of all those interviewed (12.5 per cent) were in favour of a specialist department staffed by both male and female officers. An equal number were undecided or uncommitted, including one exceptionally cynical CID constable who remarked rather caustically that he had not noticed any change at all in the role of policewomen as a result of integration, and that they were probably doing as little now as they did before!

Generally, then, current feelings about integration are that most women accept it and would not want a return to the previous limited regime, for personal, career and practical reasons. Some older women are concerned, however, about the loss of expertise but feel that this could be compensated for by a specialist department staffed by men and women. Policemen, on the other hand, were less in favour of such a department and were more likely, particularly the younger officers, to want re-establishment. Their reasons appear to reflect their perception of women's all-round ability as police officers. However, the majority do accept integration though they feel this should involve a modified role for policewomen. The attitudes underlying this perception are discussed in more depth in Chapter 7.

PATTERNS AND EXPERIENCES OF DEPLOYMENT

Having established that, in principle, integration is accepted by the majority of policemen and policewomen, the next step is to examine what it means in practice. There are two aspects to this. The first concerns the actual numbers of men and women deployed on various police duties such as patrol, traffic and CID, etc., and the second concerns the experiences of policemen and women deployed on tasks associated with these roles.

(i) Current Deployment Patterns

Women were, of course, increasingly employed on tasks other than those traditionally associated with policewomen's departments before the Sex Discrimination Act and, indeed, some were employed in departments such as the CID, the Fraud Squad and other prestigious specialist occupations. Nevertheless, in theory the Act meant that not only should the range of their day-to-day patrol duties be considerably increased to cover all those previously exclusively[5] performed by men but that women should have the same opportunities for employment in specialist departments. In other words, the Act should have increased both the range of their role occupations and the qualitative nature of their duties.

Unfortunately, it is not possible to compare the actual deployment of policemen and women immediately before the Act and at present, either nationally or in the research force, because of the problems of record-keeping. No national figures are available from the HMI reports, and the Home Office were also unable to provide them. Also, as discussed earlier, the reports prepared annually by every chief constable follow a variable format and very rarely include this depth of information. In any case, since the Act the general practice is to combine male and female figures. The questionnaire sent to all English and Welsh police forces also produced little information. Of the forces who did feel able to provide any data at all, only three provided any about deployment. This was found to be unreliable in that the breakdowns did not even approximately correspond to the total actual strength of the forces concerned.

Similar problems were encountered in the research force, though as Table 4.3 shows,[6] a relatively simple breakdown is available from the list of personnel. As can be seen from the table, there are relatively more women in the uniform department and fewer in either the CID or traffic departments. A similar pattern was also true of those forces who were able to provide information about deployment. For example, in the Metropolitan Police in 1982, there were 13.6 per cent and 7.7 per cent men and women respectively in the CID and 4.3 per cent and 0.7 per cent men and women in the traffic department.

TABLE 4.3   *Percentage of male and female officers by occupation in Medshire in 1982*

	Uniform patrol	CID	Traffic	Adminis-tration	Communi-cations	Other
Male	56·6	16·5	9·2	15·0	2·3	0·4
Female	65·8	12·8	2·4	14·0	4·8	—

Unfortunately, the classifications as displayed in Table 4.3 are rather broad and give little idea of deployment on specialist duties. For example, included under the general heading of 'uniform patrol' are those officers deployed in the collators office, on juvenile liaison and the dogs section. Similarly, the broad CID classification includes the serious crimes squad, the plain clothes department, scenes of crime officers, etc., whilst the administration classification includes people in the prosecutions department as well as senior officers on the headquarters staff.

Although the extent of the problem associated with national and local record-keeping had not been fully appreciated at the outset of the research, there was some expectation that the job titles would be 'all embracing'. For this reason more detailed deployment information was collected via the questionnaire survey. Questions were included about present and past deployment experience and work preferences. As can be seen from Table 4.4, almost two-thirds of all the officers surveyed were involved in uniform patrol duties. Although not shown in this table, 35 per cent of these were constables, 7.6 per cent sergeants and 6.8 per cent officers of inspector rank or above. The remainder (12.1 per cent) were community constables.[7]

As the data in Table 4.4 demonstrates there is very little difference in the proportion of men and women in either the uniform branch or the CID, but considerable variation exists in the other three categories. Only one woman was in the traffic department compared with 6.5 per cent of all the policemen surveyed, and there were proportionately more women in clerical or administrative jobs, though proportionately fewer in specialist jobs.

One question that arises from this analysis concerns the relative disposition of officers who joined before or after integration. Clearly, if the Act is having the intended effect then deployment patterns of men and women who joined since integration should be approximately similar, whereas it could be expected that longer-serving men and women may have become supervisors or specialists. It may even be the case that some longer-serving women have opted for particular duties through choice rather than become fully involved in an integrated role.

A cross-tabulation of role occupation by sex by time of joining is also shown in Table 4.4. This demonstrates that although roughly the same proportion of the two groups are deployed on uniform duties, there are some other noticeable differences. Overall, more women are employed in the CID or on administrative duties, whereas more men are employed on traffic regardless of when they joined the service. There is, however, a marked tendency for the 'traditional' women to be over-represented in administrative and CID posts. For example, 28 per cent of the 'traditional' women were in clerical and administrative posts compared with 6 per cent and just under 3 per cent of their

TABLE 4.4 Present deployment of police officers in Medshire (based on questionnaire sample)

	Both (n = 354) (%)	Total Female (n = 110) (%)	Male (n = 244) (%)	'Traditionals' Female (%)	Male (%)	'Moderns' Female (%)	Male (%)
Uniform branch	61·6	63·3	61·3	41·3	54·2	79·4	76·6
CID	12·2	13·8	11·5	17·4	13·9	11·1	6·5
Traffic	6·5	0·9	9·1	2·3	10·8	—	5·2
Clerical/Admin.	8·4	15·6	5·3	28·1	6·6	6·4	2·6
All specialists	11·3	6·4	12·8	10·9	14·5	3·1	9·1
Total	100	100	100	100	100	100	100

younger female and male colleagues respectively, and 7 per cent of their contemporary male officers.

A further examination of the specialist activities mentioned shows that although sixteen separate departments or squads were mentioned, policewomen were represented in only five of these. These were communications, juvenile liaison, plain clothes, the regional crime squad and the fraud squad. The only specialist department in which women were in the majority was juvenile liaison. A full list of these specialist groups and their membership is given in Table 4.5. Two points emerge from this breakdown. The first concerns the relative proportion of women in clerical and administrative jobs. The survey demonstrates that over one sixth of all policewomen are actually *formally* employed in this capacity, and as we shall see presently, there is evidence that, in addition, a substantial number are also deployed on other clerical and routine tasks even though their job title suggests otherwise. The second concerns the distribution of policewomen in specialist departments. Of the five mentioned, two were directly concerned with aspects of the traditional role. These were juvenile liaison and the plain clothes department. Of the eleven specialist departments which were not mentioned by policewomen, seven were directly concerned with the law-enforcement function (scenes of crime, serious crime squad, etc.). Even based on this partially limited data there are clear indications of differences in the deployment patterns of male and female officers, which is not restricted by reasons of choice or supervisory duties to women and men who joined the service before the Act.

(ii) Deployment History

The present distribution of occupations within the service for policemen and policewomen indicate some general differences in deployment, particularly in traffic and other specialist departments. There were, as discussed above, differences between both 'traditionals' *and* 'moderns' in the types of duties they were currently assigned to. To explore these patterns of deployment further, survey respondents were asked to give details of both the number and the nature of the departments they had worked in previously. Excluded from this analysis were the very short periods of attachment served by probationary police officers as part of their familiarisation training. The analysis does include 'aide' attachments in the CID and other

TABLE 4.5   *Membership of specialist departments in Medshire*

	Female	Male
Juvenile liaison	3	1
Crime prevention	—	1
Support unit	—	5
Plain clothes	1	3
Regional crime squad	2	2
Serious crime squad	—	3
Drug squad	—	2
Special branch	—	1
RCIO[8]	—	3
Dog section	—	1
Scenes of crime	—	4
Anti-vandal squad	—	1
Fraud squad	1	2
Others	—	2

departments since these are usually for at least three months (and are used as a way of assessing an officer's suitability for transfer to the department).

The survey showed that almost four-fifths of those questioned had worked in more than one department other than uniform patrol. Just over two-thirds (68 per cent) of the sample had experience of up to three departments, three being the modal number. As shown in Table 4.6, there was some difference in the number of previous departments for men and women, with a tendency for women to have worked in more departments than men. This difference is statistically significant, yielding a χ^2 value of 8.4, d.f. $= 2$.

Given the current assignments within Medshire, discussed above, an analysis was made of the general orientation of the previous experience of policemen and women. In other words this examination attempted to establish whether the nature of the experience of men and women was different and whether it demonstrated any particular pattern of deployment. Generally speaking, the survey showed that previous experience reflected present patterns of deployment. For example, nearly three-quarters of all policemen and women have a 'mainly general patrol' (i.e. uniform department) history of occupational experience. A further 12 per cent of men and 11 per cent of women had had 'mainly specialist crime' experience in the CID, and

TABLE 4.6   *Previous deployment experience in Medshire*

	Up to three previous departments (%)	*Over four previous departments* (%)
Total (*n* = 353)	69	28
Male (*n* = 243)	71	29
Female (*n* = 110)	64	35

just under 8 per cent of the men but less than 1 per cent of the women had had 'mainly specialist traffic' experience. About the same proportion of men and women (approximately 4 per cent) had had a mixture of previous experience which was neither mainly specialist nor generalist. In addition, as would perhaps be expected, just under 4 per cent of the policewomen surveyed had had a 'mainly specialist policewomen's' experience based on their pre-integration experience in the old policewomen's departments.

On balance, then, the survey data on occupational experience suggests that there are differences in the quantity of deployment experiences, and also reflect qualitative differences in the nature of present deployment.

(iii)   Deployment Preferences

In order to examine whether the differences in the distribution of the type of assignments between men and women were based on individual preferences (rather than differential treatment), respondents were asked to indicate the department they would most like to work in. It could be inferred, for example, that should men *or* women, in general, indicate a preference for certain kinds of police work then this could possibly be reflected in actual distributions (though, of course, preference would not in itself justify inequitable deployment patterns).

Overall 61 per cent of the men and 49 per cent of the women surveyed said that they were already in the department of their preference. Of the rest, the majority of both men (37 per cent) and women (34 per cent) would prefer to be in the CID, and an equal proportion of men and women (28 per cent) would prefer some

specialist activity. Twice the proportion of men (18 per cent) compared with women (9 per cent) would like to work in the traffic
department. This latter figure is quite interesting given the very low
representation of women in this department. It also reflects the
occupational status attached to the department (as with the CID) by
men in particular, though evidently this is to some extent shared by
policewomen. Also interesting in view of current deployment patterns
is the fact that a higher proportion of men than women (11 per cent
compared with 5 per cent) would prefer administrative duties. This
may be because many of these jobs are on a nine to five basis and
would allow a break from shift work. Also interesting is the fact that
just under 10 per cent of both men and women would like to return
from their present occupation to uniform patrol duties.

When asked to rate their chances of being able to work in their
preferred department, women were more pessimistic than men. Less
than half of the women surveyed (46 per cent) felt their chances were
'good' or 'very good' compared with 53.5 per cent of the men. Of
these, 25 per cent felt they were 'very good' compared with 18 per cent
of the women. Of the women, 24 per cent thought their chances were
'bad' or 'very bad' compared with 13 per cent of the men. So although
occupational preferences are broadly similar, there is a tendency for
expectations to vary.

Generally fewer women than men are wholly content with their
present deployment (less than half those surveyed); equal proportions
of men and women would like CID or other specialist deployment;
more men than women would prefer traffic, though women's preferences in this direction are far greater than actual deployment; and
more men than women would like deployment to duties involving
administration.

The notion of occupational preference was pursued in more depth
by asking survey respondents which aspects of police work they found
most interesting. This was to establish:

(i) whether law-enforcement duties were generally felt to be more
    interesting than those related to the service function; and
(ii) whether men and women assign different interest priorities to
    these functions.

For example, given the masculine ethos of policing and the sub-
cultural value system which views the law-enforcement function as
'real police work', as discussed earlier, one might expect that these will
be ranked higher in interest value. What is of interest is whether
policewomen subscribe equally to the 'control' notion embodied in

the 'thief-taking' or 'good capture' perception of police work, or whether they are more interested in the supposedly more feminine 'service' activities often felt to be peripheral to the 'real' job of policing.

The list of activities and their rank order of interest are given in Table 4.7. Although this is not an all-inclusive list, it does cover a fair selection of basic duties. Overall, the law-enforcement activities of interviewing suspects, making arrests and collecting evidence are ranked as the top three interesting activities. The service function of giving advice and information also has a relatively high interest value. There are, as the table reveals, some interesting similarities and differences between female and male choices. For example, both men and women find the law-enforcement activities of 'making arrests', 'interviewing suspects' and 'collecting evidence' among the most interesting activities (within the top five in rank order). However, there does seem to be a tendency for women to find service/community activities more interesting than do men. Thus, 'giving advice to the public' and 'community liaison' activities are found more interesting. The women also find 'domestic disputes' and 'working with juveniles' more interesting than do the men, though 'domestics' are ranked fairly low in interest by both groups. A Spearman rank order correlation confirms the overall similarity of male and female interests, yielding 4.7, $\rho = 0.719$ (positive correlation at $p < 0.01$).

To summarise, there are some grounds for the view that in general policewomen and men have a similar interest in the value-enhanced law-enforcement activities (and this finding adds substance to the earlier comments about occupational preferences). Nevertheless, women *do* find some 'service' type aspects of policing more interesting than do policemen, especially when they coincide with those tasks which are identified with their 'traditional', feminine gender role. Men, on the other hand, tend to find tasks such as 'foot patrol' and 'panda patrol' more interesting and show little interest in the more static duties, possibly because of the 'action-oriented' approach to policing which is a feature of some sociological accounts.[9]

THE LOCUS OF THE DEPLOYMENT DECISION

(i) Occupational Roles

The examination of deployment patterns indicates some differences in

TABLE 4.7 *Rank order of interest assigned to various aspects of general police duties*

	Total sample (rank)	Male (rank)	Female (rank)
Making arrests	2	1	2
Intervening in family crises and domestic disputes	15	17	13
Traffic management	17	14	16=
Interviewing suspects	1	2	1
General purpose motor patrol (panda)	7	6	9=
Giving advice and information to members of the public	4	5	3
Dealing with motoring offences	16	12	16=
Foot patrol	5	4	5
Observation work	6	7	6
Community liaison activities, e.g. talks in schools	8	11	8
Collecting evidence	3	3	4
Dealing with traffic accidents	11	10	14
Working with juveniles	9=	16	7
Traffic patrol	13	9	15
Police station duties	14	15	12
Preparing crime reports	9=	13	9=
Dealing with general disputes	12	8	11

the nature of male and female assignments, both from the point of view of their overall past employment history in the police service and current deployment patterns. However, there would seem to be little basis for supposing that this is entirely as a result of differences in occupational interest or preference. Certainly there are grounds which support the view that policewomen (especially the 'modern' group) share many of the same occupational value patterns, whether through recruitment or socialisation, as their male colleagues. In other words, both policemen and women share similar preferences in respect of occupational choices and have broadly similar interest in law-enforcement activities (though women also have a greater interest in service activities).

Since the difference is not due to occupational interest or preference, it is logical to conclude that these differences in the patterns of deployment for men and women are the result of management 'policy' or supervisory 'operational' decisions. Whilst, as will become apparent from the examination of male attitudes, female choices are subject to considerable peer group pressure from their male colleagues, it is the predominantly male supervisory ranks who actually have the power within the organisation to make or influence deployment decisions.

Deployment decisions about occupational roles are generally made at a relatively senior level within the organisation and during the interviews examples of this kind of decision were mentioned frequently by policewomen (particularly those who had joined since the Act) and sometimes by policemen. There was a general recognition that the range of occupational roles was restricted, and that the responsibility for this was at the senior management level of superintendent or above; but there was less agreement that this was entirely justified. Some officers even felt that it was a policy decision made at chief officer level, particularly with regard to the use of women in public order situations or in support units.

Commonly mentioned departments which either restricted or denied entry to women officers, through tradition or informal policy, were traffic, police dogs, scenes of crime, drugs squad, firearms, plain clothes and even (though not supported by this study) the CID. Sometimes it was felt that the opposition to female entry came from lower down in the hierarchy and reflected a relocation of the decision-making power. For example, one woman gave a graphic account of her three-month attachment to the traffic department. She had applied to join and been sent down for a trial and assessment period. Towards the end of this time she was told by the sergeant who was responsible for her appraisal and had the power to recommend permanent transfer:

> 'I don't like women, I don't want women down here and when you came down here I was looking for faults in you to send you back to Division, but I didn't find any so I'm going to have to recommend you stay.' I thought, 'Oh, thank you very much,' you know. That's the sort of attitude you get a lot. They don't like you; if they can fault you, they will. (Case No. FA03)

This downward relocation of decision-making is important, even if relatively infrequent, since it demonstrates the extent of the 'male' prerogative to power in the organisation and its use (and misuse) in deployment decisions regarding women. Even when 'actual' power is not relocated downwards, advice about the suitability of a candidate is frequently sought from junior officers (including constables). These 'front-line' views may be substantially influenced by the gender of the candidate. Nevertheless the function of senior management cannot be overstressed since they are most frequently responsible for these restrictive decisions. An example of the way these decisions are made occurred during the preliminary interviews for this study. A male superintendent mentioned that one of his policewomen had applied for the dog section. He had, after consultation with the senior officer in the dog section, decided that it would be too physical for a woman but, of course, could not use that as a reason for refusing her application. He had decided to use indirect persuasion, pointing out the difficulties and unpleasantness (such as having to track criminals through long wet grass!) involved in dog handling, to prevent her applying.

The complaint about the plain clothes department was a common one amongst the women interviewed. For example one woman said, 'There are departments where although we're equal they will not accept a woman ... the plain clothes department'. When asked why she replied:

> I don't know really. Their other name is the vice squad. They deal with prostitutes and pimps, etc., etc. Whether or not it's a small department and they worry about the personal aspect of a woman working with ... you know, if she's single or married, you know whether they're thrown together in a small department ... I don't know. Whether the policewomen think that because there's only been men in there it's barred and we can't apply for it. I think it's unfair if we're supposed to be equal. If we can't apply for every department, what's the point of us being equal? If we haven't got the same opportunities? (Case No. FA07)

The decision about whether women should be employed on these duties was seen to be entirely the responsibility of the local divisional superintendent or chief superintendent. As indicated by the policewoman quoted above, those who mentioned this department felt it was one in which it would be logical for them to work. This was because much of the work involves missing persons, indecent assaults, prostitution and vice, and as such it would utilise skills associated with their 'traditional' role. Some women recognised that there was a 'protective' element in the decision not to employ women on these duties in that senior supervisors did not want to expose women to the seedy side of life. However, in most instances the barriers to women's entry were seen to be based on men's reluctance to allow women into their domain.

In view of the deployment figures, the complaint about the CID would seem to be unfounded. Indeed, some policemen amongst those interviewed felt that women had a better chance of becoming CID officers than men. In part their reasons for this view were based on the commonly expressed assumption that women get preferential treatment for any 'perks' that are going (such as being allowed to change shifts to suit domestic arrangements, nine to five jobs, cushy indoor jobs, etc.) solely because they are women; but there was also a recognition that the CID needed the traditional skills of women when investigating certain offences. One officer who was interviewed felt women were more likely to get a CID job because those who do apply have the rare combination of experience gained through long service and career orientation. Nevertheless, whilst the relatively high proportion of women in the CID may only represent the presence of the 'necessary' woman, the survey figures do give some support to the policemen's view that women have a better chance of becoming CID officers. With this exception,[10] the research does support the claim of discriminatory restriction of, or exclusion from, some occupational roles which is the result of senior management decisions.

(ii) The Tasks Within Role Experience

Apart from senior management decisions, there are other levels at which decision-making can influence the deployment of policewomen. We have already seen one example (of the sergeant in the traffic department) where organisational power is located at a relatively low level within the hierarchy with potential discriminatory outcome. In addition to these kinds of decisions about occupational role there are those concerning the quality of the tasks allocated to men and women, and whether this reflects the male preference for a modified rather than fully integrated role for women. In essence the question is whether the quality of women's deployment experience reflects their legal (and preferred) role, or whether the male officer's model predominates.

In this respect the fact that only just under 12 per cent of all male sergeants and inspectors favour a fully integrated role for policewomen is not without significance. Indeed, 53 per cent of sergeants and 47 per cent of inspectors were in favour of a modified role for women officers. The significance lies in the fact that it is operationally possible for male role preferences to be converted into deployment decisions at the level of the basic work group or relief. The effect of this local decision-making could be that the actual qualitative nature of the day-to-day activities within any given occupational role may be different for policewomen than for policemen. In addition, the fact that 80 per cent of chief inspectors and superintendents are also in favour of a modified female role could have a reinforcing effect (independent of their own occupational role decisions). By tacitly approving the modified role there is reduced risk to junior line-management of their being called to account for their deployment decisions.

An examination of the activities which respondents reported as being those they are most frequently engaged in does provide evidence of a difference in the quality of male and female work patterns. For example, just over 15 per cent of the policewomen, but 28 per cent of the men, reported that their most frequent activities involved law-enforcement and/or public order duties. As would be expected given the distribution of occupational roles discussed earlier, a far higher proportion of men (10 per cent) than women (2 per cent) were involved in traffic-related activities. More men than women reported 'panda' patrol (7 per cent compared with 3 per cent) but more women (21 per cent) than men (11 per cent) reported foot patrol as their most frequent activity. This relatively higher figure most probably reflects the higher proportion of probationers in the female sample (23 per cent female compared with 6 per cent male probationers). Just over 6 per cent of the women surveyed specifically mentioned duties such as interviewing victims of alleged sexual offences and dealing with juveniles and children. However, the most frequent activities for women (reported by 24.5 per cent compared with 11.5 per cent of men) were the more general routine duties such as police station desk duties, paperwork, typing and office duties, prisoner escorts, court duties and computer duties.

This difference in duties was attributed to supervisory decisions. In response to a question about whether supervisory officers employ women on different duties than men, over half (53 per cent) of the survey sample thought this was the case. Of those who felt supervisors did employ women on different duties, more than a third (37.5 per cent) thought that supervisors avoided deploying women where there was a risk of violence, 23 per cent felt they were used for traditional policewomen's work involving women and children, 24 per cent felt that women were generally less capable and therefore supervisors did not employ them on all tasks (though these people were less specific about the tasks they thought women were employed on). A further 10 per cent felt that supervisors gave women the more mundane, less exciting, less strenuous and easier work. Just under 3 per cent actually stated that this different employment would depend entirely on the attitude of the male supervisor towards policewomen.

Although over half of the sample actually thought that supervisors did employ women differently, nearly 60 per cent felt this should not happen, though there was a clear (and significant, $\chi^2 = 6.87$, d.f. $= 1$) difference in male and female opinion on this issue. Just under 44 per cent of the male, but only 29 per cent of the women, officers surveyed felt supervisors should employ women differently. Of more salience perhaps, given their power to implement deployment decisions in practice, is the fact that 59 per cent of the male sergeants and 65 per cent of male inspectors felt that policewomen *should* be given different duties. The difference between male and female constables on this question was less pronounced with 62 per cent of men and 70 per cent of the women disagreeing with the proposition of different duties. Interestingly, a higher proportion of women of all ranks (except inspectors) felt supervisors *did* in fact employ women differently. In fact, 70 per cent of male inspectors said that supervisors do employ women on different duties.

THE QUALITY OF WOMEN'S DEPLOYMENT EXPERIENCES

These survey results indicate a substantial difference in the *quality* of male and female assignments within nominally the same role. Ample confirmation of these qualitative differences came from both the observational work and the in-depth interviews, particularly in relation to uniform patrol officers. These differences were the result of five main sets of front-line supervisory practices in the deployment of women officers. These were:

(i)   the frequent use of women patrol officers on general routine police station duties;

(ii) the allocation of women to less busy beats;

(iii) the pairing-up of women officers with male colleagues on 'panda' and foot patrol duties;

(iv) the allocation of women to different types of incident; and

(v)   the deployment of women on 'traditional' activities concerned with women victims, offenders, children and juveniles.

(i) Police Station Duties

In the case of the first of these, it has already been noted that many of
the policewomen surveyed reported that they found that they were
most often involved in routine clerical or administrative duties. At
one level, this is not altogether surprising because of the greater
proportion of women actually deployed in administrative or clerical
occupational roles. Nevertheless, the impression gained from the
observational work and confirmed by the in-depth interviews is that a
substantial number of women nominally assigned to uniform patrol
duties also find that they spend a good deal of their time on routine
police station duties. As one woman commented:

> On each shift there is an average of 22 police officers, and out of
> those 22 police constables there are only two or three policewomen
> and, more often than not, you will find the policewomen stuck in
> the office, answering the 'phone, on the desk, operating the com-
> puter and very rarely will you see two policemen. That's one of my
> gripes. (Case No. FA06)

So as well as being formally deployed in clerical and administrative
occupational roles (such as prosecutions or the collator's office), local
deployment practice means that women are also more often assigned
to routine office duties. Indeed, this can also be the case in some
specialist departments. As one female CID officer said:

> I feel sometimes that I am put upon because I'm a woman, to do the
> jobs that are expected, like the clerk goes sick and I, I mean not just
> because I know the job – it doesn't take that much to learn – but
> sometimes I feel that because I'm a woman I get the clerical side of
> the job, which I'm doing at the moment and you saw me doing.
> (Case No. FB07)

This woman officer was quite sure that it was an informal policy to
deploy women on police station duties in order to 'take women off the
streets'. Quite a few of the policemen (particularly the post-integration recruits) felt that this was a result of supervisors giving women
preferential treatment and mentioned the fact that women were more
likely to get the 'cushy' inside jobs. With the exception of those
occasions when women had been deployed on nine-to-five duties for
domestic reasons, the men were nevertheless generally in favour of the
practice. Often it was mentioned in association with the allocation of

beat duties, particularly on the night shift. As one young male constable with five years' service explained:

Obviously if you've only got about three men on the night shift, or something like that, then rather than put one of the men, they put one of the women in the office, so if there is any trouble the men are there then. (Case No. AM09)

One sergeant, with eighteen years' service, was very frank about his own deployment decisions. He associates the practice of keeping women on inside duties with particular shifts and areas and the possible risk to the officer. He explained:

If I can get it across to you, if you've got a group coming on and you're responsible for posting the beats, as it were, on Saturday nights in the city centre in ——, say, do you think a woman should walk out there on her own? I think I would make an excuse to have mine inside or only allow them out in the van. (Case No. MB07)

(ii) Allocation to Beats

The risk factor (discussed in more depth in Chapter 7) was the main factor for putting women on the less busy (and in their eyes often the most boring and unproductive) beats. One inspector explained his approach to allocating duties:

If you're looking at a list of fifteen men or fifteen numbers as they are really in this job, you will stop when you come across a number which you recognise to be the number of a woman; likewise you would stop when you come across the number of a PC who's probably been with you for four or five months and you stop. Instead of allocating the beats without any sort of question ... you would stop when you came to a WPC name, you would stop when you came to the name of somebody who is perhaps a probationer or a PC that you considered not to be too good at his job.

In the case of probationers and the less able PCs, this inspector would match the beat or the job to the officer's abilities. However, in the case of women officers he says:

likewise you stop when you come to women, because you always, in the back of your mind, perhaps you're wrong, it depends on the woman, but you always must bear in mind as I do that you could possibly be putting that woman at risk by putting her out in a sort of particularly rough area for example, or perhaps an area where you know you've got a club coming out at 2 o'clock, where you get a lot of drunks, you are exposing that woman to risk. (Case No. MB10)

Several women commented on this practice, some with approval and some without. This was particularly so with the women who had joined since the Act. As one policewoman described:

When I used to work in the town they wouldn't put me down on the busier beats. They used to shove me out of the way, where I couldn't be hurt.

When asked why, she replied:

I don't know. I don't suppose they trusted me on the pandas, didn't trust me going to situations. I had my driving test after a year or so which allowed me to drive pandas and the van and then I could take it over for an hour. Otherwise they tended to put me out of the way. I used to hate that a lot. That's why I left, that's why I went down to traffic, so that I could get involved a lot more. (Case No. FA03)

(iii)   Pairing-up with Male Colleagues

One way of overcoming the perceived problems associated with women on patrol duties is by pairing the woman officer with a man either on foot patrol or panda patrol duties. Although force orders in Medshire at the time of the research expressly disallowed 'doubling up', this is common practice with policewomen. Whilst this does sometimes happen with men,[11] it is not normal practice. Again this was condoned by the majority of the men interviewed. According to one male constable:

it's easier for me to explain if I say I was a supervisory. If I was a supervising officer, I would be wary of putting a woman out on night shift ... in my experience it very rarely happens. They normally double up, rather than put them out on the town on their own or wherever it is. The policy is that everybody will go out on their own, from the bosses. But the sergeants work closer, they're the ones who actually deploy the troops and it's very rarely they'll send a policewoman on her own. (Case No. MA06)

The 'modern' women officers were more likely to question this practice and to feel it was unnecesary. As one woman, now herself in an indoor job that she dislikes, explained:

and for some reason they don't like the girls to be out on their own during the night, which is fair comment, I suppose. I never used to mind going out on my own. I used to tell the sergeant sometimes, 'Oh, come on, let me go out on my own now. I'm fed up with you trying to protect me.' But he'd say, 'Oh but you are a woman, after all, we've got to look after you.' But more often than not they used to team me up in the car with one of the boys. (Case No. FA06)

These examples graphically illustrate the power of front-line supervisors to implement informal, and potentially discriminatory, deployment procedures which are in clear contravention of official force policy. And it should be noted that whilst such departures from official policy is known by those who formulate it, by not acknowledging the practice they are effectively condoning it. This is a classic example of 'double messages'; the 'official' and the 'unspoken'.

(iv) Allocation to Incidents

Apart from the assignment of women to station duties, 'safe' or easy beats and the practice of doubling-up, there are two other common ways in which the deployment experience of women is different from that of men. These concern the actual nature of the incidents they deal with. Of course, in some cases this is a direct result of the practices already discussed. For example, in the case of foot patrol duties, women in the urban areas of the research force were often deployed on city or town centre beats during morning or afternoon shifts. These beats are felt to be less risky because they are frequently close to the police station (and therefore to help should it be required). As a result, policewomen often mentioned that the most common incidents they dealt with were shoplifters and petty thefts. Also, as one would expect, women on inside duties are more readily available for certain kinds of duties such as escorts for female prisoners, court duties and interviewing women and children. Nevertheless, the interviews revealed a strong and consistent difference, over and above these situationally determined duties, in the pattern of the nature and the quality of incidents dealt with by women.

It is clear from the interviews that not only are supervisors selective about the assignment of duties, but that this selectivity also applies to the type of incidents they will send women to in a response situation. (In Medshire this would be in a 'panda' car or in the divisional van rather than in specially marked response units). The majority of the men interviewed (both 'traditionals' and 'moderns') were very clear about the extent of this difference, whereas opinion was divided amongst the women. About half of the women who joined since the Act felt that they were sent to all kinds of incidents and did the same job as their male colleagues (though they did nevertheless recognise the limitations placed on them with regards to situations involving physical strength). Generally speaking though, the majority of the women interviewed recognised, with varying degrees of acceptance, a difference in the nature of the incidents they commonly dealt with.

This was most apparent, as one might expect, for those incidents which might involve the risk of violence, such as a pub brawl or where the 'prisoner' might prove to be aggressive and dangerous. However, supervisors were also less likely to send women to the more unpleasant incidents. The types of incidents mentioned included bad road traffic accidents where there had been serious injury or death, the removal of dead bodies, some domestic disputes, and 'dirty' jobs such as searching through rubbish tips or in sewers, and so on. All these were felt to be unsuitable tasks for policewomen. In some ways this can be seen as an extension of the 'protectiveness' that supervisors feel in relation to women being at risk, but it is also a reflection of what is felt to be a suitable feminine role. As one detective constable with thirteen years' service explained:

> they are treated a bit differently than the men, that's certain, and anybody who says anything different is lying ... women are different from men, however much anybody wants to say they are not, and it's no use pretending. The fact that they are paid the same as men, wear the same sort of uniform and that, doesn't make them the same and I don't like it when a woman tries to be the same. I would rather women to be feminine and do the job the way they should.

Asked to explain in what way they are treated differently he said:

> Well you wouldn't have a woman carting out somebody dead in the

house, or the remains of somebody who was found. You'd have a couple of blokes on the shift doing that sort of thing. (Case No. MB05)

Sometimes the two aspects of protectiveness and feminine role are combined in what might be called 'preferential gentlemanly' treatment. One young constable, with five years' service, commented with approval on this practice:

> They think they're equal. I don't think they are ... Everybody is nicer to them, put it that way. If, say, you sent one down to a special incident or something, they get a cushier spot and things like this. You'd always look after them, anyway. It's natural. It's ... I don't know if you'd call it the gentleman in the supervisory or whatever ... And say, it's really, you know, in winter, it can be really cold outside, nine times out of ten, she'll be in the car. (Case No. MA03)

(v) 'Traditional' Womens' Duties

Finally, as referred to above, the other common difference in male and female work patterns is the traditional use of policewomen in relation to juveniles, women offenders and victims of alleged indecency. In some instances the need to have women available to perform these tasks is a *post facto* rationale given for keeping women either in the police station or on nearby beats. Current practice in Medshire is to assign at least one woman officer per shift and in larger sub-divisions there would be a woman officer per relief on each shift so that twenty-four hour availability was ensured. Women officers in the CID also have a responsibility for this type of work and are often involved in the follow-up investigation of alleged offences of indecency, etc. Since the actual number of women in any given CID office is very small (one or two on average), it is highly likely that they will find their time almost exclusively taken up with investigations of this kind.

In some places and on some shifts (for example, weekend, late evening and night shifts in busy town or city centres) there may be genuine operational reasons for ensuring that there are policewomen on hand to deal with this type of work. However, these deployment decisions rest on the assumption that women are more able or better suited than men in relation to these tasks. Most of the women and men interviewed recognised that even though policewomen no longer have a formal specialist role in relation to women and children, they are still the first choice for cases of this kind. Whether this is a wholly justified assumption is a moot point. Most of the 'modern' women felt they were no better qualified for this function than their male colleagues. Indeed, the general view was that calling upon a relatively short-service officer, and in some instances probationer constables, to conduct a delicate interview with, for example, a rape victim, purely and simply because she is a woman was seen as counter-productive. Examples were given of interviews where a distressed victim had had to be re-interviewed because an inexperienced female officer had not elicited sufficiently comprehensive information. Although most of the men interviewed felt that women should perform these 'traditional' tasks, some men also questioned the assumption that women were automatically better suited or more able. As one officer said:

> Given the same opportunity I think other men could [deal with indecency cases as well as women]. They're not given the same opportunity.

Referring to a controversial television programme recently[12] shown on the way the Thames Valley Police interview alleged victims of rape, he said:

> people now want policewomen to do the interviews for rapes and interview people who've been assaulted indecently and what they're saying is that a man is incapable of doing it. Personally, I think that's a load of rubbish. (Case No. MA08)

This, of course, begs the question of whether the suitability of a male or female officer depends on capability through experience or whether victim preferences should be paramount. It is after all quite feasible that a poorly constructed statement may merely reflect the victim's unease at being obliged to recount embarrassing experiences to an officer of the wrong sex. A recent Scottish study which examined victim comments about police officer involvement in their cases indicates that whilst a woman officer's active presence may be requested or beneficial in some cases, both 'favourable and critical comments were made with equal frequency about officers of both sexes', and that 'it was clear that qualities such as kindness and understanding when shown by police officers during investigation procedures were rated highly by complainers, whatever the sex of the officer'.[13]

Some of the women interviewed, particularly those who joined after integration, also felt that men should and could perform these duties just as well as women. The fact that they were automatically expected to take indecency or rape statements solely on the grounds of their sex was also questioned by some of these women. By way of contrast only one young male officer commented on this specific expectation, though, as noted above, several commented on their assumed suitability or capability. Apart from the implicit role segregation that this practice supports (and not only to the disadvantage of female officers), the criticism concerning women's automatic ability also raised the question of the lack of suitable specialist training for these tasks. Highlighting the unfairness of the expectation, one woman constable commented:

> So to stick us in with a victim and say, 'Right take a rape statement off her', is just as unfair as sticking a bloke in there because we didn't have any specialist training so why should we be any better than what they could do, you know ... I think they get very annoyed when we take a statement and it's a load of rubbish and they say, 'You're a woman, you should be able to do it', and you have to say to them, 'Look we didn't have any specialist training and I've never taken one before so ... if it's bad, it's bad, I'll have to do it again.' (Case No. FA02)

One consequence of being taken off normal shift work to conduct interviews or to escort female prisoners was mentioned by a number of women. This concerned their work-rate and being able to submit as many files as their male colleagues. Whether justified or not, some women clearly felt that although they were periodically called off their normal duties to fulfil the 'specialist' role, they were still expected to turn in the same amount of 'work' as men. Women with shorter service were more concerned about this, possibly because they felt evaluations of their performance were based on criteria of this type and that they were put at a disadvantage compared with their male peers. As one woman complained:

> The only thing is, when you are a policewoman you are called, say, over to the charge office, to act as Matron of the cells, because there's no Matron on, if you've got a woman prisoner, to sit in the cells, and also you are expected to do the same amount of work as the other members of the shift. But then you have to go on other runs to prisons, sit in the cells, to sit with juveniles, young girl

juveniles until their parents come in, and yet you are still expected to do the same amount of work as the others. (Case No. FA04)

One of the male sergeants interviewed was also aware of this anomoly. He said:

Some of the WPCs, now, work their ordinary duties and they tend to take specialist statements. They have a lot more work than they can cope with sometimes. (Case No. BM06)

Evidently, then, some considerable concern is generated by this 'specialist' use of policewomen, both among the 'modern' group of women officers and among their male counterparts, but (with the exception quoted above) for different reasons; and although both policemen and women who joined before the Act were more inclined to subscribe to the view that women *are* better suited for this kind of work, their qualifying reasons also varied. Whereas the men generally held the view that these duties were more 'appropriate' for women than general police work, the women stressed the specialist aspect of the work. They expressed regret at the dispersal of the expertise, built up over decades, which happened as a result of integration, to the detriment of the service that could now be offered to the public. As one woman sergeant, with twenty-six years' service, explained:

I think we've lost a certain knowledge that we used to have. Most policewomen's departments, through their dealings with certain women, families, missing girls, had built up a collection if you like, for want of a better word, of information.

She went on to echo the younger policewomen's anxiety about the inadequacy of the current specialist training in these duties, but particularly on-the-job instruction:

And I don't think young women probationers are given so much help and guidance just dealing with these sorts of things as they were when there was a policewomen's department. (Case No. FB02)

In fact, several of the women and men interviewed were concerned that most policewomen only received minimal extra training for these duties. In the case of Medshire this amounts to about two or three half-hour lessons at the Regional Training Centre as an addition to the Initial Training Course. Not only is this felt to be wholly inadequate given the widespread practice of assigning women, including probationers, to these duties, but it comes at a very early stage in a police officer's training when neither men nor women have a very clear understanding of the nature of police work. Of course many police forces, including Medshire, do run specialist courses for policewomen. In the case of Medshire, these were run very infrequently (at the time of the fieldwork there had not been a course for eighteen months, though one was about to be run). Very few of the women interviewed were aware of these courses and none of the 'modern' sample had attended such a course.

Evidently, then, whilst the deployment of women on these duties is common practice it generates concern in three major ways. Firstly, there is the question of whether women are naturally more suited and indeed more capable than men in respect of these duties. Apart from the role stereotype that this perpetuates it is patently also against the interest of those male officers who might be equally able. A second source of anxiety is the feeling of unfair disadvantage generated by being expected to take on these 'traditional' duties and to produce the same amount of 'work' from assignments associated with their generalist role. Finally, there is the question of the amount of extra training provided for these tasks. There would certainly seem to be a case for providing more courses of this kind and, given the provisions of the Act along with the views of the men and women interviewed, for extending the scope of this training to include male police officers.

SUMMARY AND IMPLICATIONS

The information presented above demonstrates that, at least at the local level of the research force, there are substantial qualitative differences in the way in which policemen and policewomen are deployed. It is also quite evident that although there is no formal force policy about the deployment of women, there are widespread deployment practices which, in effect, constitute and are recognised as, an informal policy.

As we have seen, the type of deployment decision depends on the level in the organisation at which it is made. Consequently, the range of occupational roles which women are able to fulfil is dependent on decisions made at middle and senior management level, whereas the range of duties within a particular role, and the quality and nature of work experiences, are the result of line-management decisions at inspector and sergeant level. Occasionally, authority and power to directly influence the range of role occupations that women can enter is also delegated to these lower supervisory ranks, particularly in specialist departments. Although, as is discussed in Chapter 6, the long-term consequences of women's deployment experiences may be equally dependent on both these levels of decision, it is evident from the interviews that those made at the junior level have the most immediate impact on the reality of the role women are able to fulfil. The endorsement of this informal deployment policy by the majority of operational male police officers reinforces this impact. Likewise tacit acceptance and sanction is provided by senior officers both by their own occupational role decisions (which are often shaped by the opinions sought from junior ranks) and by their failure to discourage differential practices by line management. It is these decisions which constitute the mechanism by which anxiety is lessened through 'sensible deployment'. This anxiety and endorsement is also manifest in the attitudes expressed by policemen and contributes to the social and psychological mechanisms which, as we shall see in Chapter 8, regulate the role strategies adopted by women officers.

5 Expectations and Career Choice

In Chapter 6 we shall be examining the way in which men and women develop their careers in policing. We will be interested in seeing whether or not their career patterns are similar and, if not, how they are different and why. As we saw in the last chapter on the working experiences of policewomen, the reality of integration is that there are substantial qualitative differences in the kinds of duties women are assigned to. On this basis alone, it seems reasonable to suppose that these differences might well influence the kind of career choices open to or made by policewomen.

GENDER AND OCCUPATIONAL CHOICE

However, before going on to our discussion of police careers, it seems pertinent to establish whether women and men have similar perceptions and expectations of police work as an occupation. In other words, do men and women officers have the same orientation to work, or do women officers' attitudes differ. If they do differ, this may be because of a combination of 'out of work' and 'in work' factors, the result of which Clegg and Dunkerley have described as the:

> outcome of processes over time. These processes are those of female socialisation, her choice in the labour market, her life cycle, and her adaptation and reaction to work experiences.[1]

Or, could it be that differences in gender play the major part in determining orientations to police work?

In other occupations, the evidence about womens' attitudes and orientations to work varies with, on the one hand, claims that many women, particularly married women, have no intrinsic motivation to work. This view suggests that women's interest in work is largely instrumental, their motivations being money, escaping the boredom of home, seeking the company of workmates, and so on. For these women family commitments come first.[2] On the other hand, other studies suggest that this is related to the level of work, and that for 'career women' motivation is intrinsic.[3] This view is challenged by Agassi on the basis of studies of cross-cultural and gender comparisons which demonstrate that although there are some gender-based variations in attitudes to work 'no differences are sex specific in the sense that no difference holds regardless of occupational difference'.[4]

Clearly, given the range of views that exist in occupations other than policing, it seems necessary to specifically examine this issue in relation to police work. After all, it could otherwise be argued that any variations in career patterns are the result of different gender-based outlooks and ambitions resulting from different motives for joining and expectations of police work, rather than from 'in-work' factors, such as those which might derive from women's different experiences within the police organisation.

In fact this is an argument that is commonly offered by policemen, usually in connection with a statement about women only staying in 'the job' for a short time. It is also of interest that male officers rarely offer other, possibly equally legitimate, 'in-work' explanations for what is seen as a general lack of commitment to a policing career, which it is claimed manifests itself in the comparatively shorter service of women.

Indeed, as will be discussed in Chapter 7, evidence of this commitment to a 'life' career was an essential criterion for selection in Medshire. Furthermore, the recruiting staff in this force generally felt that among serving police officers there was a qualitative difference in the commitment of male and female officers (particularly married women). As a consequence they had different gender-based expectations of applicants, thus reinforcing the salience of this criterion in the selection process. The question this raises is whether these beliefs are grounded in fact or are merely offered as justification for a selection process which limits the numbers of women recruits to an informally determined quota.

(i) Reasons for Joining

Perhaps the first way in which to begin to address this issue is to examine the reasons men and women join the police,[5] and the related point of whether there is any difference in their *intention* to make a career of policing. In the author's previous survey of police officers it was found that there were five main reasons influencing their decision to join. In order of importance, these were: the variety of work; an active job; security of employment; the opportunity to use individual initiative; and an interest in helping people.

There was no significant difference between male and female choices of reasons for joining (or indeed, in the aspects of police work which they would emphasise as attractions to a friend who might be contemplating joining). Many of these factors were mentioned by both male and female officers during the interviews, though it was also clear that there was a high degree of 'chance' in the decision to join. Boredom with a previous occupation was mentioned frequently, coupled with a desire to do something 'out of the ordinary'. Other factors such as being unemployed at the time, a careers talk at school, a chance remark from a friend about the person's suitability for police work, just happening to be in town and going into the local police station to enquire about recruitment, and the attraction of wearing a uniform were all mentioned as having a deciding influence, either on their own or coupled with discontent with their present occupation. One ex-civil servant, with thirteen years' police service explained:

Just a job. I was bored to tears working in an office all day long, writing the same sort of letters to the same sort of people. It appealed to me as a job you could get out and meet more people and have a bit of excitement in life really. (Case No. MB05)

'Modern' officers of both sexes were more likely to stress the anticipation of the variety and activity involved in police work as their reasons for joining. For example, one female officer said she joined because of a careers talk in school: 'and I thought "that sounds good, that sounds interesting, you're dealing with something different every-day"' (Case No. FA02). Another said, 'To have a career, an interesting job, something varied. To get out and about and meet members of the public more than anything' (Case No. FA03), and, giving the reasons of an outdoor life, security and being able to talk to and help people, a male colleague explained:

You go in, it's very active and it's interesting work really ... Well, generally different things happening at different times, not mono-tony and ... well, everyday's different really. (Case No. MA03)

'Traditional' women were more likely than any of their colleagues to give reasons which have an almost vocational quality. As one poli-cewoman with twenty-four years' service explained:

I just wanted to be a policewoman. I didn't think about it being a career. My grandfather was in the police force and it just seemed something I wanted to do. If somebody had said to me about three months after joining, 'Why did you join?' I don't think I could have given them a reasonable answer. (Case No. FB10)

And, of course, in some cases the reasons given for joining the police service were instrumental and based on the long-term security of the occupation: 'A good question. It offered a career basically. It just offered a job for 25 years with prospects.' (Case No. MA04).

Whilst there was considerable individual variation in the range of reasons given, overall there was no discernable difference in the quality of the reasons given between men and women officers, nor was there a more marked tendency for female officers to offer reasons which stress the more opportunistic or instrumental aspects of policing as an occupation.

(ii) Expectations of Police Work

As one might expect, the reasons given for joining the police in part reflect people's expectations of police work. In the main, where there were clear expectations about police work, it was that it would be varied and interesting, involve meeting the public and 'keeping the law'. In some cases these expectations were the result of having spoken to relatives or close friends in the police service. Even so, these expectations left some people unprepared for the reality of policing. This is demonstrated by the reply of a policewoman with seventeen years' service, who thought she knew what to expect 'until I actually came back from my initial training and found things much more different than what I'd thought' (Case No. FB08). Part of this was because, having joined a county force, she found she was not employed in a policewomen's department as were most city policewomen and as a consequence was employed on a variety of non-'traditional' tasks. As a result, her early experience was very similar to the women joining the service since the Act and it was the range and diversity involved in police work which was most unexpected. More often, however, it was the routine work involved which people were unprepared for, particularly if their expectations were based on media protrayals of police work. The amount of paperwork was often mentioned in this respect.

However, it was equally clear from the interviews that some people had only a very vague appreciation of what was involved, as well as being unprepared for some aspects. For example, asked if he knew what to expect, one young officer replied:

> None whatever, except as I said, I knew they met a lot of people. Different types of people from your villains right up to the top and I like to talk to people and I thought it'd be a way of meeting people. That was the only idea I had at all of the police force.

Asked whether he had been surprised at what was involved he said:

> Yes. There's a lot of boring things happen ... Well, I won't say boring, but run-of-the-mill things you get called to ... As an outsider I seem to remember everything seemed to be so ... all policemen seemed to be so serious. But also I suppose it's from the television more than anything, they're always investigating serious things. They're always doing serious assaults or burglaries or things of that nature, but when you actually get in the police force ... (Case No. MA06)

Likewise, a female colleague who joined at about the same time, had no idea of what was entailed:

> None whatsoever. I don't really know [what my expectations were]. I'd never spoken to a policeman, been into a police station or anything.

Asked if she was subsequently surprised at what was involved she replied, 'Yes, because it's anything and everything' (Case No. FA07).

Although there is a case for interpreting these findings with some caution (since there may be an element of in-job socialisation lending a common interpretation to their recollections), what is noticeable are the similarities in expectations on joining expressed by both the men and women interviewed, whether or not they had a realistic appreciation of the actuality of police work. This is in clear contrast to the related topic of whether police work has actually met these expectations. This produced some variation in responses between men and women with less satisfaction being expressed by the women. For example, one woman with twenty-four years' service, and only about three of those in a policewomen's department, said she felt she had been fortunate in being able to do 'proper police work' for most of her career, explaining her view by comparing her experience with that of the men. When asked whether police work had met with her expectations she said:

> At the beginning – yes, until I realised what the men were doing. Then I wanted to know if the men were doing certain jobs why couldn't I do them? (Case No. BF10)

Only one woman (a 'traditional') said it had been better than she had expected. She said, 'It's been more exciting. You never know what the day is going to bring' (Case No. BF01).

Two of the 'traditional' group and four of the 'modern' group of women felt police work had (some with qualifications) lived up to their expectations. The majority had mixed feelings, though one recent joiner admitted that as she had not known what to expect it was rather hard to make such an assessment. What is interesting about those women with ambivalent feelings was that they often explained their negative feelings in terms of their actual work experience. This was true of both the groups. One woman inspector with twenty-six years' service explained:

> On the whole I've enjoyed it. But there have been times when I've thought 'Do I want to stay in?' I have thought of going . . . Funnily enough, it's not so much when you have an unpleasant duty to do . . . but I think it's – it's mostly on perhaps a shift where not much was happening. (Case No. FB02)

The boredom and inactivity of police work featured in many of these accounts for the younger women as well. One woman with five years' service gave a graphic account of the boredom, the cold and the isolation she felt during her first three months on patrol duty:

> I went home loads of time and I said to my mother, 'I can't stick any more of this'. I was despondent in those first few months mainly I suppose because it wasn't as active as I thought it was. I spent a lot of time walking the streets, nothing going on. You know you get a lot of people talking to you but it's not as exciting as you think it's going to be. And as I said on the cold winter's nights when anybody with any sense . . .

She felt that this had been a deliberate policy of her inspector, 'to see if I would crack under the strain, being out in the cold, the boredom, you know walking the streets on your own, I suppose'. When asked specifically whether the police service had lived up to her expectations, she replied:

Yes and no ... It can be very petty and it can be ... make life very hard for you at times. I think as I saw it before and how I see it now is totally different, but having said that it gets a way of life with you. (Case No. FA02)

Although the men occasionally mentioned the boring and uninteresting aspects of police work, the image that comes across from most of their accounts is the amount of variation and, in some cases, perceived excitement in their work. The account of this officer with five years' service was almost typical:

It's been better ... A lot more varied than I expected to start off with because [then] I was dealing with traffic and then the odd minor offence, but here in —— there is such a great variety you cover all aspects of police work. It's definitely interesting although a lot of it is boring. (Case No. AM07)

Much the same sentiment is contained in his colleague's explanation, an account which provides a sharp contrast to the experience of the women quoted earlier:

You go in with a 'glory' attitude. You go in and it's very active and it's interesting work really. [Probe – Why?] I suppose speed, the fast turnover.

Asked whether it had lived up to expectations, he pointed out one aspect mentioned by several of the men which detracted from the otherwise busy and interesting work:

Yes. I did not realise it was such a workload on the paper scene. But it is and it's very time consuming and you don't seem to have the time because you've got an 8-hour shift in and, of course, you've got to deal with the incidents which are actually happening at the time. It's like every other job, there's good aspects and bad. I haven't regretted one minute of it and I still find it very interesting and I can honestly say I like coming to work. (Case No. MA03)

The enthusiasm reflected in these accounts might easily be attributed to the youth or relatively short service of the officers concerned but, although muted, much the same sentiment is expressed by the majority of their older colleagues. For example, one area constable with sixteen years' service explained why he thought it had more than lived up to his expectations:

Because as I've said, with police work, the beauty of it as far as I'm concerned, is you never know what's around the corner. You might have a day when you do nothing at all, and then the next day anything could happen and you are called on to do all sorts of things. (Case No. MB04)

Another longer-serving detective constable said:

Yes, well I couldn't imagine doing any other job really. Most of the people I know in the job, I think they're happy in it. I would find most jobs boring after the police. (Case No. MB05)

By way of contrast with the women interviewed only two of the men (both long-serving constables) expressed dissatisfaction and in both cases this could be attributed to their being bitter about specific incidents.[6] In some sense these contrasting female and male accounts of the way in which police work has lived up to their expectations could have been predicted given the difference in the kinds of duties and incidents women and men are deployed on. It is not, therefore, surprising that women, particularly the 'modern' group, have mixed feelings about whether or not police work has lived up to the expectations they had when they joined.

The survey provides more evidence that these mixed feelings derive from their experience of police work. Fewer women than men, in both groups, find police work mostly varied and interesting. For example, whereas 76 per cent of the 'modern' male officers felt this way, only 57 per cent of their female counterparts did. Just under 43 per cent of this group thought it was a mixture of interesting and boring duties, a view which was held by only 22 per cent of 'modern' males. Clearly, there seems to be a differential mismatch between expectations on joining and their fulfilment – a fact which is not without significance when considering the career patterns of police officers and which perhaps should be borne in mind when assessing the reasons for the higher premature wastage of female personnel, a topic discussed below.

CAREER ORIENTATION: COMMITMENT AND PROFESSIONALISM

It will be recalled that in a prevoius study[7] male officers expressed the view that women were not as career-minded and had less commitment to policing as a profession than men. Similar views were also expressed during the interviews for the present study. A typical view was:

> Well, I don't think that the majority of policewomen have decided to make this a career. It is a job, maybe for ten years, maybe for fifteen years, maybe for five years. But to them it is a job, whereas to a man it is a career. As I say, I am totally commited to this job until I'm 55. (Case No. MB10)

This sentiment about women's commitment was also central to the view of recruitment officers.

This study attempted to examine the basis for this assumption by eliciting information about occupational orientation and included a specific question on career disposition. This did reveal a difference in that 84 per cent of the men and 64 per cent of the women surveyed joined the police service with the intention of making it a long-term career, whereas just under 16 per cent of men but 32 per cent of women joined simply because they wanted an interesting job at the time. The difference is statistically significant, yielding $\chi^2 = 13.7$, d.f. $= 1$. Some support for the male argument that women are not as career-minded, at least when they join, is also drawn from a comparison of men and women who have joined since the Act. Although it might be expected, given a fully integrated role, that this would be accompanied by equivalent attitudes to establishing a career, 93 per cent of the men compared with 74 per cent of the women had this intention. Nevertheless, the fact that almost three-quarters of this group of women *were* career-oriented does begin to cast considerable doubt on the extent of male assertions about their long-term commitment.

There is, in any case, some indication that this is a situation in transition, with an increasing number of career-minded women joining the service. Whereas only 51 per cent of the 'traditional' women joined for a career, 74 per cent of their younger female colleagues were career-oriented. (This difference being significant at $p < 0.05$, $\chi^2 = 5.0$, d.f. $= 1$). As an indicator of intent to stay in the service, respondents were also asked whether they had seriously thought of leaving; there was no difference between men and women, with about 30 per cent of both groups saying this was something they had considered.

Another source of questionnaire information about possible sex differences in attitudes to careers is that concerning officers' views of police work as an occupation. More specifically, the survey respondents were asked to indicate whether they thought that policing was a

vocation, a well-paid job, or a profession. The question was included
because previous work suggested that this occupational viewpoint
was an important part of the self-image of police officers. In this
context it is quite conceivable that the self-image of people committed
to a life-long professional career might be qualitatively different from
those who joined the police with a different occupational viewpoint.
And if, as has been suggested, most women have an instrumental
approach to their work, then this might be reflected in the proportion
of women who see policing as a well-paid occupation rather than a
profession.

In the Jones 1982 study there was very little difference, overall,
between male and female viewpoints with about two-thirds of each
group subscribing to the notion of police work as a profession
(though, there were some regional differences with more women in the
Southern force studied holding a 'vocational' view than in the
Northern force). Interestingly, the basis of this professionalism was
very much related to the law-enforcement 'control' function of the
police rather than their broad social-welfare or 'service' role, which is
very much in accord with the deployment preferences, discussed in
Chapter 4, which indicate that women officers do value similar
policing activities as the men.

A similar pattern of responses was found in the present study,
though the definitions used varied somewhat. In this case the extra
category of 'craft' was included, in order to include some approxima-
tion to the concept of 'practical professionalism', which is dis-
tinguished from the classic 'expert' form by its 'experiential' rather
than 'esoteric, academic' base. Just under 25 per cent of male and 32
per cent of female officers described police work as a 'well paid
occupation'; 42 per cent of men and 34 per cent of women as a
profession; and a further 22 per cent and 20 per cent respectively
opting for the 'craft' description. As with the previous study, more
women (14 per cent) held a vocational view than did men (9 per cent).
The differences were not, however, statistically significant yielding a
χ^2 value of 4.7, d.f. $= 3$. There were some interesting differences
between the 'traditional' and 'modern' groups, with more men and
women in the 'traditional' group (43 per cent and 47 per cent
respectively) subscribing to a classic view of professionalism than
their younger colleagues, of whom almost a quarter (both men and
women) were craft-oriented. Also, a higher proportion (17 per cent)
of the 'traditional' female officers held a vocational view of their work
than any other group.

The study currently being conducted by Dunkerley and Kelland provides more evidence about female career commitment. They have found that the vast majority of policewomen they have surveyed in two police forces have a strong commitment to police work. They state:

> The position we have found is of women being very committed to work outside the home and especially to police work. It would seem that many would like to make it a life-long career in the way that it is taken for granted that most policemen will.[8]

On balance, then, it would seem that the small differences that do exist are related more to the time of joining the serivce than to any sex difference and that, indeed, younger officers as a whole hold a very similar range of views of their occupation. Taken together with the information concerning the reasons for joining the service and people's expectations of police work, whilst there is some evidence of differences in male and female views about career disposition (and this itself is changing), there is little other substantive evidence to justify the extent of the prevailing male belief.

PREMATURE WASTAGE RATES

The final plank of the argument that male and female career patterns are the result of differences in outlooks and ambitions is the male assertion that women officers only stay in 'the job' for a short time. At first sight this would also appear to be substantiated by the higher turnover of female officers. As can be seen from Table 5.1, the total national turnover of female personnel is substantially higher than for males. In 1971, for example, premature wastage accounted for 12.9 per cent (500) of the total female personnel but only 2.2 per cent (2110) of the total male personnel. As the table demonstrates, the percentage of female personnel resigning (relative to the total female strength) is four or five times higher than for male officers. As indicated earlier, this is generally attributed to the fact that women (i) leave in order to have families, (ii) have different, more instrumental reasons for joining the police service (better pay and conditions, etc.) which prove to be inadequate compensation for the realities of police work, (iii) show a lack of commitment to policing as a life-long professional career; or to some combination of these reasons.

The present research suggests that at least two of these reasons are

TABLE 5.1   *Turnover of male and female police officers in England and Wales since 1971*

	Total no. females	Total wastage of females* (%)	Total premature wastage† (%)	Total no. males	Total wastage of males* (%)	Total premature wastage† (%)
1971	3 865	13·7	12·9	92 869	3·5	2·2
1972	4 165	13·6	12·9	95 385	3·7	2·3
1973	4 394	14·5	13·6	96 061	5·1	3·0
1974	4 767	16·8	15·8	97 213	5·1	3·0
1975	5 840	10·8	10·0	101 195	4·4	2·0
1976	7 066	13·0	12·0	102 303	6·4	2·3
1977	7 866	16·9	16·0	100 231	7·7	3·9
1978	8 555	15·6	14·9	100 415	5·6	3·4
1979	9 472	12·9	12·0	103 731	4·5	2·4
1980	10 430	10·5	9·8	106 889	4·1	2·1
1981	10 772	8·7	8·1	108 696	2·6	1·8
1982	11 015	8·3	7·6	109 830	3·6	1·5

*Includes retirements.
†Includes dismissals and officers required to resign.

unfounded in that women appear to join for the same kinds of reasons as men and, apart from some difference in career disposition, have a similar level of professional commitment. It also demonstrates one reason which does not appear in male accounting for early resignation: the mismatch demonstrated between expectations and actuality – a mismatch which may be in part due to the reality of deployment experiences for women. Later in this chapter we shall also consider the contribution of other factors to this phenomenon.

On a more positive note it is noticeable from the table that since 1971 this percentage dropped appreciably from 12.9 per cent to 7.6 per cent in 1982 (compared with 2.2 per cent to 1.5 per cent for policemen over the same period). Apart from the unsettled period between 1976 and 1979 (where total wastage was higher for reasons already discussed, for both males and females) this is indicative of an encouraging downward trend.

It is perhaps more difficult to discern the reasons for this decrease. It may be that contrary to the effects of the frustrations discussed above, it is possible to attribute the decline in wastage to the integrated and more varied role made possible by the Sex Discrimination Act. There is also the fact that it may also reflect female satisfaction with the pay and conditions of service as well as changing attitudes towards work outside the home.[9] Many of the women interviewed noted that, as relatively educationally or professionally unqualified women, it would be hard to match their present salary levels outside of the police service. Although this is also true for men, it is particularly the case for women. Nevertheless, these data do suggest a downward trend in female premature wastage which is all the more interesting when it is remembered that, given the influx of women in 1976–7, one might reasonably expect a substantial proportion of these women to have reached their marriage and child-bearing years and thus be contributing to the more 'familiar' cycle of resignations. What these figures do suggest is that mechanisms other than marriage and child-bearing influence female resignations.

In the case of Medshire[10] the loss of personnel through premature wastage is much lower for both males and females than the national average. In 1971, 1.75 per cent (42) of the total number of policemen resigned (or were dismissed or required to resign) in Medshire, compared with 2.2 per cent nationally. The higher figure for females at 17.9 per cent (13) compares unfavourably with the national average of 12.9 per cent, but this was an unusual year for the research force and in any case only represents an actual number of thirteen women resigning. In 1972, female premature wastage was 6.3 per cent (5) compared with a national figure of 12.9 per cent. In 1975, female and male premature wastage were 4.2 per cent (5) and 1.8 per cent (52) respectively compared with 10 per cent and 2 per cent nationally. The same figures for 1982 were 6.5 per cent (10) female and 0.5 per cent (16) male, compared with 7.6 per cent and 1.5 per cent nationally. Undoubtedly one important reason for the lower than average resignation rate in Medshire is the higher than average level of unemployment in the region.

This relatively low wastage rate is reflected in the length of service statistics for Medshire. Although a high proportion of females were still in their probationary period (24.6 per cent compared with 6.4 per cent males) this reflects the 1982 intake of women. (It will be recalled that there was an equalling out in successful applications in this year, see Table 3.6). Surprisingly, 60 per cent of the female personnel have served over five years and half of these have served over ten years. Whilst the percentage of men serving over five years is considerably higher (82.7 per cent), the belief expressed by a recruiting officer in this force that women rarely serve more than five years is evidently not entirely based in fact.

Whilst it is undeniable that there is some justification for the 'short service' criticism of policewomen, it is also the case that on a national basis there is evidence of a decline in the rate of premature wastage. Indeed, in Medshire the wastage 'problem' is not as pronounced as it is nationally, if one also bears in mind the proportion of women in the force who have served more than five years (though unfortunately national length of service statistics are not available for direct comparison). It is a moot point whether these comparisons could be used to argue that the 'extra' stringency applied to women applicants at the selection interview (Chapter 3) is successful in that the susbsequent premature wastage rate is low; or whether, by screening out women at the 'selecting in' stage, Medshire is pre-empting the 'problem' – a sort of reverse Catch 22 situation.

There is evidence to suggest that the concern about the shorter service of women officers derives more from the thirty-year or life-commitment ethos of policing than from a considered comparison with other occupational wastage rates. Such a comparison demonstrates that the actual wastage rate for males is unusually low in the police service,[11] and that the turnover of female officers is more typical of general trends in other occupations. This notion of a 'thirty-year commitment', the attitudes it gives rise to, and their implications for the selection process are discussed further in Chapter 7.

SUMMARY AND IMPLICATIONS

As a prelude to a more thorough examination of the careers of men and women in the police, this chapter has sought to establish whether there is any substance in some of the more common beliefs about what might be termed 'motivations' for both joining the police and establishing a career within it.

Whilst there are some differences, most notably in female wastage rates, male and female motivations are, perhaps surprisingly, similar. There are no discernible differences, for example, in the reasons given for joining the police, or people's initial expectations of police work. Men and women expected, with similar degrees of accuracy ranging from naive to realistic, a mainly interesting, varied and active occupation. Men and women alike were surprised by the actual experience of police work, particularly the amount of mundane and routine work, which did not match up to the more glamorous media images.

However, what is disturbing is the difference between female and male accounts of the degree of fulfilment of expectations. These suggest that there is a differential mismatch of expectations on joining and their fulfilment which can be attributed to the different qualitative experiences of police work between men and women. Further, it is the 'modern' group of women who are the most affected by this, despite the fact that this particular group has much the same kind of career disposition and professional commitment as their male colleagues. Such differences as are shown on these dimensions could be mainly attributed to time of joining the police service, with the 'traditional' women exhibiting less career disposition or professional commitment.

Whilst marriage and child-bearing is no doubt a prime factor in the higher rate of female resignations (and in the next chapter we will indicate ways in which the organisation might reduce this loss of experienced personnel), one must also ask whether these disappointed expectations also make a significant contribution to this phenomenon.

6 Getting On

Alongside the day-to-day experiences in the working lives of police officers, another aspect of the 'reality' of police work is the relative way in which careers develop for women and men officers. In the police service, the patterns of career development are an inevitable function of the 'one point of entry' philosophy discussed in relation to recruitment. As we have seen, not only does this aim to recruit individuals who are capable of attaining chief officer rank, there is a need for select people who will remain at the 'sharp end' of policing for all of their career. For these people patterns of career development will reflect different personal requirements, such as job enrichment and enhancement, whereas for the relatively few officers who do want and achieve promotion, career patterns will have a different emphasis.

PATTERNS OF CAREER DEVELOPMENT

Broadly speaking career development can be thought of as three related strands of occupational activity: individual development within an existing role; movement between different roles; and upward progression to positions of greater responsibility and power. In other words, career development can occur either by increased specialisation, greater variety of experience or promotion to a higher rank, though these are not mutually exclusive courses. Indeed, one would expect any individual career to be characterised by some unique combination of these activities.

It is the way in which these unique combinations differ between women and men which is the focus of this chapter though, because of the implications for individual power within the organisation, the particular emphasis is on promotion. As with the examination of recruitment and deployment, the task is to evaluate the impact that the equal opportunities legislation has had on the prospects of women officers and to analyse the reasons for any differences which may exist in terms of the practices which result from police organisational structure and culture. It is also evident from the differential practices already discussed in relation to deployment that there are fundamental experiential variations for men and women. The question which remains concerns whether these substantially affect general career development and specifically diminish promotion prospects.

Before the Sex Discrimination Act these issues were of relative insignificance because of the mainly specialist role of women officers and the separate career and promotion structure that existed. At the time of the Act it was claimed on the one hand that career prospects, including promotion, would be enhanced and on the other that women would be disadvantaged by having to compete on unfair terms with men. Some indication of the nature of this debate has already been given (Chapter 2). The contrary view, frequently expressed by men during the interviews, was that it was they who had become disadvantaged. The substance of their argument was that if a woman qualified by passing the examinations, she would automatically be promoted because of the need to demonstrate equality to the outside world by promoting 'token' women. Clearly, then, there is a considerable divergence of views on the benefits and disadvantages of integration on this aspect of the relative career development of men and women which deserves examination.

A further related set of issues, which derive from a consideration of career development, centre on the provisions made by the organisation. Although these provisions do not solely concern women, there are some which are very pertinent, such as maternity leave, provision made for women with responsibility for children (though, of course, this can apply equally to men) and opportunities for re-employment after a career-break for child-rearing. Factors of this kind may have a contributory effect on the careers that women are able to develop within the police service. They may be especially salient given the nature and organisation of police work, which is structured around the need to provide a twenty-four hour service, and the implications this has for coordinating child-rearing responsibilities with shift work.

CAREERS: INTEGRATION AND PROMOTION

The most direct way of appreciating the effect that the Act and the subsequent full integration of women has had on careers is through an examination of promotion both before and after the legislation. Conflicting views were expressed at the time about the likely consequences on promotion prospects and opportunities, some of which have already been outlined. The following section includes an examination of the national figures on promotion against which the information from Medshire is compared. The discussion then moves on to consider possible reasons for the prevailing patterns and the way in which these data are reflected in people's beliefs about the relative promotion prospects for women officers.

(i) National Trends

There are two available types of official statistics which are pertinent to this examination. The first, displayed in Table 6.1, is the breakdown of personnel by rank and gender; the second concerns the actual numbers of male and female officers promoted to each rank annually. These data are given in Table 6.2. The use of both sets of figures enables some allowance to be made for wastage through retirements, premature resignation and other reasons (such as dismissal or death in service).

Several interesting points emerge from an examination of Table 6.1. Of particular note are the trends revealed by the each rank's proportion of the total male or female workforce for each year. In the first instance, it is clear from the table that before the Act the actual proportions of women in the ranks above constable are smaller than those for men. There are two major reasons for this, both of which have been discussed previously, namely the higher premature wastage rate for women than for men (meaning, in effect, that in order to maintain establishment more women will be present in the lowest rank), and the steady increase in the annual rate of female recruitment during the five years before the Act.

It is also the case that *before* integration the proportion of women in higher ranks had begun to decline. Three reasons might begin to account for this. Firstly, although the total authorised strength had steadily increased this may not have been reflected in the proportion of women suitably qualified for promotion to sergeant and inspector rank (through length of service and passing the qualifying examinations). Secondly, as we have already noted, a number of women (of all ranks) left the service rather than face reorganisation. Finally, the process of integration had already begun in some forces with women officers being deployed on duties outside of the policewomen's departments in roles where, as a rule, they would not have been considered eligible for promotion.

TABLE 6.1 *Composition of police service of England and Wales displayed by rank and gender*

Rank	1971 M	1971 F	1975 M	1975 F	1976 M	1976 F	1980 M	1980 F	1982 M	1982 F
Constable	68 706 (73.98)*	3 213 (83.1)	74 111 (73.2)	5 109 (87.4)	74 952 (73.2)	6 390 (90.4)	77 728 (72.7)	9 788 (93.8)	80 258 (73.0)	10 323 (93.7)
Sergeant	15 970 (17.2)	433 (11.2)	17 092 (16.8)	469 (8.0)	17 356 (16.9)	431 (6.0)	18 351 (17.1)	425 (4.0)	18 484 (16.8)	482 (4.3)
Inspector	4 572 (4.9)	134 (3.5)	5 607 (5.5)	158 (2.7)	5 678 (5.5)	143 (2.0)	6 225 (5.8)	127 (1.2)	6 447 (5.8)	129 (1.1)
Chief Inspector	1 845 (2.0)	47 (1.2)	2 220 (2.2)	56 (0.95)	2 207 (2.15)	54 (0.76)	2 301 (2.15)	51 (0.48)	2 303 (2.0)	49 (0.44)
Super-intendent	939 (1.0)	38 (0.98)	1 332 (1.3)	39 (0.66)	1 295 (1.2)	37 (0.52)	1 462 (1.36)	36 (0.34)	1 509 (1.3)	24 (0.21)
Chief Super-intendent	673 (0.7)	—	676 (0.66)	9 (0.15)	666 (0.65)	11 (0.15)	666 (0.62)	3 (0.02)	672 (0.61)	8 (0.07)
ACC**	164 (0.17)	—	157 (0.15)	—	149 (0.14)	—	156 (0.14)	—	157 (0.14)	—
Totals by gender	92 869	3 865	101 195	5 840	102 303	7 066	106 889	10 430	109 830	11 015
Total	96 734		107 035		109 369		117 319		120 845	

* The figures in brackets represent the number in each rank as a proportion of total males or females in the service.
**Includes commanders in the Metropolitan and City of London Police.

TABLE 6.2 *Promotions actually made in England and Wales displayed by gender (including the Metropolitan Police)*

Promotion	1971		1972		1976		1980		1982	
	M	F	M	F	M	F	M	F	M	F
To Sergeant	1 360	52	1 886	50	2 681	28	1 407	45	1 504	58
To Inspector	496	18	694	14	1 091	12	707	7	817	17
To Chief Inspector	237	11	332	4	595	11	383	7	402	9
To Superintendent	125	14	182	—	371	8	277	5	284	1
To Chief Superintendent	63	—	57	2	209	2	148	—	123	6

The next point of interest concerns the fact that after the Sex Discrimination Act, the decline in the proportion of women holding ranks other than that of constable continues. So although 11.2 per cent of the female workforce held the rank of sergeant in 1971, this proportion had dropped to 8.0 per cent by 1975, to 6.1 per cent by 1976, and, to 4.3 per cent in 1982. Women holding the rank of inspector had dropped from 3.5 per cent of the female workforce in 1971 (compared with an equivalent figure for men of 4.9 per cent) to 1.1 per cent in 1982 (compared with 5.8 per cent for men). The pattern is similar in the more senior ranks.

These figures are calculated as a percentage of the total male *or* female personnel. Clearly, calculations based on the total workforce, a perfectly legitimate exercise given the abolition of the separate female establishment, show these differences in a more dramatic fashion. For example, male sergeants constituted 15.8 per cent of the total workforce of 109 369 in 1976, compared with an equivalent figure of 0.39 per cent for female sergeants. The proportion of male inspectors was 5.2 per cent compared with 0.13 per cent female inspectors. Indeed, the *actual* numbers of men sergeants increased by 1128 between 1976 and 1982, whereas for women the increase was only 51. In fact there have only been 49 more women sergeants since 1971 compared with an increase of 2514 men. There were actually *fewer* women inspectors in 1982 (129) than in 1971 (134), and this figure had dropped from 158 just before the Act in 1975. As shown in the table, the same is true of all other senior ranks – the number of women has actually dropped since before the Act. By way of contrast, the proportion of male officers in each rank has remained remarkably constant both before and subsequent to integration, and is roughly in line with the proportions recommended by the Police Advisory Boards of England, Scotland and Wales in 1972.[1]

This picture of differential promotions is confirmed by the numbers of actual promotions made. As can be seen from Table 6.2, overall there has been a steady increase in the numbers of male officers achieving promotion at all ranks, with a peak immediately after the Act. In the case of women officers, however, there were only six more promotions made to the rank of sergeant in 1982 than were made in 1971; and in the year of integration there were only 28 compared with 50 the year previously. The number of women achieving the ranks of inspector and chief inspector was about the same in 1982 as in 1971. In all cases above the rank of sergeant, the actual numbers of women promoted are very small. Only one woman achieved superintendent rank in 1982 and six were promoted to chief superintendent.

Even when these actual numbers are expressed as a percentage of the number of men and women in the previous rank (Table 6.3), there is little indication of any growth in female as compared to male promotions. For example, whereas male promotions to sergeant as a percentage of male constables is almost 2 per cent in 1971 and 1.9 per cent in 1982, the comparable figures for female promotions to sergeant are 1.6 per cent and 0.6 per cent (with a steady decline in the intervening years). Likewise, male promotions to inspector as a percentage of sergeants was 3.1 per cent in 1971 and 4.4 per cent in 1982 (with a peak of 6.2 per cent in 1976), compared with female promotions to this rank peaking at 4.1 per cent in 1971 and recovering, after a low of 1.6 per cent in 1980, to 3.5 per cent in 1982. At the higher ranks a similar, though less straightforward pattern emerges, with a generally lower proportion of women achieving the next rank as compared with men. As the table shows, the trend is complicated by some years in which there is a glut of promotions made to a particular rank, most likely because of reorganisation (for example the extension of the rank of chief superintendent to women in 1975), or more posts of these higher ranks becoming authorised on the establishment.

Given these two sets of national figures it is apparent that integration has not resulted in a greater number of promotions for female officers (despite their greater representation in the total workforce). Indeed, the 'open' competition provided by the disbandment of the policewomen's departments, which in theory meant that women were eligible for all positions (rather than those solely within the policewomen's departments), has not resulted in the increased opportunities anticipated by some women.

(ii) Local Trends

How are these national trends reflected in Medshire? Table 6.4 displays the composition of Medshire by rank and gender for the years 1971, 1975 and 1982. Also included in this table are the actual promotions made for each of those years. As can be seen from the table, the local situation is much the same. Whilst some allowance must be made for the very low numbers involved, it is clear that both before and after the Act a higher proportion of women officers are in

TABLE 6.3 *Promotions made expressed as a percentage of male and female officers in the previous rank*

Promotion	1971		1972		1975		1976		1980		1982	
	M	F	M	F	M	F	M	F	M	F	M	F
To Sergeant	2·0	1·6	2·1	1·7	2·5	1·0	3·6	0·4	1·8	0·4	1·9	0·6
To Inspector	3·1	4·1	3·3	1·7	4·0	3·0	6·2	2·8	3·8	1·6	4·4	3·5
To Chief Inspector	5·2	8·2	5·8	1·5	5·9	2·5	10·5	7·7	6·2	5·5	6·2	6·9
To Superintendent	6·8	29·7	12·6	6·5	8·2	—	16·8	14·8	12·0	9·8	12·3	2·0
To Chief Superintendent	6·7	—	6·0	—	4·2	5·1	16·1	5·4	10·1	—	8·1	25·0

the rank of constable, and their representation in the higher ranks, as a proportion of the total number of women in the force, is lower at all ranks than for men in the force.

As with the national figures, the proportions of men represented in each rank have been maintained and, for some ranks, actually increased between 1971 and 1982. Accordingly, there were 404 sergeants (16.8 per cent of the male personnel) in 1971 and this figure had risen to 520 (17.6 per cent) in 1982. The equivalent figures for women officers were 8 (11.9 per cent) and 10 (6.5 per cent) representing a proportional decrease. Similarly with inspectors, 54 male inspectors had been created by 1982 (from 5.1 per cent to 6.0 per cent of the male personnel) compared with just one extra female inspector (again representing a proportional decrease).

The pattern is repeated for the other senior ranks. The growth in the overall size of the force during this period would, in fact, justify an increase in the numbers in the rank above constable. However, it is also the case that during this period the percentage increase in *male* personnel was 22.9 per cent, whereas for female personnel the increase over the 1971 figure was 128 per cent. As we have already seen, the premature wastage rate for female personnel is much lower than the national average (see Chapter 5). This, combined with the relatively favourable female length of service statistics, indicates that it would be difficult to use these factors in sole explanation of the low promotion rate amongst women officers in Medshire.

It would, of course, be unrealistic to expect a dramatic equalisation of the proportions of men and women in each rank at either a national or a local level, since it might be expected that any equal opportunities policy would take a few years to make a substantial impact. It is also necessary to take into account the fact that there was some loss of female officers in the mid-seventies and an initial influx immediately after integration (for reasons which had little to do with the legislation, see Chapter 3). Due to the 'one point of entry' system it might be expected that there would be a time lag before a proportion of these female recruits were suitably qualified for promotion. This being so, the question still remains as to why the existing 'pool' of experienced women did not produce promotable material. Though one could argue that, at least for the first two or three years after integration, many of these women might lack relevant deployment experience (that is, on duties other than traditional policewomen's tasks) and/or be considered unready to supervise male officers, one might quite

TABLE 6.4 Composition of Medshire by rank and gender and actual promotions made

		1971				1975				1982			
		Composition		Promotions		Composition		Promotions		Composition		Promotions	
		M	F	M	F	M	F	M	F	M	F	M	F
Constable	(no.)	1 766	56			2 080	106			2 125	138		
	(%)	(73.7)	(83.1)	32	1	(73.1)	(90.5)	72	—	(72.2)	(90.2)	55	1
Sergeant	(no.)	404	8			477	7			520	10		
	(%)	(16.8)	(11.9)			(16.7)	(5.9)			(17.6)	(6.5)		
Inspector	(no.)	124	1	8	1	167	2	23	—	178	2	31	1
	(%)	(5.1)	(1.5)			(5.8)	(1.7)			(6.0)	(1.3)		
C/Inspector	(%)	46	1	5	1	61	1	8	—	60	2	18	1
	(%)	(1.9)	(1.5)			(2.1)	(0.8)			(2.0)	(1.3)		
Superintendent	(no.)	38	1	3	—	42	1	4	—	41	1	13	—
	(%)	(1.5)	(1.5)			(1.4)	(0.8)			(1.4)	(0.6)		
C/Superintendent	(no.)	12	—	1	—	13	—	2	—	14	—	4	—
	(%)	(0.5)				(0.4)				(0.4)			
ACC	(no.)	4	—	—	—	3	—	—	—	4	—	—	—
	(%)	(0.1)				(0.1)				(0.1)			
Total		2 395	67	49	3	2 843	117	109	—	2 943	153	121	3

reasonably have expected to have seen some substantial increase by the end of 1982.

Again, it is highly likely that the higher turnover of female officers has both directly and indirectly contributed to this phenomenon (as discussed below). However, as already noted, this premature wastage rate has steadily declined since the equal pay and opportunities legislation and this factor now has far less salience than previously when, paradoxically, the proportions of women in the ranks above constable were substantially higher. Clearly the higher wastage rate does not account for the discrepancy.

In any event, it should also be remembered that there have also been considerable fluctuations in male officer wastage and recruitment rates. These could have been expected to have had similar, though proportionately smaller (given the difference in the actual numbers of male and female personnel) consequences for the male rank structure.

Two important concerns arise from this examination of rank and gender comparisons: Why has it been possible to maintain the proportions of male but not female officers in all the ranks above constable in the face of often dramatically changing patterns of recruitment and wastage? And, why, in the light of the equal opportunities legislation, has there not been even a marginal improvement in actual promotions for women officers? Indeed, the evidence demonstrates an actual decrease in promotions for women officers, particularly in the more senior, responsible and, ultimately, powerful ranks.

(iii)   Ability, Ambition and Opportunity

How can we begin to account for these promotion figures? Is it the case that women officers are consistently less able or less ambitious? Or can their lack of progress through the ranks be attributed to a system in which their opportunities are restricted either deliberately or unknowingly? These two sets of explanations are usually offered in a polarised fashion to either justify or declaim the apparent lack of achievement, through promotion, of women officers. What in fact does appear to be happening, and perhaps not unexpectedly, is that there is a complex, sometimes subtle, interaction between these two sets of factors which results in an adverse effect on career chances.

From what we already know about the ability of women on appointment it would seem difficult to sustain the argument that they are generally less fitted for promotion. This *prima facie* argument derives from the fact that there is evidence that women have better academic qualifications on appointment and that there is, in any case, extra stringency in their recruitment and selection. And, since theoretically the same selection criteria are supposed to be applied, women should fare as well as their male colleagues. Yet, during the interviews, lack of ability was claimed in explanation of poor promotion performance. What was also evident from these interviews, however, was that it is not the 'academic' ability of women which is questioned. Indeed, their 'cleverness' was often offered as a rationale for their frequent deployment on administrative duties. What was questioned was their *practical* ability. As one male inspector, explaining what junior ranks expected of a supervisor, put it:

> they have to be confident in your ability to do the job. If they're not, they can't cope. They have to know that if a supervisor arrives at a situation ... If it were me, I would expect, if I were being supervised, them to make a decision quickly. (Case No. MB10)

In other words, alongside the more general scepticism about the practical relevance of academic knowledge (and the frequently expressed doubts about the recruitment of graduates also stems from this) is a specific concern about the particular ability of women to supervise in practical situations.

For front-line officers this is especially important and is manifested in male fears about women's ability to cope with operational duties involving physical stamina or strength.

In relation to promotion, the focus of these doubts becomes subtly relocated. In this case, although the practical task is not as overtly physical as in the front-line patrol and law-enforcement duties, it does involve the supervision of *men* engaged in them. Alongside the more obvious issue of dominance and authority, and the assumption that women are unable to 'control' men, is the belief that in order to supervise effectively it is necessary to have 'shared experiences'. This is one of the virtues attributed to, and assumed to derive from, the 'one point of entry' recruitment philosophy. The implication is that women lack a 'natural' empathy, and hence understanding, and as a consequence are unable to manage or supervise.

Clearly, one element in this equation is the respect 'earned' by supervisors (especially at the sergeant and inspector level) by being seen to be (or to have been) a good practical officer. This is the nearest equivalent to the American notion of being 'street-wise' and carries the same high value in the sub-culture (though 'street-wise' women are perversely considered to be unfeminine or 'not quite nice'). This is almost bound to be a source of doubt in the case of women since there is a widespread awareness of the different nature and quality of women's deployment experiences. The element of self-fulfilment in these expectations is obvious. Applying their own argument, practical ability for both men and women comes through rehearsal of policing skills in a variety of deployment situations; restrictions on the chances to rehearse by limiting deployment practices leads to a lack of 'street' credibility, empathy and doubts about 'natural' ability.

This provides a classic example of a situation where deployment opportunities and ability considerations interact to enhance existing doubts about the suitability of women for promotion. The additional fact that the average length of service for women is shorter casts doubt on their commitment to policing as a career and amplifies these doubts. What is less clear in this particular instance is which is the cause and which the effect, since it is easy to see how perceived lack of chances in both deployment and promotion could itself generate less commitment on the part of women – a phenomenon which has been observed in other organisations.[2] As outlined in Figure 6.1, doubts about women's ability and commitment in a male-orientated work setting, both on operational duties and as supervisory officers, results in qualitative differences in deployment duties and fewer promotions for women. This leads to a perceived lack of chances amongst women officers and generates a decrease in confidence in their own ability. As a result women become less committed and fewer women attempt achieving promotion. In one sense the psychological stakes become higher since failure to achieve promotion, even when the chances are seen to be unequal, is a threat to self-esteem. This 'feeds' the cause and effect spiral since it reinforces the male stereotype about ability and lack of commitment or ambition, and gives them justification for perpetuating the existing relationship. In relation to promotion, the irony is that the highly valued practical law-enforcement skills, around which the doubts about women's ability are formulated and sustained, are not central to the supervisory and management tasks of higher ranks.

The dynamic described in the figure introduces the notion of ambition into the analysis and demonstrates how failure to achieve promotion can reinforce the stereotype that female officers have less ambition. The obvious question that this raises is one concerning the validity of the assumptions underlying the stereotype. In other words,

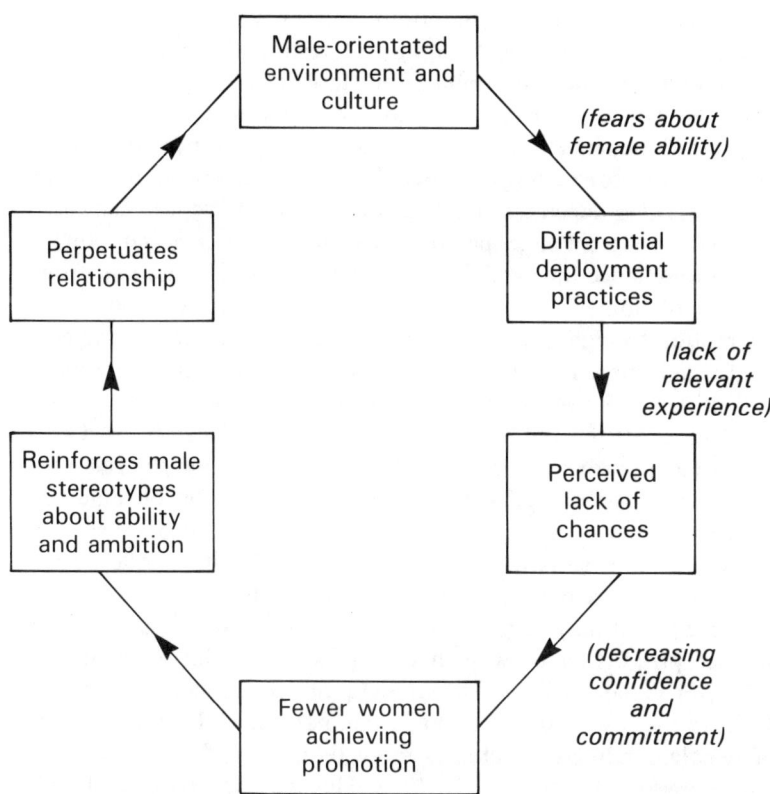

FIGURE 6.1. Cause and effect spiral

is there evidence to suggest that women are substantially less ambitious, or does the process described in the figure provide a more viable explanation of their relatively poor promotion performance?

In this instance there is some evidence which indicates that women officers are comparatively less ambitious. For example, the earlier information about relative career disposition suggests that, in general, women are less career-minded (though this was a situation in transition, particularly amongst the younger women). And, whilst it is a truism to say that career-development may take different forms for different individuals, there are nevertheless common-sense grounds for supposing that people who are less committed to policing as a career may also be less ambitious and as a consequence be less interested in promotion. One way of testing this possibility is to examine the promotion examination statistics.

In the police service, promotion to the ranks of sergeant and inspector is dependent on the individual having first passed qualifying examinations for each rank. Eligibility to take the promotion examinations is also dependent on length of service. Except in the case of the Metropolitan Police, passing the examination is no guarantee of promotion, since the candidate has then to pass at least one promotion board (some forces hold divisional *and* force promotion boards). Promotion to higher ranks within a force is the result of a system of annual appraisal and promotion boards. For promotions to sergeant and inspector however, the information about the numbers of men and women sitting and passing these examinations can be used as the basis of an approximate index. The relative proportions (in relation to the total police strength) thus gives some indication of 'ambition'. These national data are displayed in Table 6.5, and because of the special arrangements that apply in the Metropolitan Police, figures for that force are omitted from the calculations.

Three points may be made about the table. Firstly, it is clear that a smaller proportion of women officers sit both the sergeant's and inspector's examinations. The second point concerns the trends since 1975. In the case of the sergeant's examination, whilst the proportion of female candidates fluctuates more than that of males, there is a narrowing of the difference by 1982. This may be partly attributable to the fact that women recruited during the 1977–9 'bulge' are now eligible (and presumably motivated) to apply to sit the examinations. Whatever the cause, the trend since integration is upward with 7.4 per cent of all the candidates sitting this examination being women in 1982 compared with 4.8 per cent in 1975.

However, the trend is in the opposite direction for the inspector's examination, with a steady decrease in the proportion of women sitting it. For this examination, the gap between male and female officers has grown since integration, with only 1.5 per cent of women officers applying to take it in 1982, compared with 4.6 per cent of male officers. Of all candidates for this examination in 1975, 3.6 per cent were women compared with 3.2 per cent in 1982 (though this did rise to 3.6 per cent in 1983). In the intervening years this proportion was even lower (see Appendix C).

The final point concerns examination results. Here again there is no evidence to suggest that women are less able in formal terms. If

TABLE 6.5 Promotion examination statistics since integration (excluding the Metropolitan Police)*

		1975 M	1975 F	1976 M	1976 F	1980† M	1980† F	1982 M	1982 F	1982‡ M	1982‡ F
Total sergeants		13 465	413	13 674	378	14 611	345	14 614	353		
Total inspectors		4 443	135	4 499	123	4 966	107	5 080	110		
Total workforce		80 657	4 958	81 142	5 797	85 272	8 356	85 884	8 551		
Candidates for sergeant's exam	(no.)	12 615	639	12 668	448	10 447	762	10 222	818	375	6
Passed**	(no.)	1 066	66	1 909	74	1 753	135	1 188	85	189	3
	(%)	8·5	10·3	15·1	16·5	16·8	17·7	11·6	10·4		
Candidates for inspector's exam	(no.)	4 118	154	4 208	135	4 604	103	4 019	133	81	1
Passed	(no.)	854	24	532	18	1 816	46	1 250	60	47	—
	(%)	20·7	15·6	12·6	13·3	39·4	44·7	31·3	45·1		
Workforce sitting sergeant's exam	(%)	15·6	12·8	15·6	7·7	12·2	9·1	11·9	9·5		
Workforce sitting inspector's exam	(%)	5·1	3·1	5·1	2·3	5·4	1·2	4·6	1·5		

* A selection of years are represented in the table. Further details for the years 1973–83 can be found in Appendix C.
** Includes referrals.
† The format of the sergeant's examination altered in 1979 as did the inspector's examination in 1980.
‡ Medshire figures for this year.

anything a higher overall proportion of female candidates pass the examinations, though as we have seen this does not seem to be reflected in the numbers of women actually achieving promotion. It is difficult to make direct comparisons here, since people who qualify for promotion in one year may have to attend several annual promotion boards before being recommended for a higher rank. Also, once recommended there may be a delay (of years in some cases) before a suitable vacancy arises and the officer is actually appointed or 'made up' to the next rank. Unfortunately, the in-depth examination of male and female experiences of these stages was beyond the scope of this study. Nevertheless, it is clear that the promotion interviews are crucial to the final decision about who is appointed.

A rough comparison of examination performance and actual promotions made demonstrates this point. Between integration, when women became eligible for consideration for *all* posts in the service, and 1982 a total of 12 366 male officers passed the examination to sergeant; 13 007 men have been promoted to that rank.[3] In the same period 756 women passed the examination but less than half of these (303) survived the subsequent promotion boards. Even allowing for the effect of the higher turnover rate this would seem to be indicative of a differential selection process at the board stage. Similarly, 8132 male officers passed the inspector's examination and in the same period 3975 men were promoted to that rank. This compares with 232 women actually passing the examination but only 76 achieving promotion. In other words roughly a third of the qualified women but a half of the men are promoted to inspector rank. Clearly, there is a need to examine the promotion board process in more depth to establish why qualified women are ultimately less successful in achieving appointment to higher ranks. It is a question of some importance since subsequent promotions to the rank of chief inspector and above are *wholly* dependent on subjective appraisal and interview procedures.

This examination of the national examination and promotion statistics suggests that there is some substance to the argument that women are less ambitious. It also indicates that the chances of qualified women surviving the subsequent interview processes are also considerably less than for men. It is this discrepancy which, if recognised by women as an unfair lack of promotion chances, could influence the cause and effect spiral. Although it is not possible to directly examine the processes subsequent to the examination stage, the research does provide local information about male and female perceptions of promotion opportunities and processes. But it is instructive, first, to set the local situation at the time of the research in context.

In Medshire, only six women officers sat the sergeant's examination in 1982, compared with 375 male officers. Only one of these women passed the examination (bringing the total number of women in the force qualified to sergeant rank to three) compared with 81 male officers (the total of male officers qualified to sergeant rank was 301). Similarly, whereas 189 men sat the inspector's examination (47 passed, bringing the total qualified to 191), only three women actually sat the examination. None of these passed, and in fact only one woman was currently qualified to inspector rank. These figures for women officers in Medshire compare unfavourably with the national picture, though the reverse is true for male officers. Does this mean that women in Medshire are even less ambitious than would appear to be the case from the national figures? It was against this background that the issue of comparative male and female ambition was dealt with in both the questionnaire and the interviews.

In the first instance, it is clear from the survey that promotion *is* considered to be less important by the women officers. Almost 70 per cent of the men and 41 per cent of the women felt that achieving promotion was important or very important to them. Almost a third of the women, but only 15 per cent of the men, were 'not bothered either way about promotion'. However, as with career orientation, time of joining the police service is a crucial factor for both men and women. Almost 86 per cent of the younger male officers and 61 per cent of their female colleagues were interested in promotion. Of the 'traditional' males 62 per cent but only 19 per cent of the pre-integration women, felt promotion was important. What is interesting here is the size of the difference between the two groups of women officers: the 'modern' group, whilst still not displaying as much commitment to promotion as their equivalent male colleagues, nonetheless do feel it is important.

There is less difference between 'modern' men and women on the question of promotion prospects. Whereas 37 per cent of *all* the men who felt promotion was important, compared with 21 per cent of the women, rated their chances of obtaining promotion within the next five years as 'very good' or 'good', for the two younger groups the margin narrows to 40 per cent and 30 per cent respectively. And, asked to rate their chances of obtaining promotion within ten years, male and female views were almost equally optimistic at 73 per cent and 70 per cent respectively. It was the older group of women who were the least optimistic (or maybe in the light of their experience, realistic) about their chances. Only a third of this group (compared with two-thirds of their equivalent male colleagues) were optimistic about achieving promotion within five years.

The optimism of the younger women is also reflected in their perception of promotion opportunities: 78 per cent felt policewomen had as many opportunities for promotion as policemen (compared with 67 per cent of their older colleagues). Male officers in both groups were even more positive: 90 per cent of the 'moderns' and 85 per cent of the 'traditionals' subscribed to this view. Similarly, when asked to judge the effect of integration on promotion opportunities, 35 per cent of the 'modern' women felt there were now more opportunities for promotion, compared with 25 per cent and 13 per cent feeling there were equal (with men) or fewer opportunities than before. While 34 per cent of the 'modern' and 42 per cent of the 'traditional' men felt that women had more opportunities than before integration, a further 40 per cent and 35 per cent respectively, felt that they now had equal opportunities for promotion. Again, it is the traditional group of women who provide a different point of view. Just under 20 per cent felt there were now more, 25 per cent equal, and 35 per cent felt there were less, opportunities for promotion for policewomen than before integration. These data are displayed in Table 6.6.

TABLE 6.6   *Medshire male and female officers' perceptions of promotion opportunities since integration*

| | Male | | | Female | | |
	Trad	Mod	Overall	Trad	Mod	Overall
More	46	34	42	20	35	28
Equal	35	40	37	22	25	24
Fewer	7	5	6	35	13	22
Same as before	11	3	9	22	—	9
Don't know	—	6	6	2	27	16

The optimistic view held by the 'modern' policewomen, and their reasons for it, were evident from the interviews. The most common belief was that, provided the woman officer qualified by passing the examinations, she would almost automatically get promoted. One woman, when asked what her ambitions were, gave her version of this belief, as well as illustrating the difficulties involved in organising the studying required:

> To get promotion – if I pass. I'm studying like mad. It's getting me down . . . I thought, I won't study at night. My husband isn't in the force, you see . . . If I do enough work, I should pass I think . . . I'm going to take my exam in November. If I pass I should get a very, very good chance of promotion, if only because there's no women qualified . . . So if you get qualified, you're laughing. Far more chance than the men of getting promotion. (Case No. AF03)

Another 'modern' woman, when asked what rank she thought she might achieve, replied:

> I don't know . . . I would get as far as inspector, perhaps. But really the chances for promotion for a female are far better than they are for the male, so there's no stopping you once you take that first step and pass your exams. (Case No. AF05)

Only two of the younger group of women interviewed expressed a more down-to-earth opinion. One of these was actually fairly sceptical about the nature of the promotions made:

> . . . but it's not very often that you hear of policewomen being promoted . . . I know of one who's qualified to sergeant and she has a white paper. She should be made up pretty soon . . . I think a woman will stand far more chance of being promoted into a desk job like juvenile liaison. (Case No. FA08)

Clearly, for this woman promotion is seen as another mechanism by which women can be 'safely' deployed!

As one might expect given the survey data on this topic, the policemen interviewed, both 'modern' and 'traditional', shared the optimistic view of the younger women. As one officer with five years' service commented:

> It always seems to me that when you read the orders of promotions that when a woman police officer has passed her exams, she's automatically considered. I think there's more vacancies initially made for them. (Case No. MA07)

This latter comment highlights a distinction in the kinds of reasons offered by men and women for this apparently favourable (but inaccurate) view of the promotion prospects for women. In the case of the younger women the most frequent explanation was the scarcity of suitably qualified women. If a woman qualified she would compete on equal terms and would be viewed favourably precisely because so few women did qualify. The most common view held by the men took this 'positive action' hypothesis a stage further by inferring that because the organisation was anxious to demonstrate it offered equal opportunities, special vacancies were created and kept for 'token' women.

The disparate views on promotion opportunities expressed by the 'traditional' policewomen as compared with all the other men and women interviewed and surveyed demonstrates the consequences of the cause and effect spiral proposed earlier. It was suggested that the realisation that the chances of surviving the promotion boards are considerably less for qualified women might trigger the dynamic involved in the cycle. Although the actual numbers of pre-integration women are small, it is clear that the national picture is replicated in Medshire. In Medshire, just over half of the women who had passed their examinations had been before a divisional promotion board but none of them had been selected to go on to a force board. By way of contrast, 74 per cent of the men who passed their examinations had been selected to attend a divisional board. Of these, 52 per cent went on to a force board. A quarter of these men were finally recommended for promotion.

The net result of the older women's experience of this reality is that they have both a pessimistic view of their own chances and also have a general perception that there are fewer chances for women since integration. To complete the analysis in the terms postulated earlier we would, of course, need to know whether their ambitions had been adversely affected, through a possible loss of confidence, because of their experiences. In other words, was the lack of interest in promotion, as demonstrated by the survey data, a cause or an effect? Some evidence that it is an effect comes from the fact that although 19 per cent of these women said that promotion was 'not important' to them, nevertheless 63 per cent of them had at some time or other gone to the considerable trouble of studying for, and sitting, the examinations.

We can only speculate about how the 'modern' policewomen will view their chances of promotion should the trends already observed continue. It is highly probable, however, that unless more women are seen to survive the promotion process (and, in particular, the various boards) the mismatch of expectations, already evident amongst the younger women in relation to their deployment experiences, will continue to fuel the 'cycle of disadvantage'. It is clear from this analysis that as judged by the *officially* recognised criteria, women do have the ability to achieve promotion; there is also evidence of their increasing ambition. What appears to be lacking is the opportunity for them to achieve.

CAREERS: MARRIAGE AND CHILDREN

One of the explanations explored in relation to the higher turnover of female personnel was that a substantial number of women leave the service when they marry or subsequently decide to have children. Indeed, 81 per cent of the men and 64 per cent of the women agreed with the proposition that 'most policewomen' leave the service for these reasons. While this may not be the only reason for the loss of women from policing, it certainly appears to be the major one. The fact that women do leave for these 'personal' reasons is often cited both as the cause of women's lack of achievement and as justification, on economic and practical grounds, for practices which are to their disadvantage. When this study was planned, the notion of women combining marriage, children and a police career did not seem to be very widely accepted by police officers as a plausible proposition. Somehow policing, unlike other professional occupations, was seen as not only unusually difficult to combine successfully with marriage and child-rearing, but also one which married women officers *should* leave when they have families. It was for these reasons that this topic (and related issues) was included in the questionnaire and the interviews.

(i) Marital status of male and female officers

A comparison of male and female questionnaire respondents illustrates a marked difference in the marital status of male and female police officers. Only 31 per cent of the women, but 84 per cent of the men, were married. A further comparison of the 'traditional' and 'modern' groups reveals some other interesting differences. For example, 62 per cent of the younger women, but only 34 per cent of their male counterparts, were single. No doubt this is partly because of the much higher proportion of younger, probationer women, which is reflected in the age distribution. Of the women in this group, 62 per cent were aged between 18 and 24 years compared with 31 per cent of the men. On age grounds alone, one might reasonably expect a higher proportion of married officers in the 'traditional' group and, in fact, 95 per cent of the men were married. However, the proportion of married women officers in this group is about the same, at 32 per cent, as for their younger female colleagues. Again, the age distribution of men and women in this group does differ somewhat, with a higher proportion (57 per cent) of women than men (32 per cent) in the 25–34 year-old group. Nevertheless, this on its own could not account for the difference in marital status between the two groups since this is the 'prime' age group for marriage and child-bearing. Besides, a substantial 40 per cent of these women are in the higher age group (35 to 55 years old).[4]

The lower proportion of married officers in both groups of women confirms the view that married women leave once they decide to have their families. It also indicates that very few women return to policing once their families grow up. Only 10 per cent of all the women surveyed, for example, compared with 76 per cent of the men, had children. The overall higher proportion of older, single women might also be taken as indicating that policing as a career is incompatible with marriage for women, but not for men. In this respect, it is interesting to note that almost twice as many women with between ten and twenty-five years' service were single rather than married. These facts give support to the existence of the situation embodied in the suggestion reported by Heller and McGill that:

> if women want to make a career for themselves in the police force then they ought not to get married – or at least ought not to have children.

They go on to argue that:

> this is discriminatory, since presumably male officers get married and have children without jeopardising their careers.[5]

These comparisons prompt several questions. First and foremost, why is it that, at a time when the general trend is for more women to combine careers and family responsibilities,[6] such a significant proportion of women choose to leave the police service? And, related to this, what is it about a police career which, in Medshire at least,[7] marks it as a 'single woman's' pursuit? Is it because of the particular way in which police work is organised, as compared to other professions? Or, is it the result of the qualitative nature of policing, part of which is the constant exposure to the adverse results of family disruption? Does the culture of the organisation contribute to this phenomenon through the perpetuation of gender-based expectations of policewomen, both inside and outside the workplace?

In the case of the organisation of police work, the disturbance to family life caused by shift work and irregular hours (such as those experienced by CID officers) is a relevant factor; though this has not proved to be such a drawback in other professions, most notably in the female-dominated occupation of nursing. Nevertheless, 74 per cent of the 'traditional' women felt that shifts and irregular hours did disrupt their personal lives. Over half of this group (54 per cent) also felt it was more difficult to combine a police career with marriage and children since integration. These general questions were only asked of this group and were offered for comment as one of a series of post-integration 'changes' which might have affected them.

As for the nature of police work, police officers are often the 'first-aid' providers in situations involving domestic disputes and cases involving missing, neglected or deliberately brutalised children. Quite apart from the impact that these repeated (though, it must be stated, skewed) experiences have on attitudes to family life, it has long been recognised that, as a group, police officers tend to be conservative, 'status quo maintainers', with strong beliefs about traditional family values. In keeping with this was the finding from previous research that 'lack of discipline in the home' was more strongly perceived by police officers than by the public to be a primary cause of crime.

Whilst these alone may be very powerful reasons, they may be given extra potency by the additional pressure of male expectations of the 'female' role of policewomen. The interviews provide illustrative evidence of this latter factor both in relation to the attitudes which underpin deployment decisions (see Chapter 4) and directly in relation to family responsibilities. For example, one younger policewoman reported that since her marriage there was an expectation by her male colleagues that she would soon be leaving, and, on her annual appraisal interviews she was routinely asked when (not if) she would be leaving (Case No. FA05). This raises for consideration the question of how much positive encouragement women receive to persuade them to continue their careers, both directly through the appraisal system, or indirectly through their supervisors and peers. Not one of the women interviewed was able to recall specific instances of positive formal encouragement, though some did feel their colleagues, rather than their supervisors, were supportive. Another 'modern' woman said she thought that married policewomen were often given ultimatums to leave 'the job' by their husbands, particularly if, as often happens, they had married policemen. When asked why, she said she thought it was due to a combination of what they expected from their wives and knowledge of the working practices of police officers. This latter category would include exposure to the more unpleasant or dangerous aspects of policing and perhaps more significantly, from a husband's point of view, some of the dodges or cover-up practices employed by police officers for their 'extra curricular' activities!

The interviews with the male officers also reflected their expectations that married women would eventually leave the service. One went as far as to suggest that even a fairly senior female officer on his division, despite a long and evidently successful career, would leave 'if she ever met a man who fitted the bill' (Case No. MA06).

Male expectations may also indirectly influence female resignations for family reasons. The mismatch between career expectations and reality (see Chapter 5) may in some cases become another reason to conform to gender-based stereotypes and, by providing women with a legitimate excuse to leave, substantial conflict concerning role expectations is avoided.

The range of consequences to which this comparatively unusual situation gives rise is both varied and has substantial impact. The consequences include the economic loss to the organisation of trained personnel (and probably at a time when their accrued experience is becoming increasingly valuable); the loss to the community of this expertise; the perpetuation of gender-based expectations and their translation into adverse recruitment, deployment and career decisions; and, importantly, the personal consequences to women who may wish to combine marriage and motherhood with their police careers or to return to their careers after a break for child-rearing. Certainly, given the present comparatively high police salaries, it is likely that combining career and family responsibilities will become an increasingly attractive economic proposition. Inasmuch as we have already seen a substantial growth in the career disposition among 'modern' women officers, the resulting combination of economics and career commitment may well result in a desire to change existing female career patterns.

Clearly, there are issues of 'justice with fairness' as well as economic grounds for examining possible methods or actions by which these consequences and their effects can be offset or avoided. There would seem to be two possible kinds of organisational response which may be effective at both the economic and personal levels. These are organisational provision and rejoining policy.

(ii) Organisational Provision

This concerns the practical provision made by the organisation to enable people, male and female, to successfully combine career and family commitments. It is important to emphasise that, apart from the obvious exception of maternity leave provision, some possible responses are, and should be, to the benefit of male officers and their families as well. Just as some women officers are attempting to combine careers and families, so too are some policemen and their wives (who may or may not be police officers). Similar difficulties are faced by widowed, divorced or separated fathers who find they have to combine child-care responsibilities with their careers. Much of the resentment expressed in the interviews about the 'cushy' indoor, nine-to-five jobs being reserved for married women might be defused if policy statements and organisational practice reflect concern with both men and women. Whilst the following discussion will, in the main refer to policewomen, the principle outlined above is implicit.

In order to establish the extent to which police officers felt that the police service should make provision of this kind, the police officers surveyed were asked how far they agreed with the proposition that the police service should do more to make it possible for women to combine a police career with marriage and children. There was a clear difference of opinion between male and female officers. Over half of both groups of policewomen, with 55 per cent of the 'traditional' and 58 per cent of the 'modern', agreeing that this should be the case. By way of contrast only 22 per cent of the 'traditional' and 31 per cent of the 'modern' policemen felt this way.

The interviews revealed two main reasons for this male response. The first focused on the notion of equality. In particular the feeling expressed was that it would be wrong for women to receive preferential treatment over men. Typical comments concerned the perceived preferential allocation of nine-to-five jobs to married women mentioned above (though, paradoxically, this same solution was offered by some men interviewed as a way of reducing women's exposure to 'risk'). Another source of resentment was the matching of married policewomen's shifts with those of their husbands, should he also be a police officer. The second focused more on individual freedom to choose. In this case the common argument offered was that if a person joined the police service they knew what to expect, that the organisation should not make concessions, that people could leave if they could not cope, and that 'the job' was more important than the individuals doing it.

Some of the women interviewed also expressed similar, if less hard-line, sentiments both about preferential treatment and the freedom to choose. However, most recognised the special difficulties faced by married women and, although sceptical about the organisational 'will' to consider various changes in working practices on these grounds, were concerned that some flexibility should be allowed.

Possible ways of achieving this flexibility which were raised during the interviews included child-care provision, part-time opportunities, regular hours rather than shifts, different shift patterns, and deployment in specialist departments such as juvenile liaison. Clearly, some of these met with more enthusiasm than others. Indeed, the notion of child-care provision, although considered seriously by some women who felt that it might be possible for off-duty policewomen to organise, administer and run a creche, was met with considerable scepticism and, it must be said, derision, particularly by male officers. The two possibilities which received the most support from women officers were the possibility of regular hours and part-time work.

Regular hours had undoubted attractions for some women since they felt it would allow them to plan child-care provision more effectively. Shift work, particularly the continental system worked in Medshire, made it extremely difficult to organise family responsibilities. One younger married woman, whose husband also worked shifts (though not as a police officer) said that they 'often felt like ships passing in the night' (Case No. FA03), and, although she personally enjoyed working shifts she could not see how she would be able to cope if she were to have children.

Although the advantages of regular hours seem obvious, there are some important disadvantages. Not least of these is the hostility, already evident, that would be caused by women getting preferential treatment, even though this might be for a limited period of their careers and men might also be eligible for such provision in the same circumstances. A long-term consequence of this could well be the hardening of 'anti' policewomen attitudes within the service. If the provision of regular hours was also coupled with deployment in specialist departments, the patterns of deployment already in evidence could also be perpetuated.

Another serious consideration concerns promotion. Women with a background of regular working hours may be considered too inexperienced for supervisory roles and, indeed, the need to work regular hours may debar some people from promotion since it is customary that promotion (at least to the ranks of sergeant and inspector) usually means a period of shift work. This dilemma is highlighted by an article about a woman in the Metropolitan police, in their in-house magazine *The Job*. She resolved the problem by moving to a larger house in order to be able to employ a residential nanny. This rather expensive solution allowed her to return to shift work and so not jeopardise her career.[8]

In the case of part-time work, this was sometimes linked to the notion of rejoining the police service (see below) at a later date once their children were less dependent. The idea of part-time work has several attractions since, if properly negotiated, it could fulfil the needs of both the organisation and the officer concerned. An obvious example might be weekend working, where demand is highest for police services but when the possibility of the officer's spouse being able to take on the responsibility of child-care might also be greatest. It would also allow continued familiarity with police work by the officer concerned so that if and when she or he was able to rejoin on a full-time basis there would be less need for full retraining. Another undoubted benefit would be that the police service would not loose the expertise of the officer concerned and would be continuing, albeit at a reduced rate, to receive a return for the investment in training.

The main drawbacks, often mentioned in informal discussions with police managers, concern the additional administration involved (including the costs involved in the proportioning of national insurance and pension contributions) and the fear that the additional manpower that might result would not be available at the most appropriate times, i.e. at periods of high demand or during peak leave periods.

In his inquiry into the pay and conditions of service of police officers in 1979, Lord Edmund-Davies recognised the problems faced by married policewomen and offered several suggestions about the way the organisation could enable women to meet 'reasonable home commitments while they have responsibilities for young children'.[9] His suggestions included the possibility of employment in specialist departments and adapted shift patterns. Indeed, Recommendation 82 of his report states that ways of introducing a shift pattern of normal length adapted to meet temporary family commitments should 'be studied as a matter of urgency'. This study suggests that if this shift pattern merely involves nine-to-five working (which, in the absence of these recommended studies seems to have become the dominant organisational solution) there is danger of the consequences outlined above. Likewise the movement of women into specialist departments (especially those which are less sub-culturally valued) can have detrimental effects on women's overall status in the organisation and on individual careers. And, although he discounted the possibility of part-time work on the grounds that this might lead to practical deployment difficulties and also could be said to discriminate against men, there are sufficient benefits to both the police service and individual officers for reconsidering the possibility of introducing part-time work.

(iii)   Rejoining Policy

The second type of response concerns the policy and provision made for people to rejoin the police service after a career-break. This latter issue clearly affects women officers but, again, the principle of any such policy should be such that it is equally applicable to male officers. (Possible circumstances in which this might apply would be where a couple have decided that the wife will work and the husband take on the full-time responsibility of child-rearing.) This was also a topic covered by Edmund-Davies who made the point that:

> The experience and maturity of these married ex-policewomen is invaluable, and if they cannot return to the service this represents a great loss to the community, not excepting the financial investment in their training.[10]

Current national policy on rejoining is of two kinds: rules relating to rejoining after maternity leave, and policy in respect of people wishing to rejoin the service after resignation. Rules relating to maternity leave are contained in the statutory Police Regulations of 1979 and, briefly, state that women are entitled to three months' paid leave and must return no later than nine months after the birth of the child. More pertinent to this discussion is the policy on rejoining after resignation. In this case, if a man or woman wishes to join the services again, his or her application is treated as a new one. There is no Home Office direction on this and consequently it is up to individual forces' discretion. Likewise, there is no Home Office guidance on upper age limits for rejoiners, this being left to the discretion of the chief officer. Nor is there a specific Home Office policy on female re-appointments following a break for child-rearing,[11] though some work is currently in hand which is trying to establish how many women are leaving for maternity reasons, either on leave or permanently, and how many women are applying to rejoin after a career-break.

In Medshire there had not been a case of rejoining in recent history so there was no perceived need on the part of the recruiting department to examine specific policy in this respect. In a more general sense, however, the policy was that men and women are not debarred from re-applying and are treated as ordinary applicants except that it would be necessary to examine their reasons for leaving in the first place. This would be in order to establish whether they had the necessary commitment to policing as a career.

There are two points that might be pertinent here. Firstly, if rejoiners are treated as new applicants then on the basis of normal recruitment practice, female rejoiners will have less chance of being appointed. Secondly, as will be seen in the next chapter, married female officer commitment was seen by recruiting officers in this force to be substantially less than for single or married male officers. One can only speculate as to how this might affect possible married female rejoiners since, as stated above, this is not a common occurrence in this particular force.

For rejoiners (both male and female) the policy on age limits is that previous service is taken into account. Consequently, a person wishing to rejoin who is currently over the maximum age limit of 30 years could have his or her previous service offset against their current age. For example, someone aged 34 years wishing to rejoin with seven years' previous service would be considered to be 27 years old for the purposes of the application to rejoin. Whilst this formula is generally advantageous it is possible that certain women could be disadvantaged if they wished to rejoin, since the calculation depends on a balance between length of service and age on re-application. Age on initial joining would be an important factor here, with older women joiners (such as graduates) possibly running out of time. For example, a woman joining the service at 24 years who serves the 'average five years' before resignation for family reasons, and who then wishes to rejoin after a break of seven years, would on this calculation be over the age limit, since she would only have five years to offset against her age of 36 years.

Since at the time of the research there had been no instance of a woman wishing to rejoin for some time, further information was sought from another metropolitan force. (This was on the grounds that a much larger force might be expected to have more practical experience of the issues). As anticipated the policy of this force was much more explicit. All requests to rejoin are treated as fresh applications and full application forms have to be completed. Likewise enquiries have to be made into the period that they have been out of the service with respect to references, criminal records and home enquiries. In addition, a number of other enquiries are made. These include looking at the applicant's previous service record, including reasons for leaving and the senior officer's recommendation in respect of re-appointment. Also, the file is sent out to the officer's previous division for an update from a previous senior supervisor if this is possible.

Subsequent procedures depend on the previous-length-of-service/time-out-of-service ratio. Those with little service (for example, rejoining probationers) who have quite a long time out will be interviewed in the normal way, which in this metropolitan force is a two-day extended interview and exercise programme. Those who have had less than two years out and who were confirmed (i.e. not probationary) officers before resignation are not re-interviewed but are normally posted straight back on to division. Those with between two and seven years out but with 'substantial' previous service would be expected to attend a one-week refresher training course. Those with 'little' previous service would be required to re-do their initial training which is currently a twenty-week residential course. The general rule applied is that the nearer the rejoiner has to seven years out, the more service is required to offset this and the more likely it is that he or she will be required to undertake the residential course.

Rejoiners with between seven to ten years out are considered to be new entrants, and undergo the full interview and training procedures. Likewise those with over ten years out. This group may also come up against the upper age limit of 40 years, even when, as in Medshire, length of previous service is offset against age on rejoining (though for the metropolitan forces these ratios may be treated as rough guidelines and are sometimes breached in exceptional circumstances).

The major problem for rejoining policewomen is that a married female ex-police officer who has children is likely to have had a break in service of five to ten years and will probably be required to undergo retraining. The very fact that she has children could lead to considerable difficulty in attending a twenty-week residential training course, particularly if her husband is working. A married male ex-police officer will only have problems in the same circumstances if his wife is working or if he has sole responsibility for child-rearing through being widowed, divorced or separated (and custody to the father on breakdown of marriage is still relatively unusual). In reality the residential training period is more likely to affect women.

The issues raised are whether such an extended period of training is necessary for 'career-break' rejoiners, whether a series of short in-service 'refresher' courses might not be more appropriate and benefic-ial and whether any such training has to be residential. Also, there is an issue of whether or not the development of part-time employment opportunities for police officers with child-rearing responsibilities might not be a particularly satisfactory way of keeping abreast of changes in law and operational practice until full-time employment can be resumed.

SUMMARY AND IMPLICATIONS

Three main points emerge from this analysis of comparative careers within the police service. The first is that the relative lack of achieve-ment by women in formal terms can only partly be attributed to different career outlooks. As we have already discussed in Chapter 5, although there was some difference in male and female career orien-tations, the male belief that women do not have the same kind of commitment is clearly exaggerated. It is also clear that there is an increasing number of career-oriented women joining the service and that they hold a similar range of views about police work as an occupation as their male colleagues. This increasing commitment is supported by the turnover of women officers, which demonstrates a decline in the number of women leaving the service prematurely.

This leads us to the second point. Although the rate of female resignations is slowing, this is still a problem. Not only does this have considerable economic consequences for the police service, it repre-sents a loss of expertise to the community and, importantly, it provides 'evidence' to fuel male stereotypes about women officers. There are, then, compelling reasons both from the point of view of the police service and the community, and the individual officer's long-term career prospects for developing more constructive policies and practices in respect of flexible working arrangements and rejoining, particularly with regards to retraining, after a career-break.

A final important point concerns promotion opportunities. Again it is clear that integration has not resulted in the expected increase in the numbers of women achieving promotion, though this is contrary to the beliefs that many younger women have about their opportunities. This analysis indicates that there are two important factors which contribute to this aspect of women's careers. The first factor is the smaller proportion of women actually sitting the examinations, and it is clear that the time needed to study is a major hurdle here. There is a case also for providing more encouragement for women to study for and sit the examinations. Secondly, as with the recruitment process, the interview stage of the promotion process is crucial and it is evident that fewer women survive this part of the process than men. There is a need to examine in more depth the nature of these interviews to determine how this situation arises. The consequences are obviously important in determining women's career paths, but also have far-reaching effects on sustaining the cause and effect spiral of disadvantage and lack of achievement.

7 Ritual Arguments and Constraints

This chapter attempts to draw together the various beliefs and attitudes about women in policing which produce, sustain and encourage the differential treatment to which they are subjected in spite of the equal opportunities legislation. As the analysis of recruitment, deployment and careers illustrates, the practices to which these attitudes give rise have substantial consequences for the modern policewoman's role, her opportunities and her aspirations.

Some flavour of the nature and quality of the arguments presented in defence of these practices and their underpinning attitudes has already been given in the text both in relation to this and previous research. Part of the complexity of the police world is that this is inevitable and unavoidable: fact, fiction and folklore are often inextricably interwoven. However, where the previous discussion has already strayed into the realm of affect and belief, it has not fully assessed or evaluated their extent or interrelationships. An appreciation of just how widespread and powerful these ritual arguments are in defining the modern policewoman's role can only be gained from such an exercise. This chapter will examine some of the ritual arguments based on these attitudes in more depth, particularly those concerned with the operational role of policewomen; it will attempt to establish how widespread they are and also how far they are operationally justified.

In other words, we shall attempt to establish how far these recruitment, deployment and career decisions are based on a real assessment of the comparative abilities of male and female officers rather than on some sub-culturally defined concept of what constitutes a suitable gender-based role for policewomen. In real terms what constraints on the policewoman's role are justified? Are these decisions given organisational, if not legal, legitimacy or otherwise by virtue of equally shared attitudes held by male and female officers and by those who joined before and after integration? While this latter question may have little direct relevance to the political/legislative implications of a police service which does not operate a policy of equal opportunities, it may be crucial to the understanding of the etiology and the development of effective remedies.

The major focus of this analysis is, then, on the ritual arguments concerning deployment, since it is these which determine subsequent career decisions; but, since they also have a direct effect on the chances of women being able to enter the police world (with all the considerable economic consequences this entails), the discussion opens with a look at how these attitudes become the unwritten criteria for selection.

RECRUITMENT: THE UNWRITTEN CRITERIA

It will be recalled that the locally determined selection criteria, derived from the recruitment policy and statement of desirable qualities in a police officer, do not place an undue emphasis on 'control', nor do they, as stated, put female applicants at a disadvantage. It was argued that the 'translation' of these locally defined requirements, combined with assessment on unwritten additional criteria (either conscious or unconscious) during the selection interview would have the greatest influence. The national and local statistics support this argument. It was demonstrated that it was at the selection interview where these informal barriers (themselves a legacy of male attitudes against the full integration of policewomen) to equality of opportunity arise. As we shall see informal and formal interviews with staff in the recruiting and training department in Medshire[1] provide evidence for the existence and impact of these attitudes.

Additional information from both the in-depth interviewing and the questionnaire survey demonstrates that these attitudes are not isolated to recruitment staff but that they reflect those generally held by male police officers, and by some policewomen. What is important is their impact on the selection process. Not only are the recruiting staff, by virtue of the local autonomy of police forces, able to influence selection, they can also reinforce and help perpetuate these attitudes by selecting male officers who have 'the mark of affinity'. In other words, in the same way as recruitment using job descriptions based on the characteristics of the present job-holder rather than the requirements of the job can promote unfair and even discriminatory selection practices, it is quite feasible that selectors (not only in the police) will recruit those people who appear to have the same or similar attitudinal characteristics ('people like us' criteria) as the incumbent job-holders. In the case of job descriptions, if the job has in the past always been performed by a man or a woman then selectors will often look for a recruit of the same sex. In one study of clerical vacancies, for example, it was found that 'the sex of the previous job-incumbent seems strongly to influence the sex of the new appointee'.[2] The 'mark of affinity' argument would seem to have a compelling relevance to the police service, given the masculine occupational sub-culture discussed earlier (see Chapter 2).

(i) Unofficial Quotas

Two major threads of argument emerged from the interviews with recruiting staff, each of which reflect a cluster of interrelated attitudes about policewomen and their role within the service. However, before discussing these, some attention should be paid to the notion of the 'desirable' proportion or 'quota' of policewomen in the service. As we saw in Chapter 3 it is noticeable from the national and local figures that the proportion of women in most police forces varies between 5 and 10 per cent.

Although there is no *official* policy, either nationally or locally, about the ideal proportion of women (since this would, of course, be in contravention of the Sex Discrimination Act), several officers, both male and female, believed it was an informal policy in Medshire to keep the proportion of women below 10 per cent. This belief had also been expressed by police officers of two other police forces during a previous research study.

In Medshire the existence of an unofficial policy was firmly denied during an interview with a senior officer in the Recruitment and Training Department, on the grounds that it would be unlawful. When asked why in relation to other forces, the proportion of women was so much smaller, this officer reported that he was unable to comment on the practices of other forces but that the policy of Medshire was that if a woman meets their high standards she will be selected. This same rationale was given in explanation of the differ-ence in male and female appointments. Thus the quality of the female applicants rather than an official or unofficial policy was given as an explanation of the discrepancy in appointments.

Although the presence of such a policy was denied, it is quite clear from the other research data that there are strong beliefs about what is considered to be the optimum proportion of policewomen within the force. The majority of both male and female officers surveyed felt that the desirable proportion of policewomen should be 20 per cent or less, with almost 80 per cent of male and 61 per cent of female officers subscribing to this view. Of these men over 50 per cent actually felt there should be 10 per cent or less (compared with 36 per cent of women holding this view).

This issue was not raised directly in the in-depth interviews but was mentioned on several occasions by both men and women, with both groups believing such a policy does and should exist. An atypical reason given for restricting the proportion was given by a male detective inspector, but is of interest because it links into the height question, already mentioned (Chapter 3), and the credence given to certain 'objective' recruitment criteria such as being able to command authority. He said:

> They need to be a person that everybody else turns to and recognises as a figure of some form of authority, and the best way to do that psychologically is in height, and overall, I just think they're (policemen) better suited. Women I would say, probably on a percentage basis, I wouldn't like to see the proportion above 20 per cent. (Case No. MB06)

Generally, the reasons given were related to the operational requirements of the job, and echo those detailed by Edmund-Davies, which were given as evidence to his inquiry, mentioned previously. Briefly, the problem outlined in his report, and also considered by Smith and Gray, is that although the total proportion of women officers in a police force may be 10 per cent or less, the proportion deployed on operational beat duties is considerably higher.

In many, though as we have seen not all, forces this is because of the sheer increase in numbers in the relatively short period since integration. One effect of this has been that most women officers are still relatively young in age, service and experience and, like young male officers, are performing basic patrol duties. The actual proportion of women doing these duties is often quoted at 30 per cent or more and stories of turning out a mainly female relief,[3] often embellished by accounts of the dire consequences that have resulted, are legion. Whilst there is no doubt that this has happened in the past (especially in the period of the pay dispute) its frequency probably owes more to folklore than to fact. Indeed, as the discussion of deployment has amply shown there are a variety of strategies used to ensure that these dire consequences are minimised. Perhaps it is somewhat ironic that the virtue associated with the practice of 'one point of entry', which requires and values the fact that all officers serve as beat constables, should be used as a reason not to recruit a larger proportion of women.

The folklore aspect is also present in the equally paradoxical argument often advanced for the re-introduction of policewomen's departments. This is the lack of availability of women officers to deal with traditional policewomen's tasks, especially alleged sexual assaults. Before integration, the availability of a policewoman was guaranteed, it is said, because there was a central pool of women in the policewomen's department who could be called upon, even at night. Availability now depends on shift patterns, rest days, etc. and there is not guaranteed twenty-four-hour female cover. Rather like an echo of the oft-heard public lament, these officers believe that 'you can never find one when you want one'.

(ii) The 'Unfeminine' Nature of Police Work

The assumption underlying this anxiety about the proportion of women deployed on operational beat duties carries with it an implicit doubt about their capability. It is this anxiety which is the source of the first cluster of attitudes and which, in the case of recruitment personnel, influences the interview stage of the selection process. Although the standard regulations exclude both men and women who fail to meet height and physical standards, nevertheless the anxiety about the capability of women in an operational sense stems directly from the physical demands of policing. The concern is that these minimum requirements do not take account of the essentially unfeminine nature of police work.

There are two aspects to the argument in respect of women's physical ability. The first concerns the actual physical stamina needed to perform routine patrol duties, which can involve spending a whole tour of duty (about six hours after briefing, mealbreaks, etc.) actually walking a beat in all weathers. The second evolves from the risk of violence and is a synthesis of attitudes concerning:

(i) the 'morality' of exposing women to all unpleasant situations but especially those involving violence;

(ii) women's ability to deal with violence, especially arresting violent prisoners, breaking up a violent disturbance such as a fight and public disorder situations, and/or their ability to defend themselves;

(iii) the extra risk to which their male colleagues are exposed as a result of the natural 'male' instinct to protect women rather than to concentrate on defending themselves in violent situations.

This latter concern is associated with the essential trust, placed in a male colleague, that he will provide 'back up' should a dangerous situation arise.

A common element to the components concerning the physical ability of women is the 'physical appearance' dimension and its relationship with the authority of office and 'respect for the uniform'. This manifests itself in doubt as to whether members of the public are convinced by, and abide by, the authority of the policewoman as compared with her more physically impressive male colleagues. This is not only felt to be important in the case of violent encounters but also during the course of routine patrol duties, and represents the mainly masculine preoccupation with the 'control' rather than 'service' distinction in the policing function. The underlying belief is that, in general, women do not have the physical presence to command the respect due to the uniform and are therefore not even able to control routine patrol situations.

All these doubts were expressed in one form or another during the discussion and interviews with recruiting staff. For example during an interview with a senior recruiting officer it became clear that male applicants were felt to have a distinct advantage because:

> men have a better chance of coping with life in the trenches. It is a hard physical life for a girl. We're looking for a good strong girl with a background of physical involvement. It's no good if they played hockey at school if they're not active in sport at the moment. We are more and more looking for the physical side ... Men have more chance of getting past the first hurdle because of the rough and tumble of sport. It is important to remember the sheer hard work of patrolling.

Whilst he also stressed other desirable qualities (such as the ability to communicate and self-motivation) the importance of physical ability was paramount. This was true also for male applicants. This officer felt that those who played regularly for a rugby club would also have an advantage, on grounds which include recognition of the control element of policing:

You know that they have to train regularly, at least twice a week.
You know that he'd be able to handle himself if the need arose.

Indeed, during discussion of the comparative educational standards
of male and female recruits he ventured the opinion that in his
experience females were better qualified. The reason given for this was
that girls tended to study harder at school, whereas the boys would be
'distracted by sports'. He felt that another contributory reason was
because boys leave school earlier in order to 'do something' and
pursue a 'more active' occupation. Evidently a more passive role is
attributed to females from school age. There was no recognition that
this educational difference between recruits could be the result of
stiffer criteria being applied during the selection process!

As we shall see presently, attitudes about the physical requirements
of policing (both stamina and the risk of violence) were a common
theme throughout the observational work and the in depth interviewing. These attitudes were, in the main, shared by the recruiting and
training staff, and evidently played a significant part in determining
the unwritten criteria for selecting applicants.

One point should be made at this stage about the stress on the
physical requirements of operational police work. There is, at present,
no formal test of the physical fitness of applicants other than the
medical examination, though it was proposed to build physical fitness
assessments (Step Tests) into the probationer training programme,
from January 1984. There has, by tradition, been a heavy emphasis on
physical training in initial training courses, partly as an adjunct to,
and as a way of instilling, the disciplined nature of the police service.
Apart from drill, the initial training course includes swimming,
running and gymnasium exercise for both male and female recruits.
Some techniques of self-defence are also taught. Under the new
scheme, final assessments are to be conducted at the end of the two-
year probationary period by the Regional Training Centre.

However, after the end of the probationary period there is very
little emphasis on enforcing physical standards. The chief constable
does have the power to have a police officer medically examined but in
practice this is very rarely used. There would seem, then, to be a direct
contradiction between the relative disinterest in physical fitness after
completion of the probationary period and the importance accredited
it by Medshire at the selection interview. Also, the introduction of
physical fitness assessments during the probationary period requires
careful monitoring, particularly since recruits can be dismissed

(usually after warnings and counselling) at any stage if they are felt to be unsuitable. The relevance of these tests and their design to take account of the differences in male and female physiology are of crucial importance if women are not to be disadvantaged.[4]

(iii) Women Officers Are 'Uneconomic'

The second group of attitudes which contribute to the unwritten selection criteria have an economic base deriving from the relatively high turnover of women police officers and the consequent additional cost incurred in recruiting and training women. The dominant themes in this respect are:

(i) policewomen leave to get married and/or to have children after only a short period of service;

(ii) most policewomen do not join for a police career, but just for a job, presumably until they leave and get married, etc. (The totally cynical view being that they join in order to find a husband); and

(iii) women are not committed to serving thirty years.

The consequence of these female behaviour patterns is a high wastage rate which means that the considerable cost involved in initial training is lost to the police service. Women officers are, in this sense, uneconomic.

The first of these topics (marriage and children) was mentioned spontaneously in the interview with the senior recruiting officer. During discussion of selection interview criteria and the physical requirements of policing, he made the unsought statement that he personally ignored the physical attractions of female applicants even though this made it more likely that she would leave the service to 'get married and have babies'. The spontaneous nature of this comment suggests at least that the financial implications of employing 'short service' women were a factor of some importance to this officer.

Later in the same interview the question of commitment was raised and it was clear that it was felt that there were different expectations of male and female applicants. In the case of men the thirty-year ethos[5] was extremely important. In other words, if the applicant could convince the selection board during interview that he was going 'to serve the distance', he was more likely to be successful. There is an understandable, and desirable, element concerning the relative pay-off from long serving officers, both of a strictly economic (the cost of training) and experiential nature (as expressed in the notion of infinite apprenticeship where the craft of policing is learnt actually doing 'the job').

More important than these considerations is that this is a measure of the applicant's commitment to a life career, or to policing as a way of life. Without this commitment a man [*sic*] was unlikely to survive 'the hurdles and brick walls', the illustration given being 'out on patrol all night in the freezing cold or pouring rain when nothing is happening, and all you want to do is go back to the station for a cup of tea, and wondering why you ever joined the job'. In an interview with another senior officer in this department the question of whether an applicant was likely to serve thirty years was the only important interview-based selection criteria offered by him for discussion.

For female applicants, on the other hand, there was usually no expectation of a life career commitment, which was succinctly summed up in this telling remark: 'If we get five years out of them, we're lucky.'

As we have already seen, there is some foundation for the 'short service' criticism of policewomen. But it was equally clear from the information on wastage that in Medshire the 'problem' was far less acute than nationally; that, in any case, wastage rates for women were on the decline; women do have a similar level of professional commitment; and there may be important factors other than marriage and child-bearing which influence female resignations.

These reasons for female resignations are currently the subject of the research, already quoted, by Dunkerly and Kelland. This is concerned with examining whether and how far factors directly attributable to the perceived (and actual) inequalities of role and status influence the decision to leave the service.

Even if a woman stayed in the service after marriage and child-bearing, her commitment was likely to be different than that of a man. She is more likely to be a homemaker first and police officer second, unlike married men whose wives were there in the background freeing them from the bulk of minor home responsibilities. Whilst this is a recognition of the 'double job' dilemma which faces many working women, the argument involves an assumption about the priorities women attach to each of these, and a value judgement about the choice they are assumed to make. Furthermore, unlike the married female officer, the married male retains his commitment. Evidently for this officer (and these views were echoed in informal discussion with other staff in the department) although the influence of wastage through marriage and child-bearing on selection was denied, it was nevertheless a consideration, a fact amply borne out by the above remark in relation to the differing expectations of men and women.

The argument that women are 'uneconomic' is a particularly potent one especially given the prevailing doctrine of efficiency, effectiveness and economy. The national and local recruitment patterns demonstrate how powerful such informal considerations have already been in regulating the intake of women into the service. Clearly, there is a danger that during a period of increasing financial constraints, recruitment decisions based on the so-called economics of employing women will disadvantage women applicants. There is a case for emphasising that whatever the economic implications of the wastage rates, they by no means endorse these attitudes, since the spirit of the legislation is such that each application, male or female, should be considered on its merit alone.

A final point should be made about the implications of these unwritten selection criteria. Allowing generalised considerations about women's capabilities in respect of the physical nature of 'the job' to influence recruitment decisions, illustrates that there *is* a local emphasis on the 'control' rather than 'service' view of police work (see Chapter 2) which was not evident from the written statement of desirable qualities in recruits. When economic arguments concerning female resignations are also brought into these judgements, the net result of the combination is virtually an approved form of gender screening.

WOMEN IN POLICING: ATTITUDINAL CONSTRAINTS ON THEIR ROLE

As with the attitudes underlying selecting-in decisions in the recruitment process, those relating to women performing the same role and duties as men tend to fall into identifiable though not mutually exclusive categories. These include attitudes about the general ability of women which are based on a non-specific feeling that they are less effective police officers, beliefs about their emotional disposition, the discipline 'problem' presented by women and concern about the physical suitability of women. Related to the issues of emotional and physical disposition is the more ambiguous set of beliefs about the unfeminine and therefore unsuitable nature of police work for women.

(i) General Ability of Female Police Officers

In Chapter 2 it was noted that during a previous research study considerable resistance was found to the idea that women should perform general police duties, or that they could do so as effectively as men. These specific beliefs were, as already documented, central to one of the two major clusters of attitudes held by recruitment staff. The extent to which this is true of police officers in the research force is an issue which was addressed in both the in-depth interviews and the questionnaire survey. The sentiment expressed by the detective inspector quoted below sums up this general attitude:

> what I'm saying is, basically I don't think that policewomen in general do the basic job of policing as well as men; to put it in really basic terms that is what I'm saying. Generally speaking women are not cut out to perform a basic policing role. (Case No. MB10)

Of course, not all the men interviewed held this view. Some men felt women were as capable as men, but generally qualified this by excluding situations where physical strength might be necessary (a topic discussed in more depth below). The following comment typifies this argument:

> Yeah, apart from that [violence], for everyday policework there's no difference between a man and a woman, there are occasions when women deal with things a lot better than men but it's just those situations where violence occurs. (Case No. AM07)

It should be recorded that this is a view that several of the women agreed with. However, the negative view prevailed amongst the men and several other examples of this type of expressed attitude, from the interviewing, have been illustrated in relation to deployment practices and are given emphasis by the responses to the Likert items in the questionnaire. For example, in reply to the attitudinal statement, 'Policemen find it hard to accept that women should perform the same duties as they do', just under half (49 per cent) of the male officers, but 68 per cent of the female officers, surveyed agreed or strongly agreed with the proposition, an overall difference which produced a χ^2 value of 14.03 (d.f. = 1, signficance > 0.01).

This difference of opinion was even more pronounced between the women (76 per cent) and the men (43 per cent) who joined after integration, with only 9.5 per cent of the women but 42 per cent of the men actually disagreeing with the statement. Interestingly though, male and female 'traditionals' held similar views on the topic, with just over half (57.5 per cent female, 52 per cent male) agreeing. Fewer (43 per cent) of the younger male officers felt that acceptance was hard for male officers and the difference between them and their female peers is of note, since it is evident that the group of 'modern' female officers feels most strongly about this issue in that they are more confirmed than other groups in their belief that there is a greater reluctance among male officers. The response of their male peers is interesting in that one interpretation might be that it reflects their relative (though incomplete, since an almost equal number of them disagreed with the statement) acceptance of the situation if not the principle. This would seem to be a reasonable explanation given the earlier discussion on deployment preferences (Chapter 4) and the fact that only 28 per cent of this group actually supported a fully integrated role for women.

However, it is equally clear from replies to the questionnaire item 'Policewomen are deployed on exactly the same duties' that this acceptance is based on a hypothetical, rather than real, situation. Only 35 per cent of all the women and 27.5 per cent of the men surveyed agreed with the statement, and there was little difference between 'traditional' and 'modern' groups on this issue. Of interest though is the fact that 61 per cent of the 'modern' male officers (compared with 43 per cent of their female counterparts) actively disagreed with the proposition. In other words, their view is that in reality women are not deployed on the same duties as men and this is largely supported by the female officers interviewed. Some indication of the strength (rather than the extent) of feeling on this issue can be gauged by responses to the proposition that women should be paid less because they do not perform all the same duties. Almost a third of the 'traditional' male officers agreed that women should receive less money. Implicit in this response is the belief that the 'different' work that women officers are deployed on is somehow of less value to the organisation. The information revealed by the interviews, and the observational work about the different nature (and to some extent different value) of female deployment experience, is thus borne out on a wider scale by these responses to the questionnaire.

One reason often cited for this difference in the nature and quality of deployment experience is, as we have seen from the interviews, supervisors' attitudes to female officers. Again the questionnaire item on this topic testifies to the extent of this, and also examines a possible consequence of supervisors' lack of faith in female officers' abilities.

Almost half (49 per cent) of the 'traditional' and 42 per cent of the 'modern' women agreed with the statement, 'Because supervisors doubt the ability of women to perform all police duties, policewomen often find they do the most uninteresting jobs'. Predictably, perhaps, fewer (34 per cent 'modern' and 22 per cent 'traditional') male officers felt this was the case; and just under 60 per cent of all the male sergeants (compared with 30 per cent of female sergeants) actively disagreed with the statement, which is interesting given the fact that they are mainly responsible for front-line deployment decisions.

Clearly, the survey data testifies to the widespread doubts amongst male officers, in particular, about female officers' general ability to perform police duties as effectively as men; a view which is not equally supported by female officers, particularly those who joined in expectation of an equal role. It also suggests that this has consequences with regard to the quality of the deployment experiences they are able to undertake, and again supports the qualitative and observational data already documented. There is a Catch 22 quality about this belief. Without the full range of deployment experience, it is impossible for women officers to develop proficiency; and lack of ability is used as a justification for limiting the range of experience. But this very situation emphasises the paradox that if women are prevented from acquiring experience it is also impossible for policemen to base their judgement on fact, rather than opinion.

(ii) Emotional Unsuitability

There was a general belief amongst some of the policemen interviewed (formally and informally) that policewomen were too emotional to be able to carry out their duties properly. Anecdotal stories of situations where women had 'burst into tears' were frequently offered as evidence of this temperamental unsuitability, both in relation to unpleasant and distressing duties such as sudden deaths, and to reprimands from supervising officers. Reactions of this kind are taken as evidence of women's inability to cope with unpleasant duties. As one 'traditional' officer explained:

the unpleasant things that we've got to do, road accidents, where you turn up and there's a hell of a mess. I think men cope with that a little bit better than women ... I think it has a marked effect on women, because women are more prone to shock, aren't they, than men?

Using this as an argument against their full deployment as police officers (and as an inspector he was in a position to act upon his convictions) he said:

> emotionally they just lose their control, that's why I said their tolerance level is lower than a man's, and they're in all sorts of stress situations ... it's in their makeup.

Asked how he thought this had come about and whether in his opinion appropriate training could offset it, he pointed to the ways in which boys and girls are brought up and said:

> It's in their formative years ... what chance have we got of changing all that to make them ... or create this sort of psychological profile the same as men. (Case No. MB10)

Evidently, for this officer, the male response is the more appropriate and, like Professor Higgins, he would like women to be more like men. This was an extreme view, however. The more usual comment was of a more moderate kind indicating that one could not rely on women not to panic.

Occasionally this perceived feminine 'emotionality' was used to justify a protective attitude towards policewomen, though this response was restricted to the older pre-integration policemen. (One of the younger men did actually associate the stress of the job, emotionality, and the 'physical' aspects of being female, presumably menstruation, with the greater frequency of sick leave taken by women officers). As we have seen in Chapter 4 this protectiveness is manifest by supervisors tending not to deploy women on the more unpleasant duties as frequently as men. A detective constable, also a 'traditional' gave his 'emotionality'-based rationale for exceptions to the general rule that women should do all the same duties as men:

> I think they should do the same job, I think I said earlier they should do everything the same, but there are the odd exceptions ... I mean why chuck them into something you know is going to upset them, if you've got a bloke you know is not going to bother two hoots. (Case No. MB05)

Some of the women did report incidents which had been particularly distressing, though they were quick to point out that you became hardened to unpleasant or disturbing sights as a police officer; but then, so did some of the men. One view expressed by some of the women interviewed turned this argument on its head by claiming that women were by nature better at handling stressful situations. As one woman constable with fourteen years' service explained:

> I feel as if maybe women can handle it a bit more, again, because its a woman's nature to handle stresses. In all the fourteen years I've been in, I've only broken down once and that was over animals and the way they were treated. I've dealt with children and not cracked. Men tend to get emotionally involved [where children are involved] I think more than maybe the women do. (Case No. FB07)

A few of the women also recalled incidents with supervisors which they had found upsetting, though not to the point of being reduced to tears (at least not in the workplace). The positive face of this emotionality was also mentioned in the context of women's compassionate nature and how this suited them for the more traditional tasks.

Only one item in the questionnaire directly concerned this issue, but it clearly distinguishes between male and female officers' beliefs. Of all the male officers, 40 per cent, but only 20 per cent of the female officers, agreed with the statement, 'Women are more likely than mean to leave the police service because they cannot cope with the stress of the job'. In fact, 65 per cent of the women (compared with 29 per cent of the men) disagreed with the proposition. Whilst there was very little difference between 'traditional' and 'modern' women officers, male 'traditionals' were more likely to agree with this view than their younger male colleagues.

There is no clear factual evidence about the existence or consequences of alleged female emotionality for the police service. The most that can be said is that it is a view subscribed to by some, though not the majority, of the male officers and by fewer female officers. But although not a majority belief, it still has influence, not least because of the power of the supervisors among the minority. It would certainly be surprising, and perhaps alarming, if police officers (both male and female) did not find aspects of their job unpleasant, distressing or disturbing. Undoubtedly part of the professionalism of the police as a service must rest on the manner in which they cope as caring people with such incidents.

The important point here is not the presence of emotional reaction but what this is taken to signify, i.e. a general feminine weakness which is seen as reinforcing and underpinning the belief in the 'natural order'. The fact that this view is used as a justification against the full integration of women can be seen as a manifestation of an order-maintaining rather than service-oriented professional ideology.

(iii)   Women and Discipline

Several times during the interviews it was argued that women present a discipline problem to the police service. There are three main threads to this belief. The first assumes that women are less naturally inclined to accept discipline and as a result they question the orders they are given. Men, it is claimed, respond to discipline more readily than women. Although this was not a commonly expressed opinion (only three of the men interviewed, and none of the women, mentioned this as a problem) it is included in this discussion because it is further evidence of the belief that women are naturally unsuited for the policing role. One inspector gave this graphic account:

> I remember a WPC in a station refusing to go and deal with a dangerous dog. The dog had bitten somebody and she refused to go because (a) she didn't like dogs and (b) she was afraid she might get bitten. Now that is something I wouldn't expect of a PC.

Asked whether that kind of behaviour would be tolerated of a man, he replied:

> No, it wasn't tolerated of the woman either, because she was sent ... she didn't want to go. Well that absolutely astounded me, you know. I'd never expect a man to say, 'Well I'm not going' ... I said, 'Well you've got to go and deal with it', and then I think the close of the matter was, 'Well, if I get bitten it'll be your fault'. I find that type of thing totally ... (Case No. MB10)

Whilst the belief expressed above was relatively rare, the second of the three was common to the experiences of most of the men and admitted to by a few of the women. This concerned the application of discipline by supervisory officers. Although there was a consensus view that breaches of discipline were dealt with in an equitable manner, there was a prevailing belief that supervisors were less stern with the female officers. This was related to the fact that they were often given easier jobs but, in addition, if they made a mistake or failed to complete their paperwork on time, or had not completed enough work, supervisors were more lenient with women. One constable said:

> I don't think they get told off as much, put it that way ... When I say disciplined, I mean for a late file or something like that. We get threatened [laugh]. The women definitely have an easier time. (Case No. MA03)

A supervisory officer confirmed this. Although he was clear that the disciplinary code was applied equally he differentiated between the cool, calm way cautions and 'bookings' were handled from the run-of-the-mill bawling out for work badly done. When asked whether supervisors were easier on women he replied:

> That's true. Yes. It is true, because you know, I can't give a girl ... it's not in my bloody nature. I start to, and then I dry up. I can't do it, you know. I suppose with a lot of men it's, well, they can't; they can't do it, you know. They are too soft. (Case No. BM07)

Clearly this officer found applying the same standards to men and women embarrassing. In explanation of why he thought women had an easier time from supervisors, one constable gave reasons which combined the rationale of women not accepting discipline as readily as men with the supervisory reluctance displayed above:

> Even if they do the same as us, they don't do as much as us ... It's very easy for them to say, 'Oh, I don't like dealing with that' or they'll say, 'I don't fancy that' ... so after a while it's easier for the sergeant to turn round and say, 'G——' or 'B——' or whatever your name is, 'Go and deal with that', rather than put up with the hassle off her. As I say, it's very difficult for a sergeant to enforce discipline when he works so closely ... It's very difficult for him to enforce discipline and still be liked.

Asked why he thought women were privileged in this way, he replied:

> It's the old sort of thing, I suppose, that they're chauvinistic. I know you don't like me to say that ... I don't know whether it's that or perhaps the sergeant fancies the policewoman and he doesn't want to push her into doing something that might offend her, and make her dislike him. (Case No. MA06)

The implicit belief behind this type of explanation is that physical attraction interferes with the supervisor's judgement and ability. An extreme version of this view is that women deliberately use their femininity to get their own way. It is this latter point which leads us to the third argument concerning women and discipline, namely, the belief that the presence of women by their feminine nature is disruptive. Put quite simply, men and women working in the same environment is considered a recipe for disaster. As the same officer explained:

> Another thing too, when you've got a policewoman working on a shift is that when you've got one woman and nine guys on a shift – it could cause problems.

When asked what sort of problems, he replied:

> Well, relationshipwise. Relationships grow, problems grow and it causes problems. Especially, say, with a girl whose single and the married men. The old machoism comes out and 'Have I still got it', touch, and you know. It happens. Everybody's normal and nine times out of ten someone gets moved and there's a reason for the move. A lot of policemen's wives tend not to like policewomen working shifts because there's that threat.

This officer clearly saw the presence of women on a shift as providing a temptation to otherwise happily married men.

Although other policemen were not as extreme or as vocal about this topic, it was clearly an issue. It was pointed out, for example, that the police service was somewhat unique in that officers work for long periods alone together and need to build up a special relationship based on trust. This alone could lead to more intimate relationships when men and women work together. The women interviewed were more sceptical about their temptress role. One woman felt the oft-voiced proverbial fears about men and women 'alone in panda cars' was ridiculous because:

> Uh, what's so great about a car. I mean we've got a great big building here. If that's what they intend doing, they are going to do it, whether or not you put them out in a car. They can go and find a master key, and lock themselves away in a room on the third floor. I mean they are less likely to be found up here, quite honestly, than they are in a panda car. (Case No. FB05)

It would be relatively easy to dismiss these claims and fears on the basis that women and men work together successfully in many other occupations and that relationships which develop between men and women are an undeniably essential 'fact of life'. However, as the recent case of *De Launay* vs *The Metropolitan Police* clearly demonstrates these beliefs underlie discriminatory practice. In that case WPC De Launay was banned from working with her married male partner on traffic patrol because a supervisor suspected a possible relationship between the two. The chief superintendent made a general ruling that women police officers should never be given permanent patrols with married men. Explaining his decision to her, he is claimed to have said:

> Of course, if you were a man I would not have to make this decision. If you had a face like the back of a bus it would be better. But you are both attractive people.[6]

The chief superintendent is also claimed to have said that although he did not believe the officers were having an affair, he thought one might start if they continued their partnership. Although WPC De Launay won her case for sex discrimination, the chairman of the Industrial Tribunal dealing with the case saw fit to criticise her behaviour on the grounds that:

> Miss De Launay is a member of a disciplined police force and she saw the problem of a relationship with PC Attfield and she should have understood that it was a matter of genuine concern to Chief Superintendent Brian Wallace regarding discipline at the Hampton, Middlesex, garage.[7]

Clearly, this tribunal chairman fails to understand the nature of 'discipline' in the police service and the apparent threat posed to it by 'temptresses' disguised as women officers.

(iv) Physical Unsuitability

In Chapter 3 concern about the physical suitability of women as police recruits was manifest in terms of physical appearance, stamina and risk, and was a crucial factor in the selection process. As noted there, attitudes about the physical requirements of policing were a common theme throughout the observational work and the in-depth interviewing and are a direct measure of the anxiety felt about deploying women on the same range of duties and on equal terms with their male colleagues. This is certainly the single most significant, complex and controversial issue influencing the acceptance of policewomen into a fully integrated role. Physical, as distinct from

general, inability to perform all police duties is the most often quoted
reason for limiting the actual number of women in the police service,
for restricting the roles they fulfil, and for justifying their deployment
on qualitatively different duties.

The arguments about the physical *requirements* of police duties, as
contrasted with desirable *appearance*, revolve around (i) the need for
stamina (and agility) and (ii) the 'risk factor' due to the possibility of
violence inherent in police work.[8] Those dealing with suitable physical
appearance are concerned with height and physique and their alleged
correlation with conveying the authority of the office of constable,
rather than strictly performance-based criticisms and have already
been dealt with. Since physical ability is so central to the police
officer's view of his (and sometimes her) world it was felt to be
important to estimate the extent, validity and impact of these attitudes.

(i) Physical stamina and agility

The arguments presented on this issue are that police work, particularly patrol duties, involve 'sheer physical hard work' and there are
occasions which demand physical agility (such as chasing a suspect),
with which most women are unable to cope. It will be recalled that the
'hard physical life' was a reason given by a senior recruiting staff
officer for the need to select 'a good strong girl'. Similarly an example
has been given (Chapter 4) where the physical difficulties and unpleasantness associated with dog-handling were used to persuade a female
officer not to apply for that department. The hard work associated
with policing is in part a consequence of patrolling in all weathers but
is exacerbated by the added inconvenience and disruption caused by
working shifts (which is seen to be particularly important in the case
of married women with families). Referring to their ability to cope
with shifts in the same way as men, one of the officers interviewed
explained:

> Maybe some may be a bit more stronger than others but I think
> men seem to have more endurance, you know, seem to last a bit
> longer than women. I don't know if it's the shifts, or maybe I think
> they get more tired than the men. From experience I'd say one out
> of four women I've worked with has been strong enough to last the
> whole shift. (Case No. MA03)

Needless to say this was not a view supported by the women interviewed (some women pointed with pride to the fact that they coped as well as men with shiftwork, for an example see p. 54).

Physical agility becomes an issue since women are claimed to be less fit as well as less naturally active and agile, plus the added difficulty of giving chase or scaling over walls wearing a skirt. (Whilst some police forces have introduced the choice of trousers for women officers, this was not the case in the research force.) When one male sergeant was asked how he felt about women doing the same work, he replied:

> They don't do it – they try, it's not for the want of not doing it, they try, but they can't. They are not physically capable of doing the same job, it's as simple as that. I'm not saying that they are not clever enough to do it, I'm saying they're not physically able to do it.

He made it quite clear that he was talking about general policing and not just in relation to possible violence:

> Any situation. I'm talking about chasing somebody across a bloody field, if you like. They are just not physically capable of doing that sort of thing, most of them. You've got the odd occasion when you've got a fast policewoman, but there are not many of them, are there?

He added: 'Some of them are a little bit overweight too, a little bit chubby.'

When it was pointed out that some policemen are too, he replied:

> Oh yes, I know, but still in a cross-section of policemen. I'm 45 so I suppose after a few hundred yards, I'm knackered as well. But I've got a few youngsters there, and they can always be there at the other end, so we can work it out between us. But if you land up with three policewomen and one man, you've got a problem, haven't you? (Case No. MB07)

The extent of the perceived lack of physical stamina was tested in the questionnaire. In response to the statement, 'Policewomen do not have the physical strength that is required for police duties', 46 per cent of the male, but only 20 per cent of the female, officers surveyed felt this to be the case (57 per cent of the women surveyed disagreed with the statement). It was the 'traditional' men who were most in accord with this view with over half (51.5 per cent) of them expressing agreement and only 26 per cent disagreeing. Only 14.5 per cent of 'modern' women, however, felt that women were not strong enough for police duties, a view shared by only 28 per cent of their older female colleagues. Interestingly, over two-thirds of both male and female 'moderns' disagreed with the statement.

It is clear that this belief is only widely held among one group of police officers, though this is precisely the group which contains the majority of supervising officers. This point is not without significance since the pattern of male responses rises with rank with 43 per cent of constables, 52 per cent of sergeants and 76.5 per cent of inspectors agreeing with this statement. It is evident that there is some difference of opinion on this issue, with those who are more likely to be at the front-line of policing being less convinced about women's lack of physical strength in relation to general police duties than are supervisory officers; and since they are consequently more often required to exhibit physical stamina and agility this may be a 'real' indication of the validity of their argument, an interesting reflection given the otherwise negative view of young male officers in relation to physical strength and violent situations. It is equally evident though, from the information on recruitment strategy and deployment practices, that the perception of supervisory officers has considerble impact.

(ii)   The 'Risk Factor'

The question of women police officers' deployment in high risk situations and their ability to cope with violent situations evokes a far more universal response from male police officers. Included in this is the use of women in public order situations. This particular debate also raises issues about the physical strength of women and, as such, shares some of the characteristics of the stamina/agility argument. In this case the reservations commonly expressed were in relation to a specific aspect of policing rather than the more general sense discussed above. Specifically it centres on whether or not they would be a weak link in a chain of officers, and most of the men and women interviewed agreed that this would be the case. The explanation given by the following officer sums up feeling on this issue:

> A man is stronger and he is better in certain situations, if somebody is having a go at you, like a demonstration, like. They don't give a damn who you are and it is better for a man. You've got a chain and you have to keep it in line. The woman is the weakest link and

they'll go for her all the time, so I think certain things, no, a woman can't handle it. And I would never entertain saying that I could. (Case No. FA03)

Incidently, as evidence of the national nature of this debate, this same argument has more recently been used by a policewoman with respect to the female officers in policing picket lines during the recent miners' strike. In a letter replying to an article in *Police Review* she states:

... and I would not like my male colleagues having to worry about myself or any other female officer, as we would be the weak link in the chain, and the miners would use this to their advantage.[9]

In the same issue of the magazine another policewoman argues just as strongly that women have proved themselves in a whole range of public order activities:

... we have been involved in race riots, football violence and other serious public disorder, all of which we have proved we can deal with more than adequately.[10]

The national importance of the issue is underlined by the fact that it was again debated at the 1984 conference of the Police Federation. The article in *Police* (June 1984) reporting the debate makes it clear that male officers are opposed to this use of women officers, although they did see the need to extend riot training to women so that if they did find themselves in a public order situation they would at least know how to use riot shields to defend themselves. However, the fear was expressed that this could lead to women being deployed in Police Support Units and that men at the front line, 'have enough on their plates without looking after the women alongside them'. One woman officer from Avon and Somerset summed up the argument for riot training for women by saying, 'Wanting to protect us is commendable, but the best way to do it is to show us how to protect ourselves'.

Indeed, during the pilot interviews for this research two senior policewomen (one of whom had successfully argued a case to get herself 'shield trained' on the grounds that she could hardly lead her men shouting 'Tally Ho' without such protection in a public order situation) put forward a strong argument in favour of using policewomen on the grounds that they often de-escalated potentially volatile situations. On balance, however, the male view (supported by some women) is that women should not be involved. Of course, even though the issue generates such heated debate there are always exceptions and during the research there were many anecdotes given about individual policewomen who were both big and brave enough to cope with public order situations and who could even inspire confidence in their ability in their male colleagues – though such complimentary remarks were often tinged with doubts about the femininity of the women involved.

One policewoman mentioned was on the sub-division where part of the observational work was conducted. She had become a legend in her own time in the eyes of her colleagues. Comments such as, 'Oh you must meet ——', 'Just wait until you meet ——, I wouldn't want to meet her on a dark night' were frequent at the beginning of the fieldwork, along with tales of how she had gone into the local gypsy camp to sort out a disturbance (two rival families were intent on shooting each other with shotguns) and had sorted it out 'no bother'. Whilst these stories were embellished with respect for her courage and ability, there was also a doubt about her femininity. Behind her back this officer was called by a derogatory nickname because her hat was too big for any of the men on the sub-division. However, there still remained a question mark over the morality of exposing women to these high risk situations even when, as in the case quoted above, they were obviously physically capable.

The morality of exposing women to violence (even when physical strength was not an important issue) was a recurrent and important underlying theme and justifying rationale and is another example of men's protectiveness (discussed earlier in relation to deployment on unpleasant duties). In this case it has more immediate urgency since it is associated with the fear of injury. This operates on at least three levels. There is the natural gender-based anxiety that a woman will be hurt. There is the genuine fear that a colleague (who happens also to be a woman) will be hurt, and this concern extends to male colleagues as well. There is also the concern that in a violent situation a woman colleague may put male officers at risk by either being unable to provide competent back-up, or by diverting the attention of male officers who will feel bound, out of chivalry, to go to her assistance, possibly at risk to himself. (This latter concern is evident in the comment from the conference debate quoted above.) In addition, supervisors have the anxiety that if a woman gets hurt they might be held responsible to a greater degree than if a male officer is hurt since it is the supervisor's responsibility to ensure that all officers are sensibly deployed.

The urgency associated with these morality issues derives from a set of beliefs about the dangerousness of general police work. In response to an item on this topic in the questionnaire, 68.5 per cent of respondents agreed that 'Some policework is too dangerous for policewomen'. There was, however, a marked difference between male and female officers on this item, with 82 per cent of the men compared with 38 per cent of the women in agreement. Women who joined before integration were more in agreement (49 per cent) than 'modern' female officers of whom 54 per cent disagreed with the proposition. Nevertheless, despite the reservations of the older group of women officers it is quite clear that this is a belief which is much more widely subscribed to by male officers regardless of the time of joining the service: 85 per cent of the 'traditional' and 77 per cent of the 'modern' male officers were of this opinion.

The in-depth interviews along with the questionnaire provided ample illustration of the extent to which the belief about the dangerousness of police work is shared amongst police officers, but particularly amongst the men. For example, when asked to estimate what proportion of their work involved the possibility of physical violence, just under a quarter of all the men surveyed felt that 50 per cent or more of their work could do so (compared with 8 per cent of the women). Of the policewomen, 67 per cent compared with 50 per cent of the men, felt that less than 10 per cent of their work might possibly result in violence. In addition, nearly every male officer interviewed was able to recount incidents in which they had been directly involved in violence, usually as the result of a fight, domestic incidents or dealing with mentally disturbed individuals, all of which to some extent arise in an unpredictable manner (though of course experience of similar situations does incline police officers to assume there will be 'trouble'). A few of these actually resulted in some considerable degree of danger or injury to the officer involved. Ironically, some of the violent incidents mentioned by women officers involved women prisoners, either at the point of arrest or when they were detained in police cells. One officer recalled being bitten in the breast by a female prisoner, and another being attacked with a knife which had been concealed in the prisoner's boot. Evidently there is some unpredictable risk even in the more 'traditional' policewomen's duties.

It is the unpredictable nature of incidents which tends to heighten the perception of the risk and which forms the basis of male criticisms of policewomen. Quite apart from the perception of risk, however, there was a subtle difference in the accounts given by the men which suggests that their response to the danger in police work has a different social–organisational function. For them, coping with violence generates a feeling of 'front-line camaraderie', status, support and cohesion; a feeling of being 'one of the boys'. Whilst this was also present in some female accounts, it was much diluted and less focused. Indeed, some of the younger women were very philosophical about the danger and felt it was over-emphasised. Whilst one officer was quite clear that she felt women could be a liability in a public order situation, purely because of their size, she also had little time for the 'dangerous work' belief and equated the unpredictability and risk of possible violence with being a pedestrian:

> That's [general police work is dangerous] not right at all. It's not dangerous for us to walk the streets, far from it. It doesn't have to be any particular time of day and you can knock on a door and someone, a nutter, can come to the door with a shotgun, can't they? You, yourself, can be knocked over crossing the road. I mean, I don't say it's dangerous at all. As long as you've got the common-sense to know, if you think you're going to a situation that's dangerous, to use your radio. (Case No. FA02)

Of course, the different female perception of the possible frequency of violence could be a direct result of deployment practices which 'protect' women. The question which remains is whether the difference in male and female perceptions is therefore due to different experiences. In other words, leaving aside the question of policewomen's ability, what factual basis is there for the perceived risk?

The only way of gauging this in the present study was by asking survey respondents to report incidents in which they had been involved, though it is recognised that self-report data is subject to the limitations of accuracy of recall and interpretation. This may be particularly true of information about physical assaults since, quite apart from any status value these incidents may confer, they are the kinds of events which tend to assume a larger than life quality. Nevertheless, on the assumption that should this enhancement process occur it affects both male and female officers in the same way, it was felt to be a worthwhile exercise.

Initially survey respondents were asked whether they had been subjected to any of a series of increasingly hostile encounters. These ranged from verbal abuse through to physical assaults. Almost all the men (98 per cent) and women (90 per cent) surveyed reported that they had experienced verbal abuse during the course of their duties.

An almost equal proportion of the men (95 per cent) but smaller proportion of the women (at nearly two-thirds) said they had had to struggle, unaided, with a violent person. A far higher proportion of the men (at 63 per cent compared with 24.5 per cent of the women) had actually been threatened by someone with a knife, gun or other weapon. There was less difference with respect to physical assault: 82 per cent of the men and 72 per cent of the women reported that they had been physically assaulted. (This lower figure for women is in part due to the greater number of female probationers in the survey sample. Probationers of both sexes were less likely, for obvious reasons, to have been physically assaulted, with about three-quarters of both male and females reporting no assaults.)

Based on this self-report data the incidence of hostile encounters was relatively high for both men and women but with men more often involved in such encounters. Men also reported a greater frequency of physical assaults than did the women, with over quarter of all the men (27 per cent), but only 7 per cent of the women, reporting assaults on six or more occasions. This same pattern of involvement was repeated in the interviews. However, whilst there seems to be a clear difference in the frequency and types of all hostile encounters, and in the frequency of physical assaults, there was only a small difference in the overall proportions of men and women who reported injuries as a result of physical assaults. Over half of the men (58 per cent) and women (54 per cent) had been injured to some degree as a result of an assault.

However, although an attempt was made to establish the serious-ness of these injuries, the usefuless of the information is diminished by the problem of equating individual perceptions. Similarly, it was not possible to accurately establish the number of occasions upon which an assault had resulted in injury. So these data remain limited. Nevertheless they are revealing in that although they appear to support the male argument about the unpredictability and risk involved in police work, they also show that, despite the deployment practices documented earlier, women are frequently exposed to hos-tile and potentially violent situations (though apparently not as often as men), they do have to cope with violent individuals unaided, and a substantial number of them have sustained some degree of injury as a result. Clearly, despite the limitations on these data, there is sufficient evidence to support the view that female perceptions of the danger-ousness of police work are not due to their lack of exposure to risk and actual experience of hostility and violence.

Closely allied to the beliefs about the prevalence of violence is the question of the ability of women to deal with potentially violent situations, and again responses to the questionnaire highlight a difference in opinion between male and female officers. Only 14 per cent of the male, but 46 per cent of the female, officers surveyed agreed that 'Policewomen are just as capable in potentially violent situations as men', with 73 per cent of the men actively disagreeing with the statement. There was very little difference between 'traditional' and 'modern' male officers on this topic, but more agreement than in the case of the dangerousness of police work between the two groups of women officers, with just under a half agreeing with the item in each group. Again the in-depth interviews provided confirmation of this male opinion, though very often it was expressed in relation to the obligation to protect a woman officer at the scene of an incident or the lack of cover provided by a female for a male colleague should it be necessary. One constable, who himself had joined shortly after integration, described a situation where he and another policeman had restrained a violent man who had attacked them with a broken bottle. The young WPC who was with them had, despite their warnings to keep away, tried to remove the bottle and ended up with a gash on her hand. He went on to say:

> I don't like them in the situation I've just explained, a fight situation. Most of the boys would agree with me there. You are subconsciously watching what's going on over there in just in case ... (Case No. AM01)

A 'traditional' constable explained this 'subconscious watching' in more detail:

> If you go into an aggressive situation, I think obviously – I mean you've got situations – domestic situations we call them – which nine times out of ten end in violence, and I think it's better to go with a man, because if it got out of hand, at least you ... Well, I would have the confidence in knowing that the man would be able to help me. I don't think a woman could. I don't think I would feel confident at all if I went to a violent situation with a woman, because I don't think she would be able to back me up, and I'd have to go out of my way – not that I wouldn't – but I'd have to go out of my way to protect her. (Case No. MB04)

Whilst this protective attitude is based on a lack of faith in women officers' abilities, the above example also demonstrates the irritation of many men who feel they are exposed to an additional unnecessary risk. However, as we have already seen (see Chapter 4) some 'modern' women questioned this attitude and the deployment practices it leads to. The following experience of one 'modern' woman reconfirms the protective and doubting attitudes of some supervisors and illustrates her regret at the fact that, as a result, she had not had the opportunity to prove she was capable:

> ... some inspectors and sergeants think that a woman can't possibly do the same things as a man. They can't deal with, say, someone who's got a knife or a razor blade, or someone who's threatening to cut their wrists, or slash their throat or whatever. Just deal with trouble, male or female.

Explaining that as a consequence she had not dealt with many serious incidents because they were left to the men, and that she was sometimes annoyed by this, she went on to relate an incident where she felt she would have been able to talk a woman out of cutting her wrists:

> There was a policeman there with her, and she cut her wrist, and I think, well, if I'd been there maybe I could have prevented it; and, you know, sometimes I wish I had been there just to prove that I could do it, but I haven't had the opportunity, because – if you understand what I mean – the circumstance hasn't arisen where I can prove that I am able to do it. (Case No. FA06)

One related argument in favour of the use of women in general police work, including patrol duties, which the above example touches upon, is that they are better able than men to defuse potentially violent situations. A more common argument, which nevertheless has declining support, is that the mere presence of women may quell the situation because people think twice about hitting a woman. Several of the officers interviewed felt that this may have been true in the past but that the stage has been reached where people do not think twice about hitting a woman.

As discussed earlier (Chapter 2) a previous study of British police-women examined women's attitudes to the possibility of violence and emphasised the positive role that negotiating skills can have in defusing violence. Whilst that study was careful to point out that these are equally important for males and females, there is an implication in much of the debate that women either naturally possess more of these negotiating or calming skills, or that because of their physique they are compelled to make greater and more effective use of them. Certainly, a version of this kind of rationale was the basis of the justification put forward by two senior women officers, referred to earlier, for the use of policewomen in public order situations.

There was some support amongst the women surveyed for this argument (37 per cent), though over half of the sample neither agreed nor disagreed with the proposition that 'Policewomen are better than men at defusing potentially violent situations'. 'Traditional' women were slightly more inclined to hold this opinion (40 per cent compared with 34 per cent). An interview with a 'traditional' policewoman which illustrates this view and the way in which this can operate also inadvertently demonstrates the value of humour:

> ... but you get a nutcase, we had one down the Docks, and he suddenly decided to ... he stripped off, took all his clothes off in front of me and stood there in all his glory. Well, the men were just about ready to explode, but you can take the steam out because I said, 'Blimey, mate, you wouldn't win an Oscar with that', you know. And it defused the situation, everybody started to laugh, and in fact we did the job far better. (Case No. FB10)

Male officers in both groups held a substantially different view on this issue. Over half of both 'traditional' (57 per cent) and 'modern' (58.5 per cent) male officers disagreed with the proposition, the equivalent figures for these two groups of women being 17 per cent and 14.5 per cent. There was very little agreement amongst the men (less than 10 per cent) that women were better at defusing violence than men. Some of the men interviewed actually felt that policewomen could make a situation worse rather than defuse it. By way of example, one 'modern' male constable said:

> I think that women very often incite other women. If you go to an incident where there is a WPC there, then I think a woman on the street who has had a few beers will start calling the WPC names ... it gets everybody going, whereas some blokes, they smile or something ... a lot of incidents where there has been a woman involved, you know when you're locking up their husband or something, all right she can scream and shout at us but when she turns round and starts shouting and calling the WPC names, it might spark off violence, you know. (Case No. MA01)

Another officer, explaining why he felt women should not be involved in general police duties because of the risk of violence, doubted both their ability to defuse a situation and the degree of protection afforded them by being women. He said:

> I don't think it's right [deployment on general duties]. All right, you may hear of instances where women say they can defuse a situation, a potentially violent sitaution just because they're a woman. But I think the instances would be far, far higher where the person wouldn't hesitate to hit a woman and there are just no qualms whatsoever about hitting a woman. Having dealt with so many incidents of husbands beating up their wives, I'm sure they're not going to worry about beating up a policewoman ... even though she's wearing uniform. (Case No. MB01)

Clearly, then, men rather than women are much more inclined to hold the belief that police work is too dangerous for women, that they are less capable of dealing with potential violence (though older women do have some reservations, but not nearly to the same extent), and to believe that women are no better than men at defusing potentially violent situations. In addition there is substantial support by policemen (but not by the women) for the view that the presence of policewomen can actually increase the risk to their male colleagues.

Several studies of policing, both in this country[11] and in the United States[12] have indicated that these attitudes are the result of the perception that police work 'involves strength, action, danger and male fellowship'.[13] During the interviews the claim was made by some women officers that men deliberately over-emphasise the risk of violence in order to regulate the number of policewomen.

There are three points which have a bearing on this discussion. The first concerns the actual incidence of violence in policing. Although the reported frequency of hostile encounters was relatively high for both male and female officers, and over half of the men and women had been physically assaulted to some degree, it should be remembered that the majority of police work is not concerned with law-enforcement. Various research methods have been used to examine the relative time spent on law-enforcement and social-welfare service activities, such as examining responses to calls from the public and consumer surveys. All of these studies indicate that only a relatively small proportion of police time is spent on law-enforcement activities. Indeed, although there are variations according to the degree of urbanisation, up to 70 per cent of police activity can be concerned with the service role. On balance the evidence would support the view, even twelve years after it was voiced, that:

There is undoubtedly an irreducible amount of danger inherent in police work ... But there is simply no solid evidence to support the notion that all, or even most, police work is just one episode of mayhem after another. Most of the work that policemen do is peaceful, non-physical and frequently dull.[14]

The second point concerns the question of physical size and its relationship to the physical and dangerous aspects of policing. Under Section 7(2)(a) of the Sex Discrimination Act a genuine occupational qualification does *not* allow the allocation of jobs to men solely on the grounds that men are more likely to have the requisite strength and stamina. Following the example of the government's White Paper on Women and Equality, the Home Office issued a circular to police forces prior to the implementation of the Sex Discrimination Act which makes this point explicit in relation to the deployment of policewomen.[15]

Undoubtedly there are situations which arise where physical size is an advantage. Policing some public order situations, such as demonstrations, is an example. Equally, there will be occasions where sheer physical size may be intimidating and actually counterproductive, particularly if it is coupled with an over-readiness to take physical action or 'mix it' before exploring other more skilful and peaceful means of action. However, it would be an injustice to both men and women if, as a matter of policy, women were unlawfully excluded from those situations which might require physical strength, on the basis of some concept of the average woman. This is for the fairly obvious reason, that on the basis that physical size is a normally distributed variable for each sex, there will be considerable overlap on the 'tail' of the distribution. By this reasoning some women are as strong as, if not stronger than, some men. The concept of the policewoman as weak, in need of protection and unable to assist her male colleagues may not only be wrong but also contribute to those 'stereotyped images' which 'treat women as a class rather than as individuals'.[16]

The final point concerns policewomen's attitudes to violence and the danger associated with policing. In relation to British policewomen the Southgate survey (Chapter 2) demonstrated that the possibility of violence was not a particular concern, a view which was generally confirmed by the present study (though as mentioned earlier, a minority of women felt they should have a modified role). Both male and female officers had a matter of fact attitude to the possibility that an incident could result in personal danger. None of the women interviewed in Medshire gave the amount or unpredictability of violence as a possible reason for leaving the service. The unpredictability is evidently a greater hazard than the quantity of violence, but nevertheless is equally accepted by women as well as men as part of 'the job'.

Given the acceptance of the majority of women of the risk, and the fact that the physical requirements of policing are not considered sufficient reason for genuine occupational disqualification, then it is essential that both men and women be properly prepared to cope with the physical aspects of policing through training *and* sufficient experience.

SUMMARY AND IMPLICATIONS

One purpose of this chapter was to document the various beliefs and attitudes which underpin the way in which the policewoman's role is shaped within the organisation. Such a systematic analysis helps us to understand why and how these attitudes come to have such power in determining the quality of policewomen's working lives. What has become clearer through this process is just how widespread and strongly held many of these attitudes are among both older and younger male officers, and often in the face of contrary evidence.

It is equally clear that these attitudes are not shared to the same extent by policewomen, even the older women who might have been expected, perhaps justifiably, to hanker after the exclusive atmosphere of the old-style policewomen's departments. Indeed, the amount of expressed disagreement between men and women officers, and particularly from the younger women, is in itself interesting since it suggests that the pressure to conform to male views of policing is acknowledged but at the same time resisted.

Nevertheless, the fact that the younger male officers share the attitudes of their older male colleagues (and often hold them to a greater degree) is perhaps one of the more disturbing aspects of this study since one might have expected some ameliorating effect from this 'modern' group. Again, one might have anticipated that older men would be especially resistant to the kind of change signalled by the Sex Discrimination Act, but that the new generation might eventually begin to displace these attitudes. As it stands it would seem that there is every prospect that the kind of deployment and promotion decisions made by the older, more powerful group, will be perpetuated as these younger male officers move up through the police hierarchy.

In the next chapter we will conclude this analysis of the working of the Sex Discrimination Act by examining the wider implications of the material and interpretations presented so far. However, just before moving on there seems no better way to close this part of the analysis than by presenting two quotations. The first is pertinent to the attitudes which clearly influence recruitment practice:

> Some women will be found unsuitable. Sometimes men are also found to be unsuitable. One police administrator has noted that this is not a compelling reason for discontinuing the use of men in policing.[17]

And, finally:

> Organisations promote their own myths; they are reinforced by incumbents who believe themselves to be served by the myths.[18]

8 Working Solutions

In the preceeding chapters we have discussed the implications of the Sex Discrimination Act for the police service as translated into formal organisational policy and the structural and organisational changes which resulted. By examining the recruitment, deployment and careers of policemen and women, we have been able to compare the effects of formal policy with the consequences of a series of informal practices for the role women are able to fulfil within the police service. What is clear from this analysis is that the behaviour 'prescribed' by the equal opportunities legislation is not reflected in the attitudes of the majority of policemen and that, in reality, informal practices which more closely follow these attitudes have a major impact on the working lives of policewomen.

On consideration, the restrictive effects of these informal practices are perhaps not surprising since they are a demonstration of the unresolved conflict generated by unwelcome legislation. As such the conflict is not unique to either the police service or to this specific piece of legislation. However, what makes the police service unique is the combination of the extent (and rigidity to change) of these practices and the trust placed in the police to discharge their law-enforcement responsibilities. It is justifiably argued that this carries with it certain moral obligations. For example, Punch states:

> Because of the socially and politically sensitive nature of their task they are enjoined to be impartial and to exemplify honesty and integrity; the rule of law maintains that precisely those who enforce justice should be held most accountable for conducting themselves in a just and legal manner[1].

As such, one might expect the police themselves to be an exemplary role model for other organisations within society. Clearly the legislation causes a dilemma, and one which lies in the difference between what might be called 'change-driven legislation' (which includes the notion of legalisation) on the one hand and 'legislation-driven change' on the other.[2]

In the case of the former of these, legislation to regulate behaviour can be seen as the formal consequence of changing social attitudes, and mirrors the process that leads to other changes in society. For example, behaviour that was once considered to be 'deviant' may become acceptable, such as the notion of middle-class women continuing to work after marriage. Of course, the process may work in reverse and against previously acceptable behaviour. In either case, the concept of 'change-driven legislation' is based on relatively widespread 'popular' support as a result of attitude changes and, as such, the legislation represents a catching-up process. The foundation of the concept is similar to Erhlich's principle that legislation should be based on social behaviour or the 'living law of people' rather than the compulsive norm of the State.[3] On the question of the timing of such legislation, Friedmann makes the point that although in these circumstances the 'social ground swell sooner or later compels legal action', such action is usually 'at length, and tardily'.[4]

By way of contrast, 'legislation-driven change' implies that certain behaviours are sanctioned or proscribed in advance of, or sometimes in conflict with,[5] general attitudes towards the required behaviour. Legislation is thus seen as a means of effecting social reform and, when considered in relation to electoral and social welfare reform, can be seen as a method of social engineering which is often based on ideological concepts of social organisation. Whilst the extension of franchise to all groups within society can readily be seen as an example of such ideological reform, the concept would also include diverse examples such as the abolition of capital punishment and the compulsory wearing of seat belts. The effectiveness of legislation to produce social change in this way is a contested issue but, from the debate, it does seem clear that it has more effect on social structure and individual behaviour than on social norms, attitudes and feelings.[6] This is a point of some significance in the context of this study.

It is easy to see how legislation to protect minority groups might be considered in this way, since very often it is the result of campaigns prompted by opinion leaders, interested parties and activists rather than from popular grass-roots movements in favour of change. The impetus for change can often be attributed to the pioneering activities of 'moral entrepreneurs' who identify the need for legislation on a moral issue and actively campaign to mould otherwise dormant or disinterested public opinion. Sometimes there is a coincidence with public opinion and the campaign is one which mobilises support. The campaign on child pornography mounted by Mary Whitehouse is one obvious successful example of this type of moral entrepreneurship.[7]

In some cases, however, the campaign and the resulting legislation do not necessarily reflect the prevailing values, attitudes and ideologies of society at large. Explaining this in the context of social change theory, Price and Gavin make the point that for change to occur it has to be assimilated at all of three different levels in society: within the social structures, in the technology, and in the culture. They state:

> Social change theory recognises that it is much easier to initiate change in the social structure or in the technical components than it is at the cultural level. In short attitudes die hard.[8]

In theory, the principles underlying democracy favour the notion that most legislation is driven by 'popular' attitude change towards particular behaviours. In reality, and in practice, the structure of our parliamentary democracy is such that where majority support exists it has often been generated as the result of initial minority campaigns. In these circumstances it is possible that not only does the legislation precede the establishment of majority support but that this support may not subsequently be achieved. (In the extreme situation, legislation generated by and on behalf of minority interests may even cause a majority backlash). In either case, attitude change lags behind the new patterns of behaviour prescribed for by the legislation.

In the specific example of the police service and the Sex Discrimination Act, the evidence of this study is that the change in the formal structure and organisation was 'driven' by the legislation in the absence of majority support from within the service. Whether the resulting resistance to the legislation reflects a division between the police culture and wider social values is debatable. On the one hand, as discussed previously (see Chapter 2), sociological studies of policing indicate this may be the case. However, more general studies of women in employment[9] suggest that similar male resistance to equality of treatment based on adverse attitudes or specific beliefs about women's role in society is a widespread phenomenon. What is apparent is that, despite possible expectations to the contrary, there is little evidence that attitude change amongst male police officers is actually following the new patterns of female behaviour (and consequent interactions with their male colleagues) which have resulted from the formal organisational change. The fact that the 'modern' policemen in Medshire in the main share their older colleagues' views about the role of women in the service amply demonstrates this point.

At first sight this appears to run contrary to the theoretical school of thought which argues that the most effective way of changing attitudes is by first producing and rewarding the desired behaviour,[10] and the related, though less interventionist, opinion within the police that as long as police officers *behave professionally* then their personal beliefs and attitudes are immaterial to their role in society.[11]

In fact, the situation is more complex than this. What appears to be happening is that, in the absence of widespread attitudinal support for the changed behavioural role of policewomen, such change that has occurred is often restricted to the visible and publicly accessible arena such as that illustrated by the disbandment of policewomen's departments and the assignment of women to (nominally) the same functions as men. It is only in this visible arena that sanctions can be seen to be applied.

Maintaining the desired behaviour in the non-visible and private domain depends not so much on external sanctions or rewards as upon intrinsic factors.[12] In other words, policemen have to believe that their working lives, both from a personal and organisational point of view, are somehow enhanced by the involvement of women in all aspects of policing for their individual and collective attitudes to change. It is legitimate to challenge, in principle, the assumption that 'men's' working lives should be 'enhanced' before women can be accepted as equals and to argue that what is possibily required instead is a re-assessment of the requirements of the police role in society. However, it is equally possible to argue that if attitude change is crucial to the elimination of informal practices, then producing 'real', as contrasted with 'nominal', change may become a practical matter of strategy and tactics, based on the knowledge of the *process* of attitude change, rather than one of adherence to strict principle. Current knowledge suggests that, in the absence of intrinsic rewards to produce attitude change, widespread informal practices will continue to represent the grass-roots working solution to 'legislation-driven change'.

At this stage it might be countered that this is precisely because there is no evidence that women in the police do contribute towards these intrinsic rewards. However, our examination of deployment practices indicate (i) that in fact women's opportunities to contribute to these intrinsic factors, and thus to change attitudes by example, are restricted, and (ii) that the differential treatment of women by supervisors (and the implicit approval by senior management) does not promote a climate which convinces men of the intrinsic value of policewomen in their 'modern' as contrasted with their 'traditional' and acceptable role.

In addition, in the non-visible world, differential recruitment and deployment practices more in line with traditional male views, are aided by the high levels of discretion, loyalty and adherence to discipline. This has, as we have seen, predictable consequences for women's careers by sustaining the cycle of ambiguity and disadvantage. In effect, it is a working solution which allows traditional attitudes to continue to flourish and to be transmitted to (or encouraged in) the younger men joining the service. Taking a broader perspective on police studies, the informal practices which constitute this working solution represent one of several kinds of 'rule bending' justified by the 'operational code' of policing which result from a perceived 'incompatability between legal and administrative requirements and the reality of working the streets.'[13]

A simple analysis suggests four categories of such informal practices. The first includes those which are often the result of disenchantment with the outcomes of formal legal procedures and institutions and represent the administration of justice without trial and/or the means to achieve a successful prosecution. These include regulating access to solicitors and the 'strategies' and 'tactics' employed to control suspects such as those documented by Holdaway. He makes the point that although these strategies are acceptable within the framework of the law, the officers themselves are 'less certain that their actions are acceptable to the courts, senior officers or the local population'.[14] Though these informal practices stop short of what Punch refers to as 'combative corruption' (such as falsifying testimony, planting evidence etc.), the motivation is much the same.[15]

The second category are those informal practices which circumvent formal organisational procedures and regulations. They are justified as necessary in order to get 'the job' done. As in other organisations this includes the plethora of devices employed to cut corners or to achieve objectives. The practice of 'cuffing' certain crimes seen as trivial and/or as generating unjustified paperwork is a classic example[16] and can serve to concentrate resources on those crimes which have a greater probability of detection or releasing resources for other activities. In the main, however, these activities are well intentioned in that they are seen to be in the interests of the organisation and to facilitate the job. These types of 'resource management' activities are included in Lipsky's comparative analysis of street-level bureaucrats and demonstrates how widespread this kind of rule-bending is among people in public service organisations.[17]

A third group consists of all those deviations from the formal rules which are to the benefit of individual officers and are seen as legitimate 'benefits'. Along with the more usual perks, such as private telephone calls and personal use of office stationery/secretarial staff, this category would include the 'easing behaviour' described by Cain,[18] which helps to relieve the monotony of patrol work.

In all the above three categories it can be argued that although the rules are bent to meet the perceived needs of justice, the organisation or the individual, fundamentally they are not in conflict with the prevailing occupational culture. At most, they are seen to be in the way of 'effective' police practice. However, the last group of informal practices, the one which includes those in relation to women police, is based on a conflict between the rules and the prevailing culture. It would include those practices which develop in situations where, although formal management policy prescribes the maximum use of discretion in law-enforcement activities (such as in inner city areas where 'softly, softly' policing tactics are thought to be in the interests of public tranquility), front-line officers feel this undermines their authority and control of 'the ground'. As we have seen in Chapter 2, in the case of women officers, the conflict also derives from specific notions of the 'masculine' prerogative of control. And, although the use of these informal practices as a working solution is often rationalised as being in the interests of operational effectiveness, the deep motivation for their development derives from this conflict.

The justifications for this working solution are the myths that surround the emotional and physical 'performance', and thus suitability, of policewomen. Apart from our own exploration of the extent and validity of these myths, there is little objective evidence about comparative male and female performances in the British context. However, there is a substantial body of research concerning policewomen's performance on patrol in the United States which is relevant, most of which also runs contrary to conventional male wisdom.

In many ways the history of women on patrol in America is similar to the experience of British policewomen, though in many instances British policewomen have been the first to break new ground. However, during the early days of women on patrol in America several substantial attempts were made to evaluate female and male officers' comparative performance in a controlled way. These studies, some of which were sponsored by the Police Foundation in America, compared a range of objective performance criteria as well as documenting attitudes towards women on patrol by male officers and citizens.

Most of these evaluations show women in a favourable light. For example, studies by Marshall,[19] and Block and Anderson[20] which compared male and female officers' patrol skills demonstrated very few differences either in objective measures or performance ratings by supervisors and administrators. Women did make fewer arrests and issue fewer traffic citations in both these studies but the second study demonstrated no difference in the number of convictions resulting from those arrests.

This study also showed that whilst men and women received similar ratings in a survey of patrol skills by police officers, managers' and administrators' scores were divided over women's general performance on patrol, with the administrators rating them less favourably than men. Importantly, female and male officers obtained similar results in handling angry and violent citizens. Contrary to expectation there were no differences in the number of days off sick, number of injuries, driving accidents or resignations. The authors of the study conclude that:

> The men and women studied for this report performed patrol work in a generally similar manner. They responded to similar types of calls for police service while on patrol and encountered similar proportions of citizens who were dangerous, angry, upset, drunk, or violent. Both men and women officers were observed to obtain similar results in handling angry or violent citizens. There were no reported incidents which cast any serious doubt on the ability of women to perform patrol work satisfactorily.[21]

Other studies which compare productivity measures, both in matched and unmatched samples,[22] and studies of arrests (including resisting arrest statistics), injuries and complaints criteria,[23] also demonstrate that women on patrol are as competent as men. Similarly, women on one-person motor patrol performed as well as men.[24]

Alongside these mainly positive performance evaluations, these studies have also pointed to the additional benefits of having women on patrol. Price and Gavin summarise the qualities that women on patrol have been attributed by these studies as:

- causing few citizen complaints;
- improving the department's image;
- improving the department's service capability, since many women possess previous training in such areas as social work, nursing, and probation;

- increasing the crime suppression capability through the use of alternative deployment strategies;
- impelling the department to re-evaluate many of its policies, especially selection and training practices.[25]

However the American studies also demonstrate that despite all these *objective* performance evaluations, and generally favourable citizen attitudes to women on patrol,[26] male officers' attitudes to their female colleagues and their *subjective* appraisals of performance were almost universally negative.

The relevance to the present study of these findings about performance and attitudes is evident; it is also clear that whatever the additional benefits of women on patrol, they are not perceived by male officers in either America or Britain as enhancing their working lives in ways that are relevant to the 'male' culture of policing. So-called female qualities, such as those often required by, and demonstrated in, the service role are not seen as essential and are not endowed with glamour. As such they lack the power that would give them the status of intrinsic factors so vital in the process of attitude change. And, as we have seen, access to the situations which would allow women to demonstrate their abilities in terms men value is restricted, and sometimes denied.

The question which this provokes is: Given (i) the extent and universality of these attitudes, (ii) the lack of effective (if not appropriate) means of changing male attitudes, and (iii) the informal practices that they give rise to, what are the working solutions women officers adopt in order to function in a male-dominated occupational culture? In other words, how do women resolve the conflict between their expectations of equality generated by formal policy and their daily experience of informal practice? How do they cope with the tensions, often voiced, as we have seen, in relation to their deployment and careers, generated by their inequality of treatment?

Some clue to kinds of coping strategies employed by women can be found in the advice given by a senior policewoman, interviewed as part of the pilot work for this study, to new female recruits. Quite simply her advice defined three distinct approaches: (i) you can do all the jobs men do, but better because you have to; (ii) you can make tea for the boys and sew on the odd tunic button or two, but not be a real police officer (a role that many men expect and prefer the women to do); or (iii) you can become an object of sexual banter and have no self-respect nor the respect of your colleagues, male or female. This officer also felt that the difficulty some women face is that no matter how hard they try (and, being realistic, she felt some did not try hard enough), they are not accepted. Some of these women resort to using their sexuality in order to gain acceptance and be liked. After all, most people want to be liked by their colleagues. She also told female recruits that being feminine must not be confused with using their sexuality. For this policewoman, femininity is essential to the police service as a whole since it has a civilising effect.[27]

The first two of these approaches parallel very closely the distinction made by Martin[28] in her observational study of women on patrol in Washington, DC. She used Hochschild's analysis of the patterns of behaviour, adopted by 'tokens' in response to the occupational dilemmas they face, as a starting point for her own interpretation of how women adapt to a male occupational culture. She distinguishes between what Hochschild[29] termed 'defeminised' and 'deprofessionalised' policewomen. Defeminised *police*women gain acceptance by being exceptional, or in the terms of the senior policewomen quoted above, 'doing all the jobs men do but better'. On the other hand, the deprofessionalised police*woman*:

accepts the men's invitation to function as a nominal equal while actually functioning as a junior partner or assistant and receiving treatment and exemptions from work tasks appropriate for a 'lady'.[30]

These role adaptations represent the polar ends of a continuum in Martin's analysis and each has an associated set of characteristics which define the way in which policewomen typically behave, and the way policemen respond to them. The *police*woman, like the majority of her male colleagues, values the law-enforcement aspects of her work. While recognising and accepting themselves as females they share the predominantly male police norms; and although they also recognise they are at a disadvantage on street patrol, they nevertheless attempt to fulfil their occupational role in all its aspects. According to Martin:

They adopt a number of coping strategies to maximise their effectiveness as officers, including a strong emphasis on 'professionalism', assertiveness, occupational achievement, and loyalty to the department.[31]

However, to be accepted as an equal the *police*woman has to be more dedicated, reliable and productive than the men. They are as critical of other policewomen as are the men. Paradoxically the more she proves her professional ability the less 'feminine' and the more 'butch' she becomes in the eyes of her co-workers, even to the extent of leading to 'suspicions' of lesbianism.

The police*woman* typically displays behaviour traditionally associated with women's roles. They are more inclined to the service aspects of policing and so make fewer arrests. 'Making tea for the boys and sewing on tunic buttons', they also act as a back-up service for the front-line troops. Included in this group are:

> apathetic women . . . who are disinterested in their work except as a source of income; and women involved in the work but struggling with discrimination, their lack of assertiveness, the desire to remain 'ladies' on the job as well as off.[32]

Although many males are less threatened and feel more comfortable working with police*women*, these women nevertheless are criticised precisely because they are unwilling or unable to perform all aspects of policework.

It is important to emphasise that these are the extreme ends of a continuum and that many women will demonstrate some characteristics of both of these role adaptations. Often they struggle to achieve a balance between the defeminised and deprofessionalised roles. Hence the comment above that femininity can have a civilising effect on the police service. It is the ones who cannot cope with the struggle or do not have the personal resources to resolve the dilemma who are likely, in their bid to be liked on any terms, to 'fall' into what Kanter terms the seductress role[33] and to confuse their femininity and sexuality.

Many of the women interviewed for this study displayed these types of role adaptations to a lesser or greater degree. As one might have expected, this is to some extent related to time of joining the service. Those 'traditional' women who most regretted the demise of the policewomen's departments and who hankered for a return to their specialist role were more likely to display predominantly police*woman* characteristics. It is this group of women who most accept their differences in role and status in the organisation. Interestingly, the small number of *police*women in this 'traditional' group had without exception found some means of leaving the policewomen's department before integration by opting for some other specialist department, most particularly the CID. During the preliminary interviews for this study, this was also apparent among the senior women interviewed. As has already been remarked, many senior women remain unmarried and this is perhaps evidence of the greater dedication that *police*women have to give to their occupation.

*Police*women adaptations were more in evidence among the younger women which explains the similarity of their expectations of policework, deployment preferences and professional commitment, to those of their male colleagues. However, although there were some women in this group who clearly had the inner resources to cope with the tensions generated by male expectations of their role – and their own – there was clear evidence from their career histories, that for many of these 'modern' women the effort was tantamount to pushing a giant boulder up a hill. Gradually, but almost inevitably, these women were finding it easier to act in the ways expected of them. In extreme cases it is easy to see how this can lead to apathy born of disenchantment and frustrated expectations and to consequent underachievement. Bryant *et al.* have linked this process to the high turnover of policewomen, suggesting that some of the women who leave to have children do so 'because of a foreseen lack of fulfilment in their police careers'.[34] Interestingly, their sample of women leavers also contained a proportion of women whom they identified as *police*women.

It is pertinent to contemplate a similar analysis of policemen's role adaptations. Such an exploration might involve asking whether there is an equivalent difference between *police*men and police*men* and what kind of role characteristics could one predict on this basis? On the evidence of this study, current law-enforcement notions of professional competence are associated with 'masculine' behaviour patterns. As such one is tempted to reverse the Martin classification and identify this with a police*man* conception of their role. In this way *police*men would have similar service-oriented expectations and role dilemmas about policing as police*women* and would also be marginalised by other officers in the organisation. Some flavour of how male officers with this type of role identity might feel is given in Holdaway's participant observer account of British policing[35] in which he describes the dilemmas he experienced and the comments he received from colleagues because of his beliefs. However, one wonders whether the impact of holding a minority viewpoint among male peers in a male-dominated organisation has quite the same consequences for a man as it has for women officers.

It is also interesting to speculate about the possible consequences for these role adaptations of the present re-assessment of the nature of the police role in society and police professionalism. As argued elsewhere[36] changes in social and economic structures coupled with a general questioning of the role and authority of professionals and their accountability to their client groups, are prompting a need to develop an alternative model of professionalism to that of the omnipotent 'expert'. This is as true of the established professions such as law and medicine as it is of the newer professions such as social work and policing. Clients for the services provided by professionals are less ready to bow automatically to their knowledge and expertise, and more ready to question both the nature of the service and the way it is delivered. In the case of the police service, the irony of this current re-appraisal is that many of the characteristics commonly (though maybe erroneously) attributed to women officers are implicit in the more service-oriented, reflective[37] and consultative model of professionalism currently being considered as a viable alternative to that of the 'expert' model.[38]

The discussion above has examined the working solutions that currently exist. On the one hand we see how informal practices generated in the non-visible world of policing constitute the male working solution in response to a 'legislation-driven change' in policy resisted from the outset; on the other, we see the variety of individual responses of policewomen as they attempt to cope with a role made ambiguous by these practices. In this final part of the discussion, consideration will be given to the variety of institutional working solutions which would limit the development and continuation of informal practice and provide an organisational climate within which women are allowed contribute on equal terms and, if male attitudes are to change, can be seen to contribute to the intrinsic rewards of police work. Such solutions would help to remove the need for women to develop occupational role adaptations in order to cope with the conflict between their own expectations and those of their male colleagues.

There are three levels, identified at various stages during this research, at which institutional working solutions could be adopted. These are in the formulation and implementation of equal opportunities policy, management and supervision procedures, and organisational provision.

(i) Equal Opportunities Policy

Most forces would claim that the integration of women into the mainstream of policing following the Sex Discrimination Act constituted tangible evidence of their equal opportunities policy in action. Likewise the fact that there are more women in the service, performing a wider range of duties, who are equally eligible to apply for promotion, would no doubt be advanced in support of this position. The statistics (corroborated in this study by male and female officers' comparative accounts of their experiences) suggest that this is only a partial truth.

It is evident that many of the practices documented in this study occur because of a lack of clear and unambiguous guidance from the top of the organisation about how the legislation applies to the police force and how it should be implemented. None of the officers who were interviewed in this study, other than the senior recruitment officer, were clear about the organisation's obligations under the terms of the Act or the difference between direct and indirect discrimination. In the absence of the understanding of these issues it becomes difficult for individuals to challenge informal practice, particularly given the disciplined nature of the police service.

What is required is a definitive statement of policy which states clearly and concisely the current legislation as it applies to the police service, interpreted in the spirit of the Act. Interestingly, at no time during the research in Medshire was any written statement of equal opportunities policy available; nor has it been offered by other forces. Such a statement should spell out the implications of equal opportunities policy for recruitment, training, deployment and careers, including promotion. A clear statement of this kind serves the purpose of informing people of their rights and obligations as well as making it apparent that the top management of the organisation support and will enforce the policy. Where exemptions are allowed for under the terms of the Act these should be described, but with clear guidelines as to what constitutes lawful and unlawful practice. Likewise the boundary between what constitutes a legitimate challenge of practice and insubordination should be made absolutely unambiguous. As Torrington *et al.*[39] have noted general equal opportunities policy has to be supported by specific guidelines for it to operate effectively.

These guidelines should be provided at all levels within the organisation. Officers responsible for recruitment, for example, must be made aware how gender-based expectations can influence their decisions. The guidelines should make it explicit that there is no quota system regulating the recruitment of women and that all individuals should be selected on their merit alone. It should be made clear that decisions based on gender are not condoned. Front-line supervisors should also be issued with guidelines about the assignment of officers to tasks and duties and should be given guidance on their responsibilities, as supervisors, to ensure equality of opportunity and treatment. Likewise, officers responsible for annual appraisals should be made aware that their subjective assessments should not take account of factors such as the married status of the officers concerned, or the likelihood of child-bearing. A whole range of specific guidelines of this kind are possible and should be provided.

The very fact that the police service is a disciplined organisation, as indicated earlier, may inhibit some people from challenging certain assumptions and practices. For this reason, but also because it would demonstrate the commitment of the organisation, it would be of benefit to assign the responsibility for ensuring that equal opportunities policy is implemented to a senior officer, possibly in the department responsible for personnel management. This person's duties would include the specification of guidelines, advising line-management of their obligations, the monitoring of practice (including the collection and analysis of information), training (see below) and, importantly, the provision of advice to individuals wishing to query current practice. Clearly, the issue of confidentiality is of paramount importance and individuals seeking advice would need the undertaking that this would not prejudice their working lives or careers in any way.

Confidence in the impartiality of the organisation in relation to specific complaints of direct and indirect discrimination, victimisation and harassment could also be achieved by the establishment of a specific grievance procedure, modelled along the lines of those in industry. Such a procedure would ensure that all complaints are investigated and where necessary disciplinary proceedings instigated. A system of this kind would have several benefits. Apart from allowing individuals to raise complaints without fear, its existence would serve to raise the status of, and help legitimise, equal opportunities policy. It would constitute a clear statement by the organisation that these policies are to be taken seriously and indicate to managers that discrimination will not be tolerated. An additional advantage is that in the first instance complaints could be dealt with internally thus avoiding the necessity for individuals to seek external advice and support.

One caveat is necessary. No policy statement or set of specific guidelines will have credibility unless the senior police officers responsible for policy formulation and implementation are themselves committed to ensuring equality of opportunity and treatment. This involves being aware of the consequences of organisational practices, particularly the informal decisions so often tacitly condoned by management. It is not enough for senior management to preach equal opportunities; they themselves have to be seen to practice what they preach. The experience of this study and subsequent discussions with very senior officers is that, all too often, pragmatism in the interests of operational effectiveness is claimed as justification for differential treatment. Not only is this unlawful but so-called pragmatic decisions deny individuals the credit for thinking for themselves and balancing the arguments. As such it is a supreme act of paternalism which in the case of women officers denies them the possession of the 'capability' to choose, by treating them as a class rather than individuals. Nor is the disciplined nature of police work a valid excuse for differential treatment since this too should apply equally to men and women. Nor can such actions be justified by claims that 'women' do not want to be involved in some duties. Maybe some women do not (and this is hardly surprising given the police*woman* role adaptation); maybe some men do not. But equally maybe some women and some men do. The important principle is to treat people as individuals and not as members of categories.

(ii) Management and Supervision Procedures

In order to ensure that policy, as specified in the guidelines, is effected, management and supervisory staff must be fully aware of their role in its implementation and enforcement. One of the most disturbing findings of this study was that very often male officers responsible for supervision held extremely negative attitudes towards the 'modern' role of women in the service and furthermore these officers quite openly disclosed that these attitudes substantially influenced their deployment decisions. Likewise management, by failing to intervene in these decisions, have legitimised such decisions.

Two courses of action are immediately evident. As well as providing supervisors with the kind of specific guidelines (appropriate to their rank and role) outlined above, their training for their duties as supervisors should include consideration of the effects of prejudice, disadvantage and discrimination and force policy on equal opportunities, and their role in its implementation (including the monitoring, management and disciplining of sexist behaviour). Likewise, managers should be provided with similar guidelines and training but in this case their responsibilities should include monitoring on a regular basis the deployment decisions made by supervisors and where necessary taking appropriate action to eliminate differential practice. They should also be given guidance on their special role in career counselling, particularly (but not only) in relation to yearly appraisal interviews.

It cannot be stressed enough that supervisors and managers have considerable power, through their authority and discretion, to determine the quality of women's working lives (including their relationships with their male colleagues), their careers and, ultimately, the quality of their lives outside of work. It is also apparent that some women officers are acutely conscious of this fact and several instances have already been quoted where women have been victims of prejudice, sometimes to their disadvantage, by managers and supervisors. Supervisory officers by their example to front-line personnel could have a substantial impact in promoting the kind of organisational climate which would allow women to contribute to intrinsic rewards. Clearly, if equal opportunities policy is to become a reality then it is at this level that maximum effort should be focused, even to the extent of applying sanctions.

(iii)   Organisational Provision

Many of the provisions which the police service as an organisation could make to enable women officers to develop their careers have been discussed in some depth in Chapter 6. For the sake of inclusiveness these will be outlined again along with some others which arise out of the discussion of policy, supervision and management; as might have been anticipated these concern training. Before doing so, however, one point should be made absolutely clear. In the true spirit of equal opportunities, these kinds of working solutions are not offered because women should be treated as some kind of 'special' case. They are offered on the assumption that at certain times in their careers different groups may need different provision. By making these kinds of provisions it does not mean that 'normal' working norms and practices (often based on the outdated gender-defined structure of work which assumes that only men go out to work) are being disrupted; but that organisations should naturally develop to incorporate the requirements of *all* personnel rather than those of one dominant group. Considered in this way it becomes evident that provision is already made for some groups such as particularly talented, or even just enthusiastic, sportsmen and women, musicians, etc., without it being considered unnatural.

(a) Enabling provisions

As discussed in Chapter 6 there are several steps which policewomen, and some policemen, feel that the organisation could take to enable women to combine their family responsibilities with their career in policing. These have obvious advantages both to the women involved and to the police service (in terms of economics and expertise). Again it should be emphasised that apart from maternity provision, many of these are equally applicable to policemen who have the major or equally shared responsibility for child-care. Given the increasing number of full-time working mothers and single parent families, it is less likely that only women would benefit from such provisions. For those officers who choose to continue work immediately after maternity leave, possible provisions include the possibility of regular hours and flexible shift patterns (not necessarily on a nine-to-five basis but predictable enough to arrange child-care); part-time work; specialist work for the period when family responsibilities are greatest; and child-care provision by the organisation. For those who choose to break their careers, the main contribution the police service can make is to ensure that rejoining policy does not disadvantage women with family commitments. One other suggestion would be to consider the possibility of weekend work so that extensive retraining becomes less of a necessity.

(b) Training provisions

These fall into two categories. Those that are specific to women officers and those which are designed to promote equal opportunities policy and its implementation in a more general way. In the case of women's training needs, four areas are evident from this study. In the first place serious consideration should be given to the nature and extent of the self-defence training women receive. It makes sense to equip people to deal with violent encounters rather than to just limit the possibility of their exposure to them. The point made repeatedly by officers interviewed for this study was that unpredictability, rather than quantity, of violence was the main danger all officers face. It is this unpredictability that makes a mockery of 'sensible' (and unlawful) deployment strategies.

Secondly, one frequent difficulty women encountered was being expected to perform 'traditional' duties involving alleged sex offences, and women and children, without any substantial prior training, merely because they were women. Women (and men) who are involved in these duties should be given adequate training.

Thirdly, the provision made for retraining following a career-break may be important in some forces. Long residential courses, such as that expected for some rejoiners in the Metropolitan Police, may not only deter would-be rejoiners but also be unnecessary. Alternative non-residential, part-time or day-release arrangements may be far more attractive, effective and economic.

The final suggested training provision in this category involves developing women's skills, insight and understanding so that they are more assertive and effective, and are better equipped to cope with working in an all-male environment. Such a training experience would also provide policewomen with a forum to discuss the difficulties individuals have encountered, in a non-threatening environment. It could also act as a focal point and lead to the development of support groups which might help counter the fragmentation caused by the dispersion of policewomen onto different shifts and reliefs.

The second category of training provisions includes the provision of equal opportunities training for managers and supervisors. The focus of this, as already outlined, would be on their special responsibilities in ensuring equality of opportunity and treatment. However, there is also a strong case for including equal opportunities issues, as they relate to policewomen and other minority groups in the police service, in the core professional training that all police officers receive. Although current recruit and refresher training does include discussion of the effects of prejudice, disadvantage and discrimination, this is usually in relation to Community and Race Relations training, and this has in any case been criticised as inadequate.[40] There is a tendency to perceive these kinds of 'problems' as being 'outside' of the organisation. As such it is recognised that racism and sexism exist in the community and affect the quality of life of those affected by them;

but there is little, if any, awareness of parallel processes within the police service.

These are the institutional working solutions at the three interrelated levels of policy, management and provision which are essential to offset the effects of informal practices and to give the 'will' to formal policy. There is no doubt that although the inclusion of the police service within the provisions of the Sex Discrimination Act is still an issue, it is now a fact of life, and there is little prospect of a return to separate arrangements for men and women. There is no doubt either that most women officers are in favour of the present system and would not welcome a return to separate arrangements. The question that this study has attempted to address is 'How is the Act working?', and the answer has had to be, 'In name only'. Most of the reasons for this come down to one fundamental cause – a lack of real commitment and will. The time has surely come for the police service to accept the Sex Discrimination Act as a fact, to stop being ambivalent and to give full commitment to equal opportunities policy and practice. Ultimately, this is the only viable working solution if policewomen are to fulfil their potential as equal and respected colleagues.

Appendix A: Research Design and Methodology

QUALITATIVE INTERVIEWS

Altogether forty in-depth interviews were conducted with a sample of policemen and policewomen. The sample was divided into two equal groups of age-matched pairs of men and women. The first of these groups consisted of men and women who joined the police service as near as possible in the same month of the same year, prior to the implementation of the Sex Discrimination Act; and the second was a similarly matched group of officers who had joined since integration. (In the text these groups are referred to as 'traditionals' and 'moderns', a title which refers to the dominant official female role at the time of recruitment rather than to individual role preferences.) This matched pair cohort sampling method was used to compare male and female expectations and career patterns, attitudes, and views on the effects of integration.

The structure of the sample also allowed comparisons between men and women who joined before and after integration. It might have been expected, for example, that women joining since integration ('moderns') would have different expectations, aspirations and deployment experiences than those of their older female colleagues ('traditionals'). Similarly, this method would allow a test of the hypothesis that younger men adopt, through a process of socialisation, broadly similar attitudes towards the role of women as those of their older male colleagues.

Several preliminary discussions with policewomen (from another force area) and an examination of the relevant literature were used to develop a schedule for these essentially open-ended and qualitative interviews. A copy of the schedule used to guide the interview can be found in this appendix. All of the interviews were tape-recorded and later transcribed for analysis.

QUESTIONNAIRE SURVEY

As a complementary exercise to the in-depth interviews a questionnaire survey was conducted in order to provide quantitative data which would be subject to more rigorous analysis. The questionnaire included items designed to examine the deployment, training and promotion experiences of men and women, and male and female attitudes towards the previous, present and preferred role of police-women. It also aimed at establishing whether, in general, men and women believed that women had equal promotion opportunities. The information from the preliminary interviews also contributed to the questionnaire design, as did the literature survey and previous re-search information on this topic. A pilot survey was conducted with a sample of fifteen policewomen and fifteen policemen in one sub-division of a different police force, in April 1983. The questionnaire was subsequently redrafted on the basis of the results of the pilot study. A copy of the questionnaire used in the main survey is set out in this appendix.

The questionnaire was sent to all policewomen in the force and a random, representative 10 per cent sample of all the policemen, selected from the computerised force personnel list. A total of 466 police officers were sent questionnaires at the end of June 1983 and, after circulating a reminder letter, the completed questionnaires were collected at the beginning of August. They were then edited, coded and prepared for computer analysis. As shown in Table A1, the overall response rate for this survey (at 75.9 per cent) was very satisfactory, particularly since it was a postal survey, which often attracts a response rate of around 60 per cent, and was conducted at the height of the summer leave period.

Interestingly, as was also the case for the pilot survey, the percent-age of male officers completing the questionnaires was higher than that of females. It has been evident throughout this (and previous) research that the role of policewomen is an issue that many male

TABLE A1   *Questionnaire response rates*

	Whole sample (No.)	(%)	Female (No.)	(%)	Male (No.)	(%)
Pilot survey (N = 30)	23	76.6	11	73.3	12	80.0
Main survey (N = 466)	354	75.9	110	70.9	244	78.4

officers feel strongly about, which in itself may contribute towards the high response rate obtained for the questionnaire.

A comparison was made between each of the samples and the total male and female personnel in the force as a check on their representativeness, using the variables 'rank', 'length of service' and 'age'. The results of these analyses are displayed in Tables A2 to A4.

TABLE A2   *Comparison of questionnaire samples with total male and female personnel in Medshire, by rank*

Rank	Male		Female	
	Total	Sample	Total	Sample
Constable	2116	172	146	95
Sergeant	536	44	12	10
Inspector	188	17	2	2
Chief Inspector	64	6	2	2
Superintendent	44	5	1	1

$\chi^2 = 0.717, d.f. = 4$ $\chi^2 = 0.712, d.f. = 4$

TABLE A3   *Comparison of questionnaire samples with total male and female personnel in Medshire, by length of service*

Service (years)	Male		Female	
	Total	Sample	Total	Sample
<2	191	14	40	25
2–5	316	24	24	24
6–10	655	58	50	28
11–15	584	59	27	20
16–20	601	43	13	7
>21	623	46	8	6

$\chi^2 = 4.163, d.f. = 5$ $\chi^2 = 2.962, d.f. = 5$

As can be seen from these tables there were no significant differences on these variables between the samples and the male and female officers in the force.

OBSERVATIONAL WORK

A short period of observational work was conducted in two sub-

TABLE A4 *Comparison of questionnaire samples with total male and female personnel in Medshire, by age*

Age (years)	Male		Female	
	Total	Sample	Total	Sample
18–24	378	24	56	40
25–34	1125	105	73	50
35–44	1012	85	27	15
45–54	426	25	7	5
> 54	29	5	—	—

$$\chi^2 = 8.261, \text{d.f.} = 4 \qquad \chi^2 = 0.457, \text{d.f.} = 3$$

divisions of the force. One of these covered a mixed geographical site of city, suburban and rural areas, with an associated diversity of residents, including students, business people, families and pensioners. The area included two large 'problem' local authority housing estates, gypsy sites, commercial/industrial sites and premises, relatively rural farmland, as well as busy shopping areas. The second was almost exclusively city centre and dockland, with a busy shopping area, civic centre, and the usual collection of clubs, cinemas, theatres and restuarants found in a medium-sized city. The observational work extended over a period of about twelve weeks,[1] and involved visits to all the police stations in the sub-divisions as well as to others all over the force area, during the course of the in-depth interviews. Apart from informal discussions with male and female police officers and general observation work in these stations, policemen and women were accompanied on patrol on all of the shifts. This work extended over a four-week period and officers were accompanied on eight shifts.[2] The purpose of this observation work was to examine the kinds of police tasks that officers are deployed on, and whether male and female officers respond and deal differently to incidents. On patrol observation, all calls and incidents were logged, as was the officer's response and the outcome (if any) of the incident. The patrol observation also provided an excellent opportunity to discuss officers' views about women on patrol and to observe policemen's attitudes and actions towards their female colleagues.

DOCUMENTARY INFORMATION

An examination was made of recruitment, deployment and promotion statistics for the period 1971 to 1983. This involved collating information at a national level to examine trends and changes since integration coupled with a more detailed assessment of local information. The information about the research force (including that from the observation visits) was set against the national perspective.

Obtaining data on both a national and local level has presented some difficulties. At a national level, this is in part due to the fact that the most readily available source of information, the *Inspectorate Reports* (published by HMI every year), use a variable format for presenting information which may or may not be broken down by sex, and in addition, the Metropolitan Police may or may not be included in these tables. It was not possible to examine the original sources of information. Similarly, the chief constables' *Annual Reports* use a variable format, and in any case it would have taken too many resources to examine reports for every one of the forty-three forces in England and Wales for the twelve-year period. Also, since integration most forces combine data on male and female officers in their annual reports. In order to overcome these difficulties a proforma requesting standard information was sent to every chief constable in England, Wales and Northern Ireland, with a covering letter outlining the purpose of the research. The response to this request was variable with the majority of forces replying, in accordance with advice given them by ACPO, that it would require a too-heavy demand on resources (personnel to collate the necessary figures) to provide the information. Following advice from the secretary of ACPO, assistance was sought from the Home Office (Fl Division) and some national information on some of the topics was provided.

Similarly, the documenting of material in the research force has been affected by the problems of collating, though some has been made available. In the main, it is the less obvious indicators, such as the number of complaints made by the public against female as compared with male officers, the numbers of days lost through sickness by men and women, injuries while on duty, etc., which have been most affected by these difficulties. Although some of these variables can be estimated from the questionnaire data, the unavailability of some of the information is an unfortunate loss to the study.

EOC INTERVIEW SCHEDULE/GUIDE

Biographical Information
Name .... Rank ....
Age.. Length of service ....
Marital status .... Children ....
Previous occupation ....
Qualifications on joining ....
Qualifications since joining...

Police Career to Date
    (i)   Initial training.
    (ii)   In-service training.
    (iii) Details of specialist training courses.
    (iv) Deployment experiences.

Expectations on Joining the Police Service
    (i)   Reasons for joining.
    (ii)   Occupational orientation.
    (iii) Promotion chances.
    (iv) Specialist/generalist orientation.

Initial Experiences and Reactions
    (i)   Initial training.
    (ii)   First posting, senior supervisory attitudes, peer group attitudes, initiation rites and ceremonies.
    (iii) Deployment and duties.
    (iv) Relationships with senior officers and colleagues.

Present Expectations
    (i)   Explore changes in occupational/promotion expectations.
    (ii)   Examine possible causes, encouragement and advice received *re* career development.
    (iii) Promotions.
    (iv) Present relationships with senior officers and colleagues/junior ranks. Societal network of working group/relief. Morale and comradeship. The effect of in-job socialisation and its influence on the treatment of new male and female recruits.
    (v)   Job satisfaction/duty preferences.

The Role of Women in the Service
    (i)   General attitudes towards integration, its effects and consequences for the police service and the public.
    (ii)   For pre-integration respondents, the way in which the change was implemented, its effects on them as individuals, feelings at the time and now.
    (iii) Personal view of women's role in the police/society, relationship between the two. Specific attitudes towards women in the service, explore the extent of male anxieties about women in relation to

violence, physical ability, the use of discipline, sickness record, deployment perks, wastage, general female attitude towards policework as a 'life' career, the role of marriage/children from the male and female officers' view

(iv)   Differential public attitudes towards policemen/women.

Implications of Attitudes to the Female Role in the Service

(i)   The preferred role from male and female viewpoints.

(ii)   The extent to which expressed attitudes are seen to be translated into organisational policy, both formally and informally.

(iii)   The consequences of formal and informal policy for policewomen with respect to deployment, specialisation, promotion. Evidence of marginality and indirect discrimination.

(iv)   Strategies adopted by males and females in relation to the same sex and opposite sex colleagues, junior and senior ranks. Differential roles developed by women and men. Explore the use/misuse of femininity and masculinity from male and female viewpoints. Presence and extent of sexual harassment.

The Effect of Police Career on Personal Lives

(i)   Unsocial hours.

(ii)   Relationships/marriage.

(iii)   Public attitudes towards policemen/women on a personal basis.

(iv)   Attitudes towards possible innovations to overcome wastage through marriage/pregnancy.
Organisational provision.

THE ROLE OF POLICEWOMEN SURVEY
Department of Social Administration
University College
Cardiff

		F. O. U. Card
Please tick the appropriate boxes		
1. Male ☐		☐ (11)
Female ☐		
2. Age		
18 to 24 ☐		
25 to 34 ☐	45 to 54 ☐	☐ (12)
35 to 44 ☐	55 and over ☐	
3. Marital status		
Single ☐	Widowed ☐	☐ (13)
Married ☐	Divorced ☐	
4. Number of children (if any)		☐ (14)
5. Rank..		☐ (15)
6. Length of service		
Under 2 yrs ☐	15 to 20 yrs ☐	☐ (16)
2 to 5 yrs ☐	20 to 25 yrs ☐	
5 to 10 yrs ☐	Over 25 yrs ☐	☐ (17)
10 to 15 yrs ☐		

7. Qualifications when you joined the police service:

		F.O.U. Card 1
CSE/O-Levels ☐	How many? ☐	☐ ☐
A-Levels ☐	How many? ☐	☐ ☐
OND ☐	Degree ☐	☐
HND ☐	None ☐	(22)
Other (please specify)		☐ (23)

8. Have you obtained any other academic qualifications
   since joining the police service?
   (Do not include promotion exams)

Yes ☐		☐ (24)
No ☐		

   If **yes**, please give details........................
   .... ☐ (25)

9. Occupation before joining the police service... ☐
   .... (26–27)

(Please state if you joined straight from
school or from the police cadets).   ☐
                                                          (28)

10. Present occupation (department) within the
     police service
     Uniformed Senior
     Officer   Specialist Squads
     (Divisional or HQ) ☐   (please specify)   ☐
                                    ....

     Uniformed Patrol
     Officer: ....

               Constable ☐   ....

                                    Administration
               Sergeant ☐   Clerical/   ☐
     Community Con-
     stable   Communications ☐
     (or equivalent)   ☐
                                    Training/
     CID   ☐   Personnel   ☐

     Traffic   ☐   Juvenile Liaison/
                                    Bureau   ☐
                                    Crime Prevention ☐
     Other (please specify)...............................   ☐☐
                                                            (29–30)

11. Which of the following departments have you worked in?   F.O.U.
     (please give the approximate length of time you spent   Card 1
     in each)
     General Uniform Patrol   ☐   ....
     Community/Home Beat Officer   ☐   ....
     CID   ☐   ....
     Traffic   ☐   ....
     Clerical/Administration   ☐   ....
     Communications   ☐   ....
     Training/Personnel   ☐   ....
     Juvenile Liaison   ☐   ....
     Community Liaison   ☐   ....
     Crime Prevention   ☐   ....
     Policewomen's Department   ☐   ....
     Specialist Squads   ☐   ....

                                                             ☐
     Other (please specify)...................................   (31)
     ....   ☐
                                                             (32)

If you have worked in any other department, please
give details below:

....

....

□□
(33–34)

12. Which **one** of these departments did you most enjoy
working in?

....

....

□□
(35–36)

**If you are already working in the department of your
preference ignore questions 13 and 14. Go on to question 15.**

F.O.U.
Card 1

13. Which department would you **most** like to work in?

....

□□
(37–38)

14. How would you rate your chances of being
able to work in the department you would
most like to work in?

Very good	□
Good	□
Neither good nor bad	□
Bad	□
Very bad	□
Don't know	□

□
(39)

15. Which of the following definitions most
closely describes how you feel about the
police service as an occupation?

Police work is a vocation which
appeals only to people who are
dedicated to providing a service to
the public. □

Police work is an active, interesting,
secure, and well paid occupation. □

Police work is a profession which
demands a high degree of personal
responsibility and ethical
commitment. It shares many of the
same features as other professions
such as medicine and the law. □

Police work is a craft which requires
a high level of technical skill. This
can best be learned by practical
experience of doing the job.   ☐   ☐
                                                                   (40)

16. When you joined the police service was
it with the intention of making a
long-term career, or was it simply
because you wanted an interesting job
at the time?
                              Career   ☐   ☐
                              Job   ☐   (41)

17. Have you ever thought **seriously** about
leaving the police service?   F.O.U.
                                                                   Card 1
                              Yes   ☐
                              No   ☐   ☐
                                                                   (42)

If **yes**, which, if any, of the following
reasons contributed to your wish to
leave the police service.
(You may tick more than one box)
          Pay and conditions of service   ☐   ☐
          Poor management by senior officers ☐   ☐
          Career prospects   ☐   ☐
          Stress of police work   ☐   ☐
          Lack of interest in the work   ☐   ☐
          Shift work   ☐   ☐
          Just general dissatisfaction   ☐   ☐
          Other reasons (please specify)............
          ....   ☐
                                                                   (50)

18. At which Training Centre did you
complete your initial training? ....
          ....   ☐
                                                                   (51)

19. Have you ever been on any specialist
training courses?
                              Yes   ☐
                              No   ☐   ☐
                                                                   (52)

If **yes**, please give details below:
Name of courses attended
          ....   ☐
          ....   (53)
          ....
          ....   ☐
          ....   (54)

20. Which *one* of these courses do you consider to have been the **most** useful to you?

   ....

   F.O.U.
   Card 1
   ☐
   (55)

21. Do you think there are enough opportunities for specialist training courses in the police service?

   Yes ☐
   No ☐

   ☐
   (56)

   If **no**, please say why ....

   ....

   ☐
   (57)

22. Do you think that policewomen have as many opportunities for specialist training as policemen?

   Yes ☐
   No ☐

   ☐
   (58)

   If **no**, why do you think this is the case?

   ....

   ....

   ☐
   (59)

   Do you think there should be more training opportunities for policewomen?

   Yes ☐
   No ☐

   ☐
   (60)

23. Do you think that since the integration of policewomen there are:

   More opportunities for training
   for policewomen ☐

   Equal opportunities for training
   for policewomen and policemen ☐

   Less opportunities for training
   for policewomen ☐

   About the same opportunities for
   training for policewomen as before
   integration ☐

   Don't know ☐

   ☐
   (61)

24. How important is achieving promotion to you?

   Very important ☐
   Important ☐
   Not bothered either
   way about promotion ☐
   Not important ☐
   Not at all important ☐

   F.O.U.
   Card 1

   ☐
   (62)

25. How do you rate your chances of obtaining promotion

	Within 5 years	Within 10 years
Very good	☐	☐
Good	☐	☐
Neither good nor bad	☐	☐
Bad	☐	☐
Very bad	☐	☐
Don't know/ not interested in promotion	☐	☐

☐ (63)

☐ (64)

26. Do you think that the promotion system within the police service works fairly?

Yes ☐
No ☐

☐ (65)

If **no**, please say why ....
....
....

☐ (66)
F.O.U.
Card 1

27. Do you think policewomen have as many opportunities for promotion as men?

Yes ☐
No ☐

☐ (67)

If **no**, please say why ....
....
....

☐ (68)

28. Do you think that since the integration of policewomen there are:

More opportunities for promotion for policewomen ☐

Equal opportunities for promotion for policewomen and policemen ☐

Fewer opportunities for promotion for policewomen ☐

About the same opportunities for promotion for policewomen as before integration ☐

Don't know ☐

☐ (69)

**Constables (Not Probationers) and Sergeants only,
answer question 29. All other ranks go on to question 30.**

29. Have you ever taken the promotion examination to
the next rank?

		F.O.U
Yes	☐	Card 1
No	☐	☐
		(70)

If **no**, please say why ....

....

☐
(71)

If **yes**, what was the outcome?

Pass	☐	
Fail	☐	☐
		(72)

If **pass**, have you been
before a divisional promotion board?

Yes	☐	☐
No	☐	☐
		(73)

If **yes**, have you been
before a force promotion board?

Yes	☐	
No	☐	☐
		(74)

What was the result of the interview?
Recommended for Promotion

Yes	☐	
No	☐	☐
		(75)

If **no**, do you feel that the
outcome was fair?

Yes	☐	
No	☐	☐
		(76)

Please give reasons for your answer ....

....

☐
(77)

30. Which of the following aspects of police work do
you find the most interesting?
(Please rank each activity in order of its interest
giving 1 to the most interesting and 17 to the least
interesting).

F.O.U.
Card 2

		Rank	
a.	Making arrests	☐	☐☐
			(11–12)
b.	Intervening in family crises and domestic disputes	☐	☐☐

c. Traffic management ☐ ☐☐
d. Interviewing suspects ☐ ☐☐
e. General purpose motor patrol ☐ ☐☐

(19–20)

f. Giving advice and information to
members of the public ☐ ☐☐
g. Dealing with motoring offences ☐ ☐☐
h. Foot patrol ☐ ☐☐
i. Observation work ☐ ☐☐

(27–28)

j. Community liaison activities, such as
giving talks to children in schools ☐ ☐☐
k. Collecting evidence ☐ ☐☐
l. Dealing with traffic accidents ☐ ☐☐
m. Working with juveniles ☐ ☐☐
n. Traffic patrol ☐ ☐☐
o. Police station duties (desk duty, etc.) ☐ ☐☐
p. Preparing crime reports ☐ ☐☐
q. Dealing with general disputes ☐ ☐☐

(43–44)

Are there any **other** activities which you find
particularly interesting? (please specify) ....
....
....

☐☐
(45–46)

31. Which police activities do you find you do most
often?

F.O.U.
Card 2

....
....

☐☐
(47–48)

32. In your opinion, do you think that the work you do
is:

Mostly varied and interesting ☐
Mostly boring and routine ☐
A mixture of the two ☐
Don't know ☐

☐
(49)

33. Do you think that supervisory officers employ
policewomen on different duties than men?

Yes ☐
No ☐

☐
(50)

If **yes**, in which way are the duties policewomen
are employed on different? ....
....
....

☐
(51)

Do you think that policewomen should be given different duties?

Yes ☐
No ☐

☐
(52)

Why do you feel this way? ....
....
....

☐
(53)

34. Compared with police officers of the opposite sex, how would you assess **your own capability** in each of the following situations?
(tick the response which applies to you for each task)

F.O.U.
Card 2

	Better	Same	Worse
a. General purpose motor patrol			
b. Clerical work			
c. Child abuse cases			
d. Motoring offences			
e. Foot patrol			
f. Questioning victims of rape/or indecency offences			
g. Writing reports			
h. Traffic accidents			
i. Interviewing female suspects			
j. Observation work			
k. Domestic disputes			
l. Getting information at the scene of a crime			
m. Dealing with a crowd of 4–6 male drunks on the street			
n. Juvenile offenders			
o. Threating situations where someone has a knife			
p. Interviewing male suspects			
q. Community liaison			

☐
(54)
☐
☐
☐
☐
(58)

☐
☐
☐

☐
☐
☐
(64)

☐
(65)

☐
☐
(67)

☐

☐
☐
(70)

35. Which of the following definitions most closely describes the way in which **you think** policewomen should be employed in the police service:

    Policewomen should take on **all** the same duties as policemen. ☐

    Policewomen should take on similar duties to policemen **except** those where violence is anticipated. ☐

    Policewomen should **not** do the same work as policemen, but should specialise in duties such as female offenders and victims, juveniles and children, and missing persons. ☐

36. Please indicate which one of the following options you prefer:

    A fully integrated role for **all** police officers such that men and women perform the same duties. ☐

    The re-establishment of **Policewomen's Departments**, with a separate career structure for women officers, which would specialise in female offenders and victims, juveniles and children, and missing persons. ☐

    The establishment of a department, staffed by both **male and female** police officers, which would specialise in female offenders and victims, juveniles and children, and missing persons. ☐

37. In your opinion what proportion of police officers should be women?

Less than 10%	☐	40%	☐
10%	☐	50%	☐
20%	☐	More than 50%	☐
30%	☐	Don't know	☐

F.O.U.
Card 1

☐
(71)

☐
(72)

☐
(73)

38. Please indicate how far you agree or disagree with
     each of the following statements by ticking the
     appropriate box.

F.O.U.
Card 3

	Strongly agree	Agree	Neither agree nor disagree	Disagree	Strongly disagree	Don't know	
Since integration there has been a serious loss of expertise in dealing with young people, female offenders and missing persons.							☐ (11)
Since integration women officers are involved in far more interesting work.							☐ (12)
Policemen find it difficult to accept that women should perform the same duties as they do.							☐ (13)
Policewomen do not have the physical strength that is required for police duties.							☐ (14)
Most policewomen leave the police service in order to get married and/or have a family.							☐ (15)

Most policewomen join the police service because they want a proper career.							☐ (16)
Some policework is too dangerous for policewomen.							☐ (17)
Policewomen are deployed on exactly the same duties as policemen.							☐ (18)
Policewomen are just as capable in potentially violent situations as men.							☐ (19)
Policemen do not feel they can rely on policewomen if they are confronted with a potentially violent situation.							☐ (20)
Women are more likely than men to leave the police service because they cannot cope with the stress of the job.							☐ (21)
Policemen are unnecessarily protective towards policewomen when they are working together on foot patrol duties.							☐ (22)

Policewomen are better than policemen at defusing potentially violent situations.							☐ (23)
Since police supervisors doubt the ability of women to perform all police duties, policewomen often find they do the most uninteresting jobs.							☐ (24)
The police service should do more to make it possible for women to combine a police career with marriage and children.							☐ (25)
Policewomen should be paid differently because they do not perform all the same duties as men.							☐ (26)

39. What proportion of your work would you **estimate** involves the possibility of physical violence:

        Less than 10%   ☐

        Up to a quarter   ☐

        Up to a half   ☐

        More than half   ☐

F.O.U.
Card 3

☐ (27)

40. Please indicate whether you have ever been in any of the following situations during the course of your duties as a police officer:

    Been threatened verbally   ☐

☐ (28)

Struggled, unaided, with a violent person ☐ | ☐ (29)

Been threatened by someone with a knife, gun or other weapon. ☐ | ☐ (30)

Been physically assaulted ☐ | ☐ (31)

If you have at some time been physically assaulted please answer the following questions:
How many times have you been physically assaulted?
Number ☐ | ☐ (32)

Did any of these assaults result in you being injured?
Yes ☐
No ☐ | ☐ (33)

If **yes**, for each occasion please indicate whether your injuries were minor or serious.

	Minor	Serious		Minor	Serious	
1.	☐	☐	4.	☐	☐	☐☐ (34–35)
2.	☐	☐	5.	☐	☐	☐☐ (36–37)
3.	☐	☐				☐ (38)

42.   Has a member of the public ever made a complaint about the way you perform your police duties?
Yes ☐
No ☐ | ☐ (39)

If **yes**, did this complaint result in formal investigation under the complaints procedure?
Yes ☐
No ☐ | ☐ (40)

The following questions are for policewomen who joined the police service before integration (before 1975)

Policewomen only
If you joined the police service before integration (before 1975) please answer the following questions

43.   Listed below are some of the changes, resulting from integration, which are said to affect policewomen. Please indicate (by ticking the appropriate box) how far you **agree** or **disagree** that these have affected you.

	Strongly agree	Agree	Neither agree nor disagree	Disagree	Strongly disagree	Don't know	
There is a greater variety of work.							☐ (41)
Shifts, night duty and irregular hours disrupt personal life.							☐ (42)
There is more chance to specialise, for example, in the CID.							☐ (43)
There is more exposure to danger and violence.							☐ (44)
Working relationships have improved.							☐ (45)
Policewomen have equal status with policemen.							☐ (46)
'Traditional' policewomen's tasks cannot be done as well.							☐ (47)
Policemen are prejudiced and rude.							☐ (48)
Policewomen have more responsibility now.							☐ (49)
It is more difficult to combine a police career with marriage and/or children now.							☐ (50)

Shift work makes personal life easier to plan ahead.							□ (51)
There is more chance to use your initiative.							□ (52)
There is more opportunity to meet people.							□ (53)
There is less chance for promotion.							□ (54)
Policewomen are more subject to sexual harassment from male officers.							□ (55)

Appendix B: Recruitment Criteria

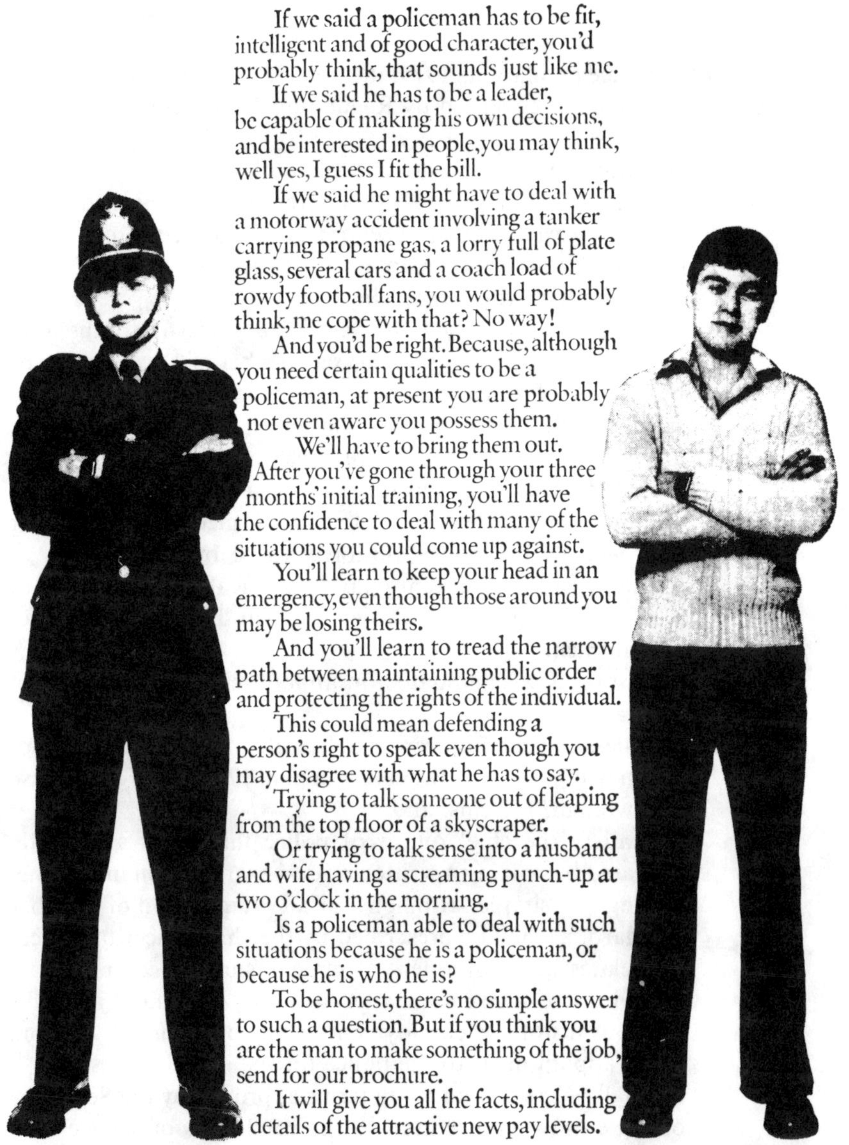

If we said a policeman has to be fit, intelligent and of good character, you'd probably think, that sounds just like me.

If we said he has to be a leader, be capable of making his own decisions, and be interested in people, you may think, well yes, I guess I fit the bill.

If we said he might have to deal with a motorway accident involving a tanker carrying propane gas, a lorry full of plate glass, several cars and a coach load of rowdy football fans, you would probably think, me cope with that? No way!

And you'd be right. Because, although you need certain qualities to be a policeman, at present you are probably not even aware you possess them.

We'll have to bring them out. After you've gone through your three months' initial training, you'll have the confidence to deal with many of the situations you could come up against.

You'll learn to keep your head in an emergency, even though those around you may be losing theirs.

And you'll learn to tread the narrow path between maintaining public order and protecting the rights of the individual.

This could mean defending a person's right to speak even though you may disagree with what he has to say.

Trying to talk someone out of leaping from the top floor of a skyscraper.

Or trying to talk sense into a husband and wife having a screaming punch-up at two o'clock in the morning.

Is a policeman able to deal with such situations because he is a policeman, or because he is who he is?

To be honest, there's no simple answer to such a question. But if you think you are the man to make something of the job, send for our brochure.

It will give you all the facts, including details of the attractive new pay levels.

Does the man make the job?

Or does the job make the man?

Figure B1 Police recruitment advertisement. (Reproduced with permission of the Controller, Her Majesty's Stationery Office)

STATUTORY REGULATIONS CONCERNING RECRUITMENT

Under the Police regulations 1979, the qualifications for appointment to a police force are governed by Regulation 14 which states:

14. (1) A candidate for appointment to a police force –
(a) must produce satisfactory references as to character, and if he has served in any police force, in the armed forces, in the civil service or as a seaman, produce satisfactory proof of his good conduct while so serving;
(b) must have attained the age of 18 years 6 months and, unless he has previous service as a member of a police force or by reason of other experience or his personal qualities is specially suitable for appointment, must not have attained the age of 30 years or, if he has previous whole-time service in the armed forces or previous service as a seaman, 40 years;
(c) must be certified by a registered medical practitioner approved by the police authority to be in good health, of sound constitution and fitted both physically and mentally to perform the duties on which he will be employed after appointment;
(d) must, if a candidate for appointment in the rank of constable –
(i) unless the chief officer of police otherwise decides, be not less in height than, in the case of a man 172 cms, or in the case of a woman, 162 cms, and
(ii) satisfy the chief officer of police that he is sufficiently educated by passing a written or oral examination in reading, writing and simple arithmetic, or an examination of a higher standard, as may be prescribed by the chief officer of police;
(e) [relates to appointment of sergeants or inspectors;]
(f) must give such information as may be required as to his previous history or employment or any other matter relating to his appointment to the police force;
(g) shall be given a notice in terms approved by the Secretary of State drawing attention to the conditions of service contained therein.
(2) For the purposes of this Regulation –
(a) the expression 'armed forces' means the naval, military or

air forces of the Crown including any women's service administered by the Defence Council, and
(b) the expression 'seaman' has the same meaning as the Merchant Shipping Act, 1894.

A further restriction on appointment is applied by Regulation 13, which states:

13. (1) Save in so far as the chief officer of police may allow at the request of the candidate concerned, a person shall not be eligible for appointment to a police force if he or a relative included in his family has a business interest within the meaning of Regulation 12, and paragraphs (6) and (7) thereof shall apply for the purposes of this Regulation as they apply for the purposes of that Regulation.

Regulation 12:

(6) For the purpose of this Regulation, a member of a police force or, as the case may be, a relative included in his family, shall have a business interest if –
(a) the member holds any office of employment for hire or gain (otherwise than as a member of a police force) or carries on any business;
(b) a shop is kept or a like business carried on by the member's spouse (not being separated from him) at any premises in the area of the police force in question or by any relative included in his family at the premises at which he resides; or
(c) the member, his spouse (not being separated from him) or any relative included in his family living with him holds, or possesses a pecuniary interest in, any such licence or permit as is mentioned in paragraph (7);
and a reference to a relative included in a member's family shall include a reference to his spouse, parent, son, daughter, brother or sister.
(7) The licence or permit referred to in paragraph (6) (c) is a licence or permit granted in pursuance of the law relating to liquor licensing, refreshment houses or betting and gaining or regulating places of entertainment in the area of the police force in question.

MEDSHIRE RECRUITMENT INTERVIEW FORM

Medshire Constabulary

Interviewed for appointment by   Date ....
....
....
Name .... Tel no........................
Occupation...................................... Availability ....
Accommodation (Type).........................
Liability explained............................. Preference...................
Driving licence................................. Vehicle ....
Languages....................................... Special skills ....
Education
Qualifications at school...
Qualifications since leaving school ....
P.I.R. test result...

Remarks

Ambitions
 Past and present
 Standards set
 Motivation
 Other careers
  considered

Appearance

Attitudes
 To present job
 Reasons for change
 To people at work
 To studying
 To this interview
 To police service

Bearing

Clarity of speech
 Oral expression
 Ability to grasp questions
 Speed and accuracy of
  answers
 Reasoned arguments

Common sense

Current affairs
 Knowledge
 Source

Determination
  Energy
  Enthusiasm

Interests and hobbies
  School sports, clubs,
    societies
  Range
  Intensity

Knowledge of police work
  Sources
  Conditions of service

Maturity/confidence

Physical fitness
  Doctor's remarks
  Team games
  Leadership at games
  Administration
  Other sports

Prejudices
  Racial
  Political

Previous convictions
  Explanations

Written expression
  Grammar
  Spelling

Domestic circumstances
Has discussed with:
  Wife
  Parents
  Friends

Possibility of moving

General observations

Recommended/Not recommended .... Superintendent

Appointment approved/Not approved ....
                                        Assistant Chief
                                        Constable

Appendix C: National Promotion Examination Statistics

POLICE FORCES IN ENGLAND AND WALES, OUTSIDE THE METROPOLITAN POLICE

TABLE C1 *Qualifying examination for promotion to the rank of inspector, comparison of results by gender*

Year	Candidates	Males Sat (no.)	Males Passed (no.)	Males Passed (%)	Females Sat (no.)	Females Passed (no.)	Females Passed (%)	Total No. Sat	Females as % of total sitting
1973	3 paper (no referred)	10 888	712	6.5	573	67	11.7	11 461	5.0
1974	3 paper	11 099	670	6.0	631	41	6.5	11 730	5.4
	referred	916	499	54.5	51	26	51.0	967	5.3
	all	12 015	1 169	9.7	682	67	9.8	12 697	5.4
1975	3 paper	11 556	487	4.2	567	22	3.9	12 123	4.7
	referred	1 059	579	54.7	72	44	61.1	1 131	6.4
	all	12 615	1 066	8.5	639	66	10.3	13 254	4.8
1976	3 paper	11 463	1 027	9.0	401	35	9.0	11 864	3.4
	referred	1 205	882	73.2	47	39	83.0	1 252	3.8
	all	12 668	1 909	15.1	448	74	16.5	13 116	3.4
1977	3 paper	11 897	783	7.0	557	22	4.0	12 454	4.5
	referred	1 244	972	78.1	34	25	73.5	1 278	2.7
	all	13 141	1 755	13.4	591	47	8.0	13 732	4.3

TABLE C1 Continued

Year	Candidates	Males Sat (no.)	Passed (no.)	Passed (%)	Females Sat (no.)	Passed (no.)	Passed (%)	Total No. Sat	Females as % of total sitting
1979*	3 paper	10 361	1 401	13.5	676	127	18.8	11 037	6.1
	referred	784	697	88.9	39	35	89.7	825	4.7
	all	11 145	2 098	18.8	715	162	22.7	11 860	6.0
1980	3 paper	10 260	1 602	15.6	752	128	17.0	11 012	6.8
	referred	187	151	80.7	10	7	70.0	197	5.1
	all	10 447	1 753	16.8	762	135	17.7	11 209	6.8
1981	3 paper	10 234	1 924	18.8	781	159	20.4	11 015	7.1
	referred	281	242	86.1	20	16	80.0	301	6.6
	all	10 515	2 166	20.5	801	175	21.8	11 316	7.1
1982	3 paper	9 908	987	10.0	801	73	9.1	10 709	7.5
	referred	314	201	64.0	17	12	70.6	331	5.1
	all	10 222	1 188	11.6	818	85	10.4	11 040	7.4

*The format of the examination was altered; objective questions and a scheme of compensation passing were introduced.

TABLE C2 *Qualifying examination for promotion to the rank of inspector, comparison of results by gender*

Year	Candidates	Males			Females			Total No. Sat	Females as % of total sitting
		Sat (no.)	Passed (no.)	(%)	Sat (no.)	Passed (no.)	(%)		
1974	3 paper (no referred)	4 197	437	10.4	149	23	15.4	4 346	3.4
1975	3 paper	3 567	513	14.4	132	13	9.8	3 699	3.6
	referred	551	341	61.9	22	11	50.0	573	3.8
	all	4 118	854	20.7	154	24	15.6	4 272	3.6
1976	3 paper	3 658	212	5.8	117	7	6.0	3 775	3.1
	referred	550	320	58.2	18	11	61.1	568	3.2
	all	4 208	532	12.6	135	18	13.3	4 343	3.1
1977	3 paper	6 071	609	10.0	144	17	11.8	6 215	2.3
	referred	346	278	80.3	11	7	63.6	357	3.1
	all	6 417	887	13.8	155	24	15.5	6 572	2.4
1978	3 paper	5 024	523	10.4	121	10	8.3	5 145	2.4
	referred	937	731	78.0	15	12	80.0	952	1.6
	all	5 961	1 254	21.0	136	22	16.2	6 097	2.2
1979	3 paper	4 550	598	13.1	127	18	14.2	4 677	2.7
	referred	779	587	75.4	23	18	78.3	802	2.9
	all	5 329	1 185	22.2	150	36	24.0	5 479	2.7
1980*	2 paper	3 993	1 250	31.3	80	25	31.3	4 073	2.0
	referred	611	566	92.6	23	21	91.3	634	3.6
	all	4 604	1 816	39.4	103	46	44.7	4 704	2.2
1981	2 paper	4 053	1 208	29.8	87	26	29.9	4 140	2.1
1982	2 paper	4 019	1 250	31.1	133	60	45.1	4 052	3.2
1983	2 paper	3 405	1 220	35.8	127	52	40.9	3 532	3.6

*The format of the examination was altered in 1980 to two papers; a combined Traffic and Crime paper plus the General Police Duties paper. Referral in one paper was not possible under the new rules but an opportunity was given to candidates referred in previous examinations to take that one paper only.

Notes and References

CHAPTER 1

1. Martin, S. E., *Breaking and Entering* (University of California Press, 1980).
2. Critchley, T. A., *A History of the Police in England and Wales 900–1966* (London: Constable, 1966) p. 217.
3. Over 4000 members of the Metropolitan Police alone served in the Armed Forces.
4. Ascoli, D., *The Queen's Peace* (London: Hamish Hamilton, 1979) p. 207.
5. Owings, C., *Women Police* (New Jersey: Patterson Smith, 1969) p. 10.
6. Ibid., p. 21.
7. Critchley, op. cit., p. 216.
8. Hart, J., *The British Police* (London: Allen & Unwin, 1951) p. 135.
9. Lock, J., 'The Extraordinary Life of Mary Allen', *Police Review*, 22 June 1984, p. 1266.
10. Lock J., *The British Policewoman* (London: Robert Hale, 1979).
11. *Bridgeman Committee on Employment of Policewomen*, Cmd 2224 (London: HMSO, 1924).
12. *Royal Commission on Police Powers and Procedures*, Cmd 3297 (London: HMSO, 1929).
13. Ibid., paras 256–7.
14. Home Office, *Police Postwar Reports* (Four Reports) (London: HMSO, 1946–7).
15. Berkley, G., *The Democratic Policeman* (Boston: Beacon Press, 1969) p. 67.
16. Lock, *The British Policewoman*, p. 183.
17. Smart, C., *Women, Crime and Criminology: A Feminist Critique* (London: Routledge & Kegan Paul, 1981) p. 24.
18. May, D., 'What Price Equality?', *Police Review*, 6 March 1981, p. 458.
19. Ibid., p. 461.
20. Or the Police (Scotland) Act 1967.
21. The minimum height requirements are laid down in S.14.1 (d)(i) of the Police Act as 'unless a chief officer of police otherwise decides, be not less than, in the case of a man 172 cms., or in the case of a woman, 162 cms.'
22. Whittaker, B., *The Police in Society* (London: Eyre Methuen, 1979) p. 122.
23. Ibid., p. 122.
24. Report on Superintendents' Annual Conference, *Police Review*, 10 March 1978, p. 337.

25. Hilton, J., 'Women in the Police Service', *Police Review*, 17 September 1976, p. 1166.

26. Bunting, A., *Police Review*, 9 January 1976, p. 39.

27. It would be impossible to quote accurate figures on this as some women chose early retirement, but some notable resignations were publicised in *Police Review*, see issues of 9 January 1976 and 6 February 1976.

28. Edmund-Davies, Lord, *Committee of Inquiry on the Police, Reports on Negotiating Machinery and Pay*, Cmd 7283 (London: HMSO, 1978).

29. Ibid., para. 384.

30. The Act specifically exempts acts which are necessary in order to comply with the requirements of statutes passed before the Sex Discrimination Act, and since 1953 women in the federated ranks have had separate representative arrangements within the Federation. These arrangements were given statutory force by the Police Federation Act 1961, and are now incorporated in the Police Federation Regulations.

31. Edmund-Davies, op. cit., p. 91.

32. Smith, D. and Gray, J., *Police and the People in London*, vol. IV, Policy Studies Institute, November 1983, p. 247.

CHAPTER 2

1. Jones, S. J. and Levi, M., 'Police–public relationships: a study of police and public perceptions of each other', unpublished research report prepared by the Department of Social Administration, University College, Cardiff, February 1983.

2. Jones, S. J., 'Police inter-rank attitudes: a study of junior and senior ranks' attitudes to the police service', unpublished research report prepared by the Department of Social Administration, University College, Cardiff, July 1982.

3. This was claimed by a PC in a letter to the *Manchester Evening News* on 6 April 1978, and subsequently reported in *Police Review*, 12 May 1978.

4. Southgate, P., 'Women in the police', *The Police Journal*, vol. 54 (April 1981) pp. 157–67. See also, Sullivan, P. K., 'The role of women in the police service – the effects of the Sex Discrimination Act 1975 – a comparison of respective positions', *The Police Journal*, vol. 52 (1979) pp. 336–43.

5. See, for example, Martin, S. E., *Breaking and Entering* (University of California Press, 1980) and Hunt, J., 'The development of rapport through the negotiation of gender in fieldwork among police', unpublished paper, Department of Sociology, Queens College, City University of New York, 1983.

6. For classic examples of studies which demonstrate the peace-keeping role of the British police see, for example, Banton, M., *The Policeman in the Community* (London: Tavistock, 1964) and Cain, M. E., *Society and the Policeman's Role* (London: Routledge & Kegan Paul, 1973). For comparisons with the American experience of policing see, Man-

ning, P. J., *Police Work: The Social Organisation of Policing* (Cambridge, Mass. and London: MIT Press, 1977).

7. Smith, D. and Gray, J., *Police and the People in London*, vol. IV, Policy Studies Institute, November 1983, p. 93.

8. See, for example, Manning, op. cit.; Bittner, E., 'The police on Skid Row: a study of peacekeeping', *Am. Sociol Review*, vol. 32 (1967) no. 5, pp. 699–715; and Holdaway, S., *Inside the British Police: A Force at Work* (Oxford: Basil Blackwell, 1983).

9. Brown, C. L., 'The effect of training and some job experience on the attitudes of recruits', unpublished PhD dissertation, University of Wales, 1983.

10. Ibid., p. 23.

11. Skolnick, J. K., *Justice without Trial* (New York: John Wiley, 1966).

12. See, for example, Skolnick, op. cit.; Neiderhoffer, A., *Behind the Shield: the Police in Urban Society* (New York: Anchor, 1967); and Leftkowicz, J., 'Psychological attributes of policemen', *J. of Social Issues*, vol. 31 (1975) no. 1, pp. 5–26.

13. This is particularly true of other male-dominated occupations such as the law and the clergy, see for example, Morris, J., *Against Nature and God: The History of Women with the Jurisdiction of Bishops* (London: Macmillan, 1973); and Spencer, A. and Podmore, D., 'Life on the periphery of a profession: the experience of women lawyers', unpublished paper presented to the British Sociological Association Conference, 1983. Other studies show that barriers exist even in occupations often classed as women's work see, for example, Novarra, V., *Women's Work, Men's Work: The Ambivalence of Equality* (London: Marion Boyars, 1980).

14. For an account of these media portrayals, and in particular the difference between the images presented of male and female police officers, see Morrison, C. M., 'A sociological analysis of the image of the British police in the media', unpublished PhD thesis, Department of Sociology, University of Aberdeen, 1984.

15. The accounts by Cain, op. cit., and Holdaway, op. cit. describe the boredom and inactivity of patrol work. My own experience in connection with the present study also confirms this view of routine policing.

16. Peter Manning makes the point that police manpower has to be available to cover peak times and the possibility of high demand. As a result, for much of the time personnel are underused. Personal communication, July 1984.

17. See, for example, Punch, M., 'The Police as Secret Social Service', in Holdaway, S. (ed.) *The British Police* (London: Edward Arnold, 1979); Ekblom, P. and Heal, K., 'The police response to calls from the public', Research and Planning Unit Paper 9 (London: HMSO, 1982); and McCabe, S. and Sutcliffe, F., *Defining Crime: A Study of Police Definitions* (Oxford: Basil Blackwell, 1977).

18. For example, Smith and Gray, op. cit. and Jones, 'Police inter-rank attitudes'.

19. For accounts of the factors influencing the detection of crime see, for example, Chaiken, J. M., Greenwood, P. W. and Petersilia, J., 'The

Criminal Investigation Process: A Summary Report' (California: The Rand Corporation, 1976); Steer, D., *Uncovering Crime: the Police Role*, Royal Commission on Criminal Procedure, Research Study No. 5 (London: HMSO, 1980); and Chatterton, M., 'Police in Social Control', in King, J. (ed.) *Control without Custody* (Cropwood Papers, Cambridge Institute of Criminology, 1976).

20. Southgate, op. cit. and May, D., 'What price Equality?', *Police Review*, 6 March 1981, pp. 458–61.

21. Hilton J., 'Women in the Police Service', *The Police Journal*, vol. 49 (1976) pp. 93–103.

22. Feinman, C., *Women in the Criminal Justice System* (New York: Praeger, 1981).

23. Fowler, H. W. and Fowler, F. G. (eds) *The Concise Oxford Dictionary*, 4th edition (Oxford: Clarendon Press, 1962).

24. *Random House Dictionary of the English Language* (New York: Random House, 1966).

25. Jones J. M., *Prejudice and Racism* (Reading, Mass: Addison-Wesley, 1972).

26. Allport, G. W., *The Nature of Prejudice* (Reading, Mass: Addison-Wesley, 1954) p. 10.

27. Wilson, E., *Women and the Welfare State* (London: Tavistock, 1977).

28. Chiplin, B. and Sloane, P. J., *Tackling Discrimination at the Workplace* (Cambridge University Press, 1981) p. 5.

29. These are the definitions given in the Home Office publication *A Guide to the Sex Discrimination Act 1975* (London: HMSO, 1975).

30. Department of Employment, *New Earnings Survey* (London: HMSO, 1983) p. 90.

CHAPTER 3

1. Based on figures supplied by F1 Division of the Home Office. These differ slightly from those extracted from the HMI reports (5777). Unless otherwise stated, national figures are derived from this Home Office data throughout this section.

2. Figures for 1983 and 1984 are not included in the percentage increase calculation because the study was conducted on the basis of the 1982 figures.

3. This information was requested but is not kept centrally. It could be collated from all the individual annual reports for this period but even then it would be impossible to judge the 'quality' of the pool of applicants because of the complication of local variations, even in objective criteria such as height, etc. The annual reports do suggest that female applications account for a quarter to a third of all those received.

4. The 1983 figure is the recruitment figure given in the HMI report for that year and excludes the Metropolitan Police. Actual appointments

made tend to be lower than HMI recruitment figures. The actual appointment data were unavailable when this section was compiled.

5. A Marxist interpretation of this process is that employers substitute women for men in order to keep wage levels down. See, for example, Milkman, R., 'Women's Work and the Economic Crisis', *Review of Radical Political Economy*, 1976.

6. For an account of these trends, see Breugel, I., 'Women as a Reserve Army of Labour', in Evans, M. (ed.) *The Woman Question* (London: Fontana, 1982) p. 280.

7. Ibid. See also, EOC *Research Bulletin*, no. 9, Spring 1985. This contains a number of articles on Occupational Segregation by Sex, including the way recruitment is affected by gender considerations.

8. Quartiles are derived from the distribution of scores around the median, which is that value at which 50 per cent of the scores occur above and below. The median is the second quartile.

9. This force was selected for this research before this was known. Nevertheless, there are no *prima facie* grounds for supposing this force is markedly different from the others in England and Wales.

10. Smith, D. J. and Gray, J., *Police and the People in London*, IV, Policy Studies Institute, November 1983, p. 246.

11. *Parliamentary Debates – Hansard*, 11 May 1984 (London: HMSO).

12. In theory, probationers are still in the process of initial training until they have completed two years' service.

13. Bunyard, R. S., *Police: Organisation and Command* (Plymouth: Mac-Donald & Evans, 1978) p. 196.

14. Critchley, T. A., *A History of Police in England and Wales: 900–1966* (London: Constable, 1966).

15. Jones, S. J. and Levi, M., 'The police and the majority: the neglect of the obvious?', *The Police Journal*, vol. LVI, no. 4, pp. 351–64.

16. Scarman, Lord, *The Brixton Disorders: Report of an Inquiry*, Cmd 8427 (London: HMSO, November 1981) para 5.6.

17. Police Advisory Board, *Report of a Working Party on Manpower, Equipment and Efficiency* (London: HMSO, 1967).

18. Although 2216 applications were received, 582 were subsequently withdrawn or not proceeded with.

19. Body proportions are also supposed to be in relation to height and weight.

20. This is because of the high level of unemployment in the area. Two exceptions are at the discretion of the Chief Constable: members of the Armed Forces wishing to return to the area, and applicants whose parental home is in the area but who have been living outside the area for education or employment reasons.

21. Though in practice, few forces having training procedures.

22. These figures are based on data extracted from the Chief Constable's Annual Reports. It should be noted that there is sometimes a lag between applications and appointments in that some applications are still being processed in the following year. These comparisons are based on the assumption that approximately the same proportion of applications are carried forward from year to year.

23. Smith and Gray, op. cit., p. 247.
24. In other words, after all the applicants rejected because of failure to meet educational, physical or age requirements and those classified as 'otherwise unsuitable' are removed from the pool of applicants. The category 'otherwise unsuitable' includes people who do not get through the vetting procedure (previous convictions, or unsatisfactory employment history, etc. contribute towards this procedure). It may also include people who have been interviewed. In this sense the data given in the table, is a conservative estimate of the local influence.

CHAPTER 4

1. Lock, J., *The British Policewoman* (London: Robert Hale, 1979) p. 202.
2. Southgate, P., 'Women in the Police', in, *The Police Journal*, vol. 54 (April 1982) p. 163.
3. The full definitions of these roles can be found in the questionnaire in Appendix A.
4. This apparently favourable advantage is based on actuarial tables which are derived on the basis of comparative male and female life expectancy rates.
5. Except where the Genuine Occupational Qualification applies such as in some observational work, or when searching people, where there is a need to preserve privacy or decency.
6. Again, it should be emphasised that these percentage figures actually mask the very small numbers of women involved.
7. The term community constable is one which became common during the time when John Alderson was Chief Constable of Devon and Cornwall and advocating community policing. Generally speaking, community constables, resident or home-beat officers (as they are sometimes called), are those officers whose role it is to be the direct link between the police organisation and the community. Each officer is responsible for almost all the policing of a specific geographical section or area and is meant to provide a focal point for people within the community for policing (and sometimes other) matters.
8. Regional Criminal Intelligence Office. Police officers from all the forces in any region are seconded to work in this office, normally for a two-year tour of duty.
9. See, for example, Manning, P. J., *Police Work: The Social Organisation of Policing* (Cambridge, Mass. and London: MIT Press, 1977); and, for an account of how this mainstream action-oriented approach influences police attitudes to white collar crimes, see Levi, M., *The Phantom Capitalists* (London: Heinemann, 1981).
10. Of course, this may in itself be a way of controlling women's deployment experience. Contrary to popular belief, CID officers are not the first at the scene of an incident and are usually allocated crimes to investigate which may (or may not) result from incidents. Putting women in CID may serve the dual function of keeping them from

front-line, possibly dangerous, incidents as well as regulating the kinds of crimes (i.e. those felt to be suitable for women) which they investigate.

11. Particularly if there is not much happening on a night shift. One inspector told me he did it so that the officers would have company but he was anxious that I would not mention this to his supervisor.

12. The programme was one of a series of 'fly on the wall' documentaries about the police produced by Roger Graff of the BBC with the full collaboration and consent of the Thames Valley Police, which was designed to give a real life insight into policing and police practice.

13. Chambers, G. and Millar, A., *Investigating Sexual Assault* (Edinburgh: HMSO, 1983) p. 117.

CHAPTER 5

1. Clegg, S. and Dunkerley, D., *Organisation, Class and Control* (London: Routledge & Kegan Paul, 1980).

2. See, for example, Carter, M. P., *Education, Employment and Leisure* (Oxford: Pergamon, 1963); and Brown, R. K., Kirkby, J. M. and Taylor, K. F., 'The employment of married women and the supervisory role', *Brit. J. Industrial Relations*, vol 2 (1964) no. 1.

3. Fogarty, M., Rapaport, R. and Rapaport, R., 'Women and top jobs: the next move', *PEP Broadsheet 535*, 1972.

4. See Agassi, J. B., *Women on the Job* (Lexington, Mass: Lexington Books, 1979); and Agassi, J. B., *Comparing the Work Attitudes of Men and Women* (Lexington, Mass.: Lexington Books, 1982).

5. Interestingly, the classic account on police socialisation by John Van Maanen, refers only to men and their reasons for joining. See Maanen, J. V., 'Observations on the making of policemen', in Blumberg, A. S. and Neiderhoffer, E. (eds) *The Ambivalent Force*, 3rd edition (New York: Holt, Rinehart & Winston, 1985).

6. One man had recently been 'put back in uniform' after an incident in the CID, and the other man made no attempt to hide his bitterness at an event (several years earlier) that had almost resulted in his resignation.

7. Jones, S. J., 'Police inter-rank attitudes: a study of junior and senior ranks' attitudes to the police service', unpublished research report prepared by the Department of Social Administration, University College, Cardiff, July 1982.

8. Kelland, G., Bryant, L. and Dunkerley, D., 'Policewomen and their work', in *Police Review*, 17 May 1985, p. 1013.

9. Ibid.

10. It should be borne in mind that in Medshire the actual numbers, especially for females, is very low and consequently a big percentage increase or decrease may represent the addition or deduction of only one or two cases. Actual numbers are therefore given in brackets after the percentage figure quoted.

11.   Office for Census and Population Surveys, *General Household Survey
        No. 11, 1981* (London: HMSO, 1983).

CHAPTER 6

1.   Police Advisory Boards for England, Scotland and Wales, *Report of
        the Joint Working Party on the Rank Structure of the Police* (London:
        HMSO, 1972).
2.   See, for example, Anderson, P., 'Influencing skills – a blue touch paper
        for women', in *Women and Training News*, Issue 18, Spring 1985,
        Manpower Services Commission.
3.   This higher number reflects men who had passed the examination in
        previous years and had finally been appointed.
4.   Another interesting difference between men and women in this age
        group which is worth noting in passing is the proportion of divorcees:
        19 per cent of the women, but only 5 per cent of the men, were
        divorced.
5.   Heller, M. and McGill, P., 'How to get the women back to work',
        Police Review, 15 February 1985, p. 335.
6.   For details, see Martin, J. and Roberts, C., *Women and Employment: A
        Lifetime Perspective*, Department of Employment (London: HMSO,
        1984).
7.   During the preliminary work for this study, interviews were conducted
        with a selection of senior women officers from other forces. Interest-
        ingly, most of these were unmarried.
8.   This example is taken from an article in the Metropolitan Police's in-
        house magazine in May 1985.
9.   Edmund-Davies, Lord, *Committee of Inquiry on the Police, Reports on
        Negotiating Machinery and Pay*, Cmnd 7283 (London: HMSO, 1978)
        para. 385.
10.   Ibid.
11.   Indeed, when I rang the Home Office to enquire about rejoining policy
        and regulations, I overheard my contact seeking advice from his
        colleague. He was told that 'officially we are silent on this, we have no
        policy and it is up to the discretion of local forces'!

CHAPTER 7

1.   Following some informal discussions with recruiting and training staff,
        formal interviews were conducted with both the senior officers in the
        department.
2.   Chiplin, B. and Sloane, P. J., *Tackling Discrimination at the Workplace*
        (Cambridge University Press, 1982) p. 45.
3.   A relief is the smallest operational patrol unit. It usually consists of a
        sergeant and a group of constables directly responsible to him or her as

a supervisor. A relief inspector will be responsible for several (usually three or four) reliefs on a particular shift. A three-shift pattern (mornings, afternoons and nights) is usual, though there are local variations.

4. Several police forces in America have physical fitness assessments of applicants and have been known to increase the standard of these tests in order to exclude women applicants.

5. The significance of the thirty years is that officers 'sign on' for this period rather like the Armed Forces, except that there is no question of them having to be 'bought out' if they want to leave. Normal notice periods of one month apply for either side.

6. *The Times*, 20 December 1983.

7. *The Times*, 22 December 1983.

8. Including public order situations, on the basis that although most public order situations do not involve violent confrontations, the *possibility* remains.

9. *Police Review*, 8 June 1984.

10. Ibid.

11. Manning, P. J., *Police Work: The Social Organisation of Policing* (Cambridge, Mass. and London: MIT Press, 1977) and Punch, M., 'The Police as Secret Social Service', in Holdaway, S. (ed.) *The British Police* (London: Edward Arnold, 1979).

12. Skolnick, J. K., *Justice Without Trial* (New York: John Wiley, 1966); Martin, S. E., *Breaking and Entering* (University of California Press, 1980); and Wilson, J. Q., *Varieties of Police Behaviour* (New York: Atheneum, 1973). In addition, for a first-hand account, Jennifer Hunt has written a graphic (unpublished) and analytic account of her experiences of negotiating her gender role when conducting a participant observation study with the New York police.

13. Flynn, E. E., 'Women as Criminal Justice Professionals', in Rafter, N. H. and Stanko, E. A. (eds) *Judge, Lawyer, Victim, Thief: Women Gender Roles and Criminal Justice* (Boston: Northeastern University Press, 1982) p. 316.

14. Sherman, L. J., 'A psychological view of women in policing', *J. of Police Science and Admin.*, vol. 1 (1973) no. 4 p. 390.

15. Home Office Circular 173/75, para. 9.

16. Flynn, op. cit., p. 317.

17. Price, B. R. and Gavin, S., 'A Century of Women in Policing', in Price, B. R. and Sokoloff, N. J. (eds) *The Criminal Justice System and Women: An Anthology of Women Offenders, Victims and Workers* (New York: Clark Boardman, 1982) p. 410.

18. Ibid.

CHAPTER 8

1. Punch, M., *Conduct Unbecoming: The Social Construction of Police Deviance and Control* (London: Tavistock, 1985) p. 3.

2. Perhaps it is worth nothing here that these concepts are offered as analytic tools rather than mutually exclusive categories. As such it is feasible that in some instance they may overlap, or more likely succeed each other as part of a cycle of events leading to legislation.

3. Erhlich, E., 'Fundamental Principles of the Sociology of Law', in *Twentieth Century Series of Legal Philosophy*, vol 4. See also, Sumner, W. G., *Folkways* (Boston: Ginn, 1906).

4. Friedmann, W., *Law in a Changing Society* (Harmondsworth: Penguin, 1964) p. 24.

5. Dicey, A. V., 'Law and Public Opinion in England', in Aubert, W. (ed.) *Sociology of Law* (Harmondsworth: Penguin, 1969).

6. For a review of the debate about whether legislation can affect social norms as well as individual behaviour, see Grace, C. and Wilkinson, P., *Sociological Inquiry and Legal Phenomena* (London: Collier MacMillan, 1978) p. 119.

7. Roshier, B. and Teff, H., *Law and Society in England* (London: Tavistock, 1980) p. 25.

8. Price, B. R. and Gavin, S., 'A Century of Women in Policing', in Price, B. R. and Sokoloff, N. J. (eds) *The Criminal Justice System and Women: An Anthology of Women Offenders, Victims and Workers* (New York: Clark Boardman, 1982) p. 408.

9. Most accounts of women in employment, whether in 'traditional' women's work or in those usually seen as mainly male occupations, document these attitudes either directly or indirectly. For more general accounts, see, for example, Whitelegg, E. *et al.*, *The Changing Experience of Women*, Part II (Oxford: Basil Blackwell, 1982); and Sanders, D., with Reed, J., *Kitchen Sink or Swim?: Women in the Eighties* (Harmondsworth: Penguin, 1982).

10. For a review of the relationship between behaviour change and attitude change, see Ullman, L. P. and Krasner, L., *A Psychological Approach to Abnormal Behaviour* (New Jersey: Prentice Hall, 1975) p. 242 *et seq.*; and Bandura, A., *Principles of Behaviour Modification* (New York: Holt, Rinehart & Winston, 1969) pp. 599–615.

11. The dangers associated with this 'professional mask' approach are outlined in Smith, D. and Gray, J., *Police and the People in London*, vol. IV, Policy Studies Institute, November 1983, where they make the point that under conditions of stress this mask might slip.

12. In this sense, intrinsic factors or rewards are equivalent to internalised reinforcers such as those discussed by Bandura, op. cit., p. 615 *et seq.*

13. Punch, op. cit., p. 2. As Punch points out, the PSI study of the Metropolitan Police (Smith and Gray, op. cit.) gives numerous examples of persistent rule-bending in the law-enforcement process.

14. Holdaway, S., *Inside the British Police: A Force at Work* (Oxford: Basil Blackwell, 1983) p. 100.

15. Punch, op. cit., p. 13.

16. An account of the various practices which make crime rates a most uncertain indicator of 'real' crime can be found in Bottomley, A. K. and Coleman, C., *Understanding Crime Rates: Police and Public Roles in the Production of Official Statistics* (Aldershot: Gower, 1981).

17. Lipsky, M., *Street-Level Bureaucracy: Dilemmas of the Individual in Public Services* (New York: Russell Sage Foundation, 1980).
18. Cain, M. E., *Society and the Policeman's Role* (London: Routledge & Kegan Paul, 1973).
19. Marshall, P., 'Policewomen on patrol', *Manpower 5*, vol. 10 (1973) pp. 14–20.
20. Bloch, P. B. and Anderson, D., *Policewomen on Patrol: Final Report* (Washington, DC: Urban Institute, 1974).
21. Ibid.
22. See, for example, Bouza, A. V., 'Women in Policing', *FBI Law Enf. Bul.*, vol. 44 (1975) no. 9, pp. 2–7.
23. See, for example, Garmire, B. L., 'Female Officers in the Department', *FBI Law Enf. Bul.*, vol. 43 (1974) no. 6, pp. 11–13.
24. Sherman, L. J., 'An evaluation of policewomen on patrol in a suburban police department', *J. of Police Science and Admin.*, vol. 3 (1975) no. 4 pp. 434–8.
25. Price and Gavin, op. cit., p. 410.
26. For a review of studies of citizens' attitudes to policewomen see, for example, Milton, C., *Women in Policing* (Washington, DC: Police Foundation, 1972); and Bell, D. J., 'Policewomen: Myths and Reality', *J. of Police Science and Admin.* vol. 10 (1982) no. 1.
27. This is a view that has also been expressed to me by a chief constable who was concerned that if women were expected to perform public order duties (which he felt they did not want to do anyway) they would leave the service, leaving behind only those women whom he considered to be the 'wrong kind'.
28. Martin, S. E., '*Police*women and police*women*: occupational role dilemmas and choices of female officers', *J. of Police Sicence and Admin*, vol. 7 (1979) no. 3.
29. Hochschild, A. R., 'Making it: marginality and obstacles to minority consciousness', *Annals of the NY Acad. of Sci.*, vol. 208 (1973) pp. 79–82.
30. Martin, op. cit., p. 315.
31. Martin, S. E. *Breaking and Entering* (University of California Press, 1980) p. 186.
32. Ibid. p. 194.
33. Kanter, R. M., *Men and Women of the Corporation* (New York: Basic Books, 1977); and Kanter, R. M., 'Skewed sex ratios and responses to token women', *Am. J. of Sociol.*, vol. 82, 1977.
34. Bryant, L., Dunkerley, D. and Kelland, G., 'One of the Boys?', *Policing*, vol. 1 (Autumn, 1985) no. 4, p. 243.
35. Holdaway, op. cit.
36. Jones, S. J. and Joss, R. 'Do police officers survive their training?', *Policing*, vol. 1 (Autumn 1985) no. 4.
37. The notion of the 'reflective professional' comes from Schon, D. A., *The Reflective Practitioner: How Professionals Think in Action* (London: Temple Smith, 1983).
38. This forms a central part of much of the work currently underway at the Centre for the Study of Community and Race Relations at Brunel

University where a multidisciplinary team is engaged in CRR training and research with the police service. It is also one of the concerns of the Centre for Applied Research in Education, University of East Anglia which is currently engaged in a review of police probationer training.

39.   Torrington, D. P., Hitner, T. and Knights, D., *Management and the Multiracial Workforce: Case Studies in Employment Practice* (Aldershot: Gower, 1982).

40.   The content, context and credibility of police CRR training were criticised in the Police Training Council Working Party Report, published in November 1983. The CRR element of the Metropolitan Police's Social Skills of Policing package for recruits was also found to be unsatisfactory in an independent evaluation conducted by Bull and Horncastle. For an account of this evaluation, see Bull, R., 'An Evaluation of Police Recruit Training in Human Awareness', paper presented at the NATO Advances Study Institute on The Role of Psychology in Police Selection and Training, held on Skiathos, May 1985. For an analysis of current CRR training, see Jones and Joss, op. cit.

APPENDIX A

1.   This took place between June and September 1983 and includes visits made in connection with the in-depth interviewing.

2.   Since there were, in fact, very few women on actual patrol duties, it seemed unproductive to continue this aspect of the study any longer. There is, however, clearly a case for conducting a more in-depth observational study of women on patrol over a period of several months.

Bibliography

Agassi, J. B. (1979) *Women on the Job* (Lexington, Mass: Lexington Books).
Agassi, J. B. (1982) *Comparing the Work Attitudes of Men and Women* (Lexington, Mass: Lexington Books).
Allport, G. W. (1954) *The Nature of Prejudice* (Reading, Mass:, Addison-Wesley).
Anderson, P. (1985) 'Influencing skills – a blue touch paper for women', in *Women and Training News,* Issue 18 (Manpower Services Commission).
Ascoli, D. (1979) *The Queen's Peace* (London: Hamish Hamilton).
Bandura, A. (1969) *Principles of Behaviour Modification* (New York: Holt, Rinehart & Winston).
Banton, M. (1964) *The Policeman in the Community* (London: Tavistock).
Bell, D. J. (1982) 'Policewomen: Myths and Reality', *J. of Police Science and Admin.* vol. 10, no. 1.
Berkley, G. (1969) *The Democratic Policeman* (Boston: Beacon Press).
Bittner, E. (1967) 'The police on Skid Row: a study of peacekeeping', *Am. Sociol. Review,* vol. 32, no. 5.
Bloch, P. B. and Anderson, D. (1974) *Policewomen on Patrol: Final Report* (Washington, DC: Urban Institute).
Bottomley, A. K. and Coleman, C. (1981) *Understanding Crime Rates: Police and Public Roles in the Production of Official Statistics* (Aldershot: Gower).
Bouza, A. V. (1975) 'Women in Policing', *FBI Law Enf. Bul.* vol. 44, no. 9.
Breugel, I. (1982) 'Women as a Reserve Army of Labour', in Evans, M. (ed.) *The Woman Question* (London: Fontana).
Brown, C. L. (1983) 'The effect of training and some job experience on the attitudes of recruits', unpublished PhD dissertation, University of Wales.
Brown, R. K., Kirkby, J. M. and Taylor, K. F. (1964) 'The employment of married women and the supervisory role', *Brit. J. Industrial Relations,* vol. 2. no. 1.
Bryant, L., Dunkerley, D. and Kelland, G. (1985) 'One of the Boys?', *Policing,* vol. 1, no. 4.
Bull, R. (1985) 'An Evaluation of Police Recruit Training in Human Awareness', paper presented at the NATO Advances Study Institute on The Role of Psychology in Police Selection and Training, held in Skiathos, May 1985.
Bunyard, R. S. (1978) *Police: Organisation and Command* (Plymouth: Mac-Donald & Evans).
Cain, M. E. (1973) *Society and the Policeman's Role* (London: Routledge & Kegan Paul).
Carter, M. P. (1963) *Education, Employment and Leisure* (Oxford: Pergamon).
Chaiken, J. M., Greenwood, P. W. and Petersilia, J. (1976) 'The Criminal Investigation Process; A Summary Report' (California: The Rand Corporation).
Chatterton, M. (1976) 'Police in Social Control', in King, J. (ed.) *Control*

without Custody, Cropwood Papers (Cambridge Institute of Crimonology).

Chiplin, B. and Sloane, P. J. (1981) *Tackling Discrimination at the Workplace* (Cambridge University Press).

Clegg, S. and Dunkerley, D. (1980) *Organisation, Class and Control* (London: Routledge & Kegan Paul).

Critchley, T. A. (1966) *A History of the Police in England and Wales: 900–1966* (London: Constable).

Department of Employment (1983) *New Earnings Survey* (London: HMSO).

Department of Employment (1984) *Women and Employment: A Lifetime Perspective* (London: HMSO).

Dicey, A. V. (1969) 'Law and Public Opinion In England' in Aubert, W. (ed.) *Sociology of Law* (Harmondsworth: Penguin).

Erhlich, E. (1936) 'Fundamental principles in the sociology of law', in the *Twentieth Century Series of Legal Philosophy*, vol. 4.

Feinman, C. (1981) *Women in the Criminal Justice System* (New York: Praeger).

Fogarty, M., Rapaport, R. and Rapaport, R., (1972) 'Women and Top Jobs: The Next Move', *PEP Broadsheet 535.*

Flynn, E. E. (1982) 'Women as Criminal Justice Professionals', in Rafter, N. H. and Stanko, E. A. (eds) *Judge, Lawyer, Victim, Thief: Women Gender Roles and Criminal Justice* (Boston: Northeastern University Press).

Friedmann, W. (1964) *Law in a Changing Society* (Harmondsworth: Penguin).

Garmire, B. L. (1974) 'Female officers in the department', *FBI Law Enf. Bul.* vol. 43, no. 6.

Grace, C. and Wilkinson, P. (1978) *Sociological Inquiry and Legal Phenomena* (London: Collier Macmillan).

Hart, J. (1951) *The British Police* (London: Allen & Unwin).

Heller, M. and McGill, P. (1985) 'How to get the women back to work', *Police Review*, 15 February 1985.

Hilton, J. (1976) 'Women in the Police Service', *Police Review*, 17 September 1976.

Hochschild, A. R. (1973) 'Making it: marginality and obstacles to minority consciousness', *Annals of the NY Acad. of Sci.*, vol. 208.

Holdaway, S. (1983) *Inside the British Police: A Force at Work* (Oxford: Basil Blackwell)

Home Office (1924) *Bridgeman Committee on Employment of Policewomen*, Cmd 2224 (London: HMSO).

Home Office (1929) *Royal Commission on Police Powers and Procedures*, Cmd 3297 (London: HMSO).

Home Office (1946–7) *Police Postwar Reports* (Four Reports) (London: HMSO).

Home Office (1967) *Report of a Working Party on Manpower, Equipment and Efficiency*, Police Advisory Board (London: HMSO).

Home Office (1972) *Report of the Joint Working Party on the Rank Structure of the Police*, Police Advisory Boards for England, Scotland and Wales (London: HMSO).

Home Office (1975) *Sex Discrimination: A Guide to the Sex Discrimination Act 1975* (London: HMSO).

Home Office (1978) *Committee of Inquiry on the Police*, Reports on Negotiating Machinery and Pay, Cmnd 7283 (London: HMSO)

Home Office (1980) *Uncovering Crime: the Police Role*, Royal Commission on Criminal Procedure, Research Study No. 5 (London: HMSO).

Home Office (1981) *The Brixton Disorders: Report of an Inquiry*, Cmnd 8427 (London: HMSO).

Home Office (1982) *The Police Response to Calls from the Public*, Research and Planning Unit Paper 9 (London: HMSO).

Home Office (1983) *Investigating Sexual Assault* (Edinburgh: HMSO).

Hunt, J. (1983) 'The Development of rapport through the negotiation of gender in fieldwork among police', unpublished paper, Department of Sociology, Queens College, City University of New York.

Jones, J. M. (1972) *Prejudice and Racism* (Reading, Mass.: Addison-Wesley).

Jones, S. J. (1982) 'Police inter-rank attitudes: a study of junior and senior ranks' attitudes to the police service', unpublished research report prepared by the Department of Social Administration, University College, Cardiff, July 1982.

Jones, S. J. and Joss, R. (1985) 'Do police officers survive their training?', *Policing*, vol. 1, no. 4.

Jones, S. J. and Levi, M. (1983) 'Police–public relationships: a study of police and public perceptions of each other', unpublished research report, prepared by Department of Social Administration, University College, Cardiff, February 1983.

Jones, S. J. and Levi M. (1983) 'The Police and the majority: the neglect of the obvious?', *The Police Journal*, vol. LVI, no. 4.

Kanter, R. M. (1977) *Men and Women of the Corporation* (New York: Basic Books).

Kanter, R. M. (1977) 'Skewed sex ratios and responses to token women', *Am. J. of Sociol.*, vol. 82.

Kelland, G., Bryant, L. and Dunkerley, D. (1985) 'Policewomen and their work', in *Police Review,* 17 May 1985.

Leftkowicz, J. (1975) 'Psychological attributes of policemen', *J. of Social Issues*, vol. 31, no. 1.

Levi, M. (1981) *The Phantom Capitalists* (London: Heinemann).

Lipsky, M. (1980) *Street Level Bureaucracy: Dilemmas of the Individual in Public Services* (New York: Russell Sage Foundation).

Lock, J. (1979) *The British Policewoman* (London: Robert Hale).

Lock, J. (1984) 'The extraordinary life of Mary Allen', *Police Review*, 22 June.

Maanen, J. V. (1985) 'Observations on the making of policemen', in, Blumberg, A. S. and Neiderhoffer, E. (eds) *The Ambivalent Force*, 3rd edition (New York: Holt, Rinehart & Winston).

Manning, P. J. (1977) *Police Work: The Social Organisation of Policing* (Cambridge, Mass. and London: MIT Press).

Marshall, P. (1973) 'Policewomen on patrol', *Manpower 5*, vol. 10.

Martin, S. E. (1979) '*Police*women and police*women*: occupational role dilemmas and choices of female officers', *J. of Police Sci. and Admin.*, vol. 7, no. 3.

Martin, S. E. (1980) *Breaking and Entering* (University of California Press).

May, D. (1981) 'What price equality?', *Police Review,* 6 March 1981.

McCabe, S. and Sutcliffe, F. (1977) *Defining Crime: A Study of Police Definitions* (Oxford: Basil Blackwell).

Milkman, R. (1976) 'Women's work and the economic crisis', *Review of Radical Political Economy.*

Milton, C. (1972) *Women in policing* (Washington DC: Police Foundation).

Morris J. (1973) *Against Nature and God: The History of Women in the Jurisdiction of Bishops* (London: Macmillan).

Morrison, C. M. (1984) 'A sociological analysis of the image of the British police in the media', unpublished PhD thesis, Department of Sociology, University of Aberdeen.

Neiderhoffer, A. (1967) *Behind the Shield: The Police in Urban Society* (New York: Anchor).

Novarra, V. (1980) *Women's Work, Men's Work: The Ambivalence of Equality* (London: Marion Boyars).

Owings, C. (1969) *Women Police* (New Jersey: Patterson Smith).

Price, B. R. and Gavin, S. (1982) 'A century of women in policing', in Price, B. R. and Sokoloff, N. J. (eds) *The Criminal Justice System and Women: An Anthology of Women Offenders, Victims and Workers* (New York: Clark Boardman).

Punch, M. (1979) 'The police as secret social service', in Holdaway, S. (ed.) *The British Police* (London: Edward Arnold).

Punch, M. (1985) *Conduct Unbecoming: The Social Construction of Police Deviance and Control* (London: Tavistock).

Roshier, B. and Teff, H. (1980) *Law and Society in England* (London: Tavistock).

Sanders, D. with Reed, J. (1982) *Kitchen Sink or Swim?: Women in the Eighties* (Harmondsworth: Penguin).

Schon, D. A. (1983) *The Reflective Practitioner: How Professionals Think in Action* (London: Temple Smith).

Sherman, L. J. (1973) 'A psychological view of women in policing', *J. of Police Science and Admin.,* vol. 1, no. 4.

Sherman, L. J. (1975) 'An evaluation of policewomen on patrol in a suburban police department', *J. of Police Sci. and Admin.,* vol. 3, no. 4.

Skolnick, J. K. (1966) *Justice without Trial* (New York: John Wiley).

Smart, C. (1981) *Women, Crime and Criminology: A Feminist Critique* (London: Routledge & Kegan Paul).

Smith, D. and Gray, J. (1983) *Police and the People in London: The Police in Action,* vols I–IV, Policy Studies Institute.

Southgate, P. (1981) 'Women in the police', *The Police Journal,* vol. 54.

Spencer, A. and Podmore, D. (1983) 'Life on the periphery of a profession: the experience of women lawyers', unpublished paper presented to the British Sociological Association Conference.

Sullivan, P. K. (1979) 'The role of women in the police service – the effects of the Sex Discrimination Act 1975 – a comparison of respective positions', *The Police Journal,* vol. 52.

Sumner, W. G. (1906) *Folkways* (Boston: Ginn).

Torrington, D. P., Hitner, T. and Knights, D. (1982) *Management and the*

Multiracial Workforce: Case Studies in Employment Practice (Aldershot; Gower).

Ullman, L. P. and Krasner, L. (1975) *A Psychological Approach to Abnormal Behaviour* (New Jersey: Prentice Hall).

Whitelegg, E., Arnot, M., Bartels, E., Beechy, V., Birke, L., Himmelweit, S., Leonard, D., Ruehl, S. and Speakman, M. A. (eds) (1982) *The Changing Experience of Women* (Oxford: Basil Blackwell and the Open University).

Whittaker, B. (1979) *The Police in Society* (London: Eyre Methuen).

Wilson, E. (1977) *Women and the Welfare State* (London: Tavistock).

Wilson, J. Q. (1973) *Varieties of Police Behaviour* (New York: Atheneum).

Index